RETHINKING RURAL POVERTY

RETHINKING RURAL
POVERTY

WITHDRAWN BY THE
UNIVERSITY OF MICHIGAN

RETHINKING RURAL POVERTY

Bangladesh as a Case Study

EDITORS

**Hossain Zillur Rahman
Mahabub Hossain**

Sage Publications
New Delhi/Thousand Oaks/London

Copyright © Hossain Zillur Rahman, 1995

All rights reserved. No part of this book may be reproduced or utilised in any form or by any means, electronic or mechanical, including photocopying, recording or by any information storage or retrieval system, without permission in writing from the publisher.

First published in 1995 by

Sage Publications India Pvt Ltd
M-32 Greater Kailash Market I
New Delhi 110 048

Sage Publications Inc
2455 Teller Road
Thousand Oaks, California 91320

Sage Publications Ltd
6 Bonhill Street
London EC2A 4PU

Published by Tejeshwar Singh for Sage Publications India Pvt Ltd, photo-typeset by Pagewell Photosetters, Pondicherry and printed at Chaman Enterprises, Delhi.

Library of Congress Cataloging-in-Publication Data

Rethinking rural poverty: Bangladesh as a case study / editors, Hossain Zillur Rahman, Mahabub Hossain.
    p.   cm.
    Includes bibliographical references and index.
    1. Rural poor—Bangladesh. I. Rahman, Hossain Zillur, 1951– II. Hossain, Mahabub, 1945–
HC440.8.Z9P6263   1995   339.4'6'095492—dc20   94–23400

ISBN: 0–8039–9205–X (US-Hb)
        81–7036–433–7 (India-Hb)

When I was leaving India people asked me which of all the sights I had seen had most impressed me. I answered as they expected me to answer. But it wasn't the Taj Mahal, the 'ghats' of Benares, the temple at Madura or the mountains of Travancore that had most moved me, it was the peasant, terribly emaciated, with nothing to cover his nakedness but a rag round his middle the colour of the sun-baked earth he tilled, the peasant shivering in the cold of dawn, sweating in the heat of noon, working still as the sun set red over the parched fields, the starveling peasant toiling without cease in the north, in the south, in the east, in the west, toiling all over the vastness of India, toiling as he had toiled from father to son back, back for three thousand years when the Aryans had first descended upon the country, toiling for a scant subsistence, his only hope to keep body and soul together. That was the sight that had given me the most poignant emotion in India.

W. Somerset Maugham,
A Writer's Notebook

Contents

List of Tables and Figures 9
Glossary and Abbreviations 16
Preface 19

PART I: INTRODUCTION

1. Rethinking the Poverty Debate 23
   Hossain Zillur Rahman
2. Study Coverage and Methodology 28
   Hossain Zillur Rahman and **Mahabub Hossain**
3. Rural Poverty Trends, 1963–64 to 1989–90 39
   Binayak Sen

PART II: DIMENSIONS OF POVERTY

4. Structure and Distribution of Household Income and Income Dimensions of Poverty 57
   Mahabub Hossain
5. Nutritional Dimensions of Poverty 74
   Omar Haider Chowdhury
6. Selected Living Standard Indicators 99
   Binayak Sen
7. Crisis and Insecurity: The 'Other' Face of Poverty 113
   Hossain Zillur Rahman
8. Gender Dimensions of Poverty 132
   Shamim Hamid

PART III: THE SOCIAL COMPOSITION OF POVERTY

9. Socioeconomic Characteristics of the Poor 157
   Mahabub Hossain

8 • Rethinking Rural Poverty

10. The Poor and the Poorest 170
    Binayak Sen
11. Female Headed Households 177
    Shamim Hamid

PART IV: ASPECTS OF POVERTY PROCESS

12. Income-Earning Environment of the Poor: Aspects of Dislocation, Adjustment and Mobility 193
    Binayak Sen
13. Ecological Reserves and Expenditure-saving Scope for the Poor 221
    Hossain Zillur Rahman
14. *Mora Kartik*: Seasonal Deficits and the Vulnerability of the Rural Poor 234
    Hossain Zillur Rahman

PART V: POLICY ENVIRONMENT AND POVERTY

15. Determinants of Poverty 257
    Mahabub Hossain and Binayak Sen
16. The Political Economy of Poverty-Alleviation 274
    Hossain Zillur Rahman

PART VI: CONCLUSIONS

17. Conclusions 283
    Hossain Zillur Rahman

    The Contributors 298
    Index 300

List of Tables and Figures

Tables

2.1	Representativeness of the BIDS Sample with Regard to the Distribution of Land Ownership in the Country	33
2.2	Indicators of Rural Economy Obtained from BIDS Sample Compared with National Level Indicators Published by the BBS	34
3.1	Sector Wise Growth Rate of GDP, 1984–85 to 1987–88 (at constant 1984–85 market prices) as prepared by the Bangladesh Bureau of Statistics (BBS) and the Planning Commission (PC)	41
3.2	Discrepancy of Annual Household Income Estimates on Account of Certain Consumption Items between Income and Expenditure Data	43
3.3	Comparison of Estimates between BIDS Household Expenditure Survey and BBS Data	44
3.4	Variations in the Rural Head Count Ratios amongst the Previous Studies	45
3.5	Rural Consumer Prices	47
3.6	Poverty Line for Rural Areas	48
3.7	Trends in Rural Absolute Poverty	48
3.8	Head Count Ratios for Rural Areas According to 'Per Household' Classification	48
3.9	FGT Measures of Rural Poverty in Bangladesh	50
3.10	Seasonal Variation in Rural Head Count Ratio, 1988–89	51
4.1	Rural Household Income and its Composition	59
4.2	Degree of Inequality in the Distribution of Income and Land: Per Capita Income Scale, 1989–90	65
4.3	Degree of Inequality in the Distribution of Income and Land: Per Capita Land Ownership Scale, 1989–90	65
4.4	Poverty Lines and Head Count Ratio: Estimates from Income Data, 1987–88 and 1989–90	67

4.5	Incidence of Poverty by Self-Evaluation Indicator	68
4.6	Incidence of Poverty by Geographical Division, 1989–90	68
4.7	Incidence of Poverty by Production Environments, 1989–90	69
4.8	Allocation of Food for Work and Targeted Employment Generation Programme	72
4.9	Trends in Real Wage Rate, 1973–74 to 1990	72
5.1	Per Capita Food Intake in Rural Areas	78
5.2	Regional Variation in Per Capita Food Intake (gm/person/day)	79
5.3	Seasonal Variation in Food Intake	79
5.4	Age-Sex Composition of Food Intake	79
5.5	Per Capita Nutrient Intake, 1962–64 to 1990–91	82
5.6	Percentage Distribution of Rural Households Meeting Different Proportions of Calorie and Protein Requirement	83
5.7	Age-Sex Structure of Malnutrition	84
5.8	Changes in Nutritional Status of Rural Children Under Five Year Age Group in Rural Bangladesh	87
5.9	Intertemporal Comparison of Nutritional Status of Children under Five Year Age Group in Rural Bangladesh	88
5.10	Nutritional Status by Gomez Classification	90
5.11	Nutritional Status under Five Year Group Boys and Girls	90
6.1	Selected Living Standard Indicators, 1989–90	101
6.2	Distribution of Rural Patients by Type of Medicare, 1989–90	103
6.3	Morbidity Status by Land Ownership Groups (1989–90)	104
6.4	Disease Pattern by Land Ownership Categories in Rural Bangladesh (1989–90)	105
6.5	Primary School Enrollment Rate	106
6.6	Housing Condition by Land Ownership Categories, 1989–90	107
6.7	Change in Housing Status by Land Ownership Categories: Comparison of BBS and BIDS Data (1988–90)	109
6.8	Change in Housing Condition: 1987–90	110
6.9	Ownership of Durable Consumer and Socially Prestigious Items by Land Ownership Categories	111
7.1	Intensity of Seasonal Deficits for Rural Households	115
7.2	Identifying Lean Seasons: Deficit Months as Reported by Households	117

7.3	Perceptions on Injustice	121
7.4	Crisis-Proneness of Rural Households	122
7.5	Major Types of Crisis Faced by Rural Households	123
7.6	Coping with Crisis	125
7.7	Change in Household Economic Status in the Eighties	127
7.8	Factors Explaining Downward Mobility	128
8.1	Percentage Distribution of Household Members by Poverty Level	134
8.2	Distribution of Members by Deficit Status of Household	134
8.3	Distribution of Members by Principal Source of Income of Household	135
8.4	Marital Status of Household Members by Sex	135
8.5	Intra-Household Distribution of Minimum Assets of Earning Members by Sex	136
8.6	Age-Specific Participation Rates	137
8.7	Distribution of Labour Force by Poverty Level of Household	140
8.8	Distribution of Labour Force by Principal Source of Income of Household	140
8.9	Minimum Labour Wages (Aman Season)	141
8.10	Types of Labour Arrangements	142
8.11	Terms of Wage Labour by Sex	143
8.12	Relationship between Age and Poverty Level of Household	143
8.13	Distribution of Widowed by Age and Sex	148
9.1	Incidence of Poverty: By Size of Land Ownership, 1989-90	158
9.2	Incidence of Poverty: By Land Tenure, 1989-90	159
9.3	Incidence of Poverty: By Education Status, 1989-90	160
9.4	Incidence of Poverty: By Occupation, 1989-90	160
9.5	Incidence of Extreme Poverty by Educational Level, Controlling Landholding Size, 1989-90	161
9.6	Incidence of Extreme and Moderate Poverty by Educational Level, Controlling Landholding Size, 1989-90	162
9.7	Incidence of Extreme and Moderate Poverty by Occupation Controlling Landholding Size, 1989-90	162
9.8	Incidence of Extreme Poverty by Occupation Controlling Landholding Size, 1989-90	163
9.9	Characteristics of the Poor and Non-Poor Households, 1987-88	164
9.10	Composition of Rural Household Incomes: For Poor and Non-Poor Households	165

12 • Rethinking Rural Poverty

9.11	Level and Changes in Agricultural Wages in Villages Classified by Land and Labour Endowment and Development of Infrastructure	168
9.12	Relationship between the Incidence of Poverty and Real Wage Rate, Regression Estimates, 1989–90	169
10.1	Distribution of Rural Households by Housing Status and by Income Measures of Poverty, 1989–90	173
10.2	Movement In and Out of the Poverty, 1987–90	174
11.1	Demographic and Economic Indicators	180
11.2	Poverty Level	181
11.3	Dynamics of Land Ownership	181
11.4	Principal Source of Income	181
11.5	Livestock Ownership	182
11.6	Ownership of Other Assets	182
11.7	Ownership of Consumer Durables	183
11.8	Ownership of Basic Clothing	183
11.9	Deficit Status	184
11.10	Standard of Living Indicators	186
11.11	Housing	186
11.12a	Classification of Female Headed Households through Clustering Exercise	187
11.12b	Analysis of Variance	187
12.1	Land Ownership Location of Deficit Households, 1989–90	194
12.2	Control Over Resources by Size of Landholding, 1983–84	195
12.3	Percentage Distribution of Livestock Ownership among Land Ownership Categories, 1989–90	196
12.4	Percentage Distribution of Non-Land Asset Ownership by Land Ownership Categories, 1989–90	196
12.5	Principal Income Sources of Households by Land Ownership Status, 1989–90	197
12.6	Access to Institutional Credit Sources, 1989–90	199
12.7	Dependence of the Land-Poor on Tenancy Market, 1989–90	201
12.8	Adjustment through Tenancy Market: Relevance of Kinship Network	202
12.9	Access to Non-Institutional Credit Sources	204
12.10	Pattern of Distribution of Credit Advances amongst Different Land Owning Groups, by Lender Types	206
12.11	Breakdown of Informal Credit Flow by Lender Types	207
12.12	Risk-Insurance through Access to Emergency Loans	207
12.13	Dependency on Lenders Supplying Emergency Loans	208
12.14	Kinship Lineages with Lenders Supplying Emergency Loans	208

12.15	Incidence of Multiple Occupation by Land Ownership Categories	210
12.16	Participation in Income-Earning Activities by Land Ownership and Surplus Deficit Status	211
12.17	Days of Labour in 1990, by Land Ownership Group	212
12.18	Composition of Annual Employment per Household by Surplus Deficit Status	212
12.19	Land Stability by Deficit Surplus Status, 1989–90	216
12.20	Land Stability by Land Ownership Status, 1989–90	216
12.21	Incidence of Land Stability by Age of Household and by Non-Land Income Status	217
12.22	Incidence of Inter-Class Mobility vis-à-vis Land Stability by Land Inheritance Group	218
13.1	Extent of Household Participation in Expenditure-Saving	224
13.2	Division-Wise Household Participation Rate in Expenditure-Saving	225
13.3	Annual Savings on Expenditure and Annual Household Income	228
13.4	Five Year Trend in Access to Ecological Reserves, 1985–90	230
13.5	Division-Wise Five Year Trend in Access to Ecological Reserves, 1985–90	232
14.1	Percentage of Labour Households Going Without any Work for 4–7 Days a Week	235
14.2	Average Daily Earning of Petty Trader Households During 10–20 October, 1991 vis-à-vis Average Daily Earning in Normal Time	236
14.3	Comparison of Daily Wage Rates during October 1991 and Normal Time	237
14.4	Impact of Flood/Excess Rain on Aman/Aus Crop: Local Estimate of Loss and Recovery	239
14.5	Expectation of 1991 Aman Production vis-à-vis Normal Year	240
14.6	Intensity of Food Intake Shortage, 10–20 October, 1991	241
14.7	Wage Rates and Market Prices, 10–20 October, 1991	244
14.8	Trend in Business Activity	248
14.9	Reasons for Lower Sale in Current Period as Provided by Traders	250
15.1	Determinants of Rural Household Income: Regression Estimates	260
15.2	Determinants of Income of the Poor and Non-Poor Households	263

15.3	The Incidence of Poverty by State of Development of Infrastructure	268
15.4	Incidence of Poverty by Irrigation: Controlling Size of Landholding	268
15.5	Incidence of Poverty by Access to Electricity: Controlling Landholding Size	270

Appendix Tables

A5.1	Comparing Average Weight between 1982–83 and 1990–91	96
A5.2	Comparing Average Height between 1982–83 and 1991	97
A5.3	Average Weight as a Percentage of Reference Weight	98
A5.4	Average Height as a Percentage of Reference Height	98

Figures

2.1	Bangladesh Map Showing Sites Under BIDS 62-Village Survey	30
3.1	Trend in Rural Absolute Poverty as per Uniform Method of Calculation (Per Capita Expenditure Classification)	49
3.2	Seasonal Trend in Rural Head Count Ratio	52
4.1	Composition of Rural Income (All Households)	60
4.2	Concentration of Per Capita Income Land Ownership, 1989–90	63
4.3	Concentration of Household Income in Per Capita Income and Land Ownership Scale	63
4.4	Concentration of Agricultural Incomes in Per Capita Income and Land Ownership Scale	64
4.5	Concentration of Non-Agricultural Incomes in Per Capita Income and Land Ownership Scale	64
4.6	Regional Variation in Moderate and Extreme Poverty (Division-wise)	69
4.7	Incidence of Poverty Under Different Environments	70
5.1	Female Food Intake as a Percentage of Male Intake	81
6.1	Poverty by Quality of Life Indicators	100
7.1	Seasonal Deficits in Rural Bangladesh	116
7.2	A Typology of Crisis Routinely Faced by Rural Households	119
7.3	Factors Explaining Downward Household Mobility	129
8.1	Male-Female Disparities	136
8.2	Age-Specific Female Participation Rate	138
8.3	Male/Female Age-Specific Participation Rate	139
8.4	Poverty Level of Household and Life-Cycle of Members by Sex	144

List of Tables and Figures • 15

8.5	Food Security of Household and Life-Cycle of Female Members	145
8.6	Food Security and Life-Cycle of Stable and Surplus Members	146
9.1	Composition of Rural Household Income by Poverty Status	166
10.1	Chronic and Transient Poverty: Inter-Class Mobility 1987–88 to 1989–90	175
11.1	Poverty Distribution in Different Types	185
13.1	The Importance of Ecological Reserves for Rural Households	229
15.1	Impact of Infrastructure on Extreme and Moderate Poverty	265
15.2	Impact of Infrastructure on Extreme Poverty	266
15.3	Comparison of Poor Household Income Under Differing Infrastructural Situations	267
17.1	The Problem of Economic Gradation: Nature of Household Mobility over the Eighties as per Self-Evaluation	293

Glossary and Abbreviations

Amon	Paddy harvested in winter
Boro	Paddy harvested in summer
Bil	Marshy land
BBS	Bangladesh Bureau of Statistics
BIDS	Bangladesh Institute of Development Studies
BRAC	Bangladesh Rural Advancement Committee
FCD	Flood Control and Drainage
FFW	Food for Works Programme
FHH	Female Headed Households
HDI	Human Development Index
HES	Household Income and Expenditure Surveys
HKI	Helen Keller International
Hogla	A Kind of Leaf
ICM	Informal Credit Market
INFS	Institute of Nutrition and Food Science
Khal	Canal
LFPR	Labour Force Participation Rate
LFS	Labour Force Survey
Lungi	Lower garment for men
PEM	Protein Energy Malnutrition
Rabi Crop	Different types of pulses which are grown in the winter months
Shawl	Upper garment for women used in winter
UNCH	United States National Centre for Health
UNDP	United Nations Development Programme

Union	Local Government tier, has an average of 10 villages
USAID	United States Agency for International Development
Upazila/Thana	Sub-district; lowest tier of central administration
VGD	Vulnerable group development, a programme for the poor
VHSS	Voluntary Health Services Society
WID	Women in Development

Preface

The study of poverty urgently requires interpretations and solutions. Lacking neither in will nor in initiatives, a majority of the rural population in the developing world nevertheless faces a bleak existence of deprivation and vulnerabilities. Such poverty is the making not of individuals but of society and history. Not the least of the objectives of a study of poverty is to understand and identify where interventions to aid the struggle for survival by the poor are best made.

This book is the culmination of an extraordinarily fruitful team effort involving researchers with diverse professional backgrounds and a dynamic field team of fresh graduates. Research and field teams came together as part of a long-term research study on the poverty process titled 'Analysis of Poverty Trends Project'. The study was undertaken at the Bangladesh Institute of Development Studies (Dhaka) and has been generously supported by aid agencies from Denmark, Sweden, Norway, Holland and Canada. All these institutional and their financial assistance is gratefully acknowledged.

Contributors to this volume also made up the research team for the study. Mahabub Hossain, then Director-General of BIDS and now Head of Social Sciences Division, IRRI provided the expertise on rural income analysis. He is the co-editor of this book. Omar Haider Chowdhury, Senior Research Fellow at BIDS provided the expertise on nutritional analysis. Binayak Sen, Research Fellow at BIDS analysed critical macro issues, including comparability of poverty statistics over time. Shamim Hamid, Research Fellow at BIDS and now at the Bangladesh Embassy in Rome provided the special focus on the situation of women. Hossain Zillur Rahman, Research Fellow at BIDS has been the Co-ordinator of the Study

20 • Rethinking Rural Poverty

and the principal editor of this book. He has been mainly responsible for the overall conceptual framework as well as for the analysis of the more unconventional non-income dimensions of poverty. While each chapter has specific author(s), the overall result has to be seen as a team effort.

This book is a direct outcome of an intensive programme of field research. The manifold demands of generating a complex range of data of high reliability was ably met by a team of fresh graduates whose enthusiasm and commitment provided much of the brainstorming stimulus which helped to carry the study forward. Syed Ziauddin Ahmed, Subodh Chandra Sarkar, Nasima Parveen, Ayesha Banu, Mahbuba Haque, Fouzia Mannan, Sabikun Nahar, Talat Sultana, Lutfe Ara Begum, Md. Sultan Mahmud, Md. Ali Akbar, Bhanu Bhusan Chakrabarty, Md. Masudul Haque, Nilufar Akhtar, Nurul Momen, Salma Khatun, Salma Begum, Md. Zobair, Md. Ziaul Islam, Muahhid Billah Faruqui, Md. Sayeed Hasan Raza, Md. Mohidur Rahman Khan, Bibhuti Bhusan Mazumder, Mozaffar Hossain, Shahida Nasreen are all gratefully acknowledged.

The final editing of this book was facilitated by an anonymous reader's report. His/her comments are duly acknowledged. Shafiqul Islam Molla and Humayun Kabir Kazal deserve appreciation for bearing the burden of typing the manuscript.

Hossain Zillur Rahman
Dhaka, May 30 1993

I

Introduction

1
Rethinking the Poverty Debate

HOSSAIN ZILLUR RAHMAN

Fifty years after the great wave of decolonisation, the discussion on poverty in the developing world has sadly lost none of its pathos or urgency. Widespread and acute rural poverty remain the single most important feature of these socioeconomic landscapes. This notwithstanding the fact that alleviating poverty has officially been the priority developmental goal of most Third World regimes since independence. It is common and easy to see here a failure of intentions. In truth, the failure has been a multiple one, a failure of political intentions but as importantly a failure of analytical understanding, a failure of policy perspective, a failure of managerial and mobilisational capacities and a failure to trust the productive energies of the people.

Developing a more meaningful discussion on poverty cannot be a matter of academic invention. Rather the starting point has to be a better understanding of the poverty experience itself. What are the vulnerabilities which make up the experience of poverty? Are such vulnerabilities reducible to a single dimension and if such is the case, is it useful to do so? Are the poor a homogeneous group or do critical differentiations exist amongst them? Is poverty a lack of resources or a lack of coping capacity or a lack of institutional/network defences or all of these? In what follows, an attempt is made to trace the broad contours of 'rethinking' which may be necessary if the poverty debate is to improve our analytical understanding and provide a better guide to action.

A large part of the problem with existing indices of poverty lies in their inadequate characterisation of the economic and social contexts in which the majority of the population pursues its livelihood. Rural households are rarely able to depend on single, substantive sources of income as in the urban, formal sector. Instead, they have to make do with a variety of petty self-employment and wage-employment activities. They have to operate in both market and non-market contexts. The economic opportunities available to them have marked seasonal variation. Their economic transactions are enmeshed in varying ties of dependence and unequal power relations which have the effect of severely circumscribing the fundamental assumptions of free choice and perfect competition. Yet, the economic modelling of household behaviour which underlie the analytical discussion of poverty more often than not is uninformed by these basic features of rural household existence.

Distinct from the question of more realistic economic modelling and as important a consideration, is the adequate cognisance of non-income dimensions of poverty. Such dimensions are often overlooked on the rationale that they are in any case reflected in the income measure of poverty. Such reasoning have two major flaws. Firstly, even if some non-income dimensions are reducible to the income indicator, a separate look at them may be worthwhile on the ground that the whole discussion of poverty is not only about counting the poor but also to understand and identify priority areas for remedial action. Thus, even if non-income indicators, such as nutrition, housing, sanitation and health are reducible to the income measure, it is definitely worthwhile to know in which of these areas poverty-alleviating action may bear the most fruit. Secondly, not all non-income dimensions are reducible to the income measure of poverty. Community facilities, such as safe water and good sanitation are a good example. Such facilities have an impact on the living standard and the nutritional health of household members and yet their presence reflects not household income but a community facility. A less familiar example is community opportunities in ecological reserves which constitute a significant supplementary source of sustenance for the rural poor. Such ecological reserves which subsume various common property resources again do not arise out of household income but exist, if at all, as a community opportunity.

A look at non-income dimensions at once extends the discussion on poverty beyond the household domain and brings attention to bear on the social and institutional environment in which the poor pursue their livelihoods and everyday life. In positing such a focus, the concern is not so much building a new hypothesis as ensuring an adequate cognition of the vulnerabilities which make up the experience of poverty. Two such vulnerabilities which are obscured in conventional thinking but are of major analytical significance are personal insecurity and susceptibility to crisis. The pervasive and routine nature of these vulnerabilities well merits a redefinition of poverty as a three-dimensional syndrome of hunger, insecurity and crisis.

The focus on crisis as a dimension of poverty unveils a critical lacuna in current debates on poverty. Insofar as the occurrence of a crisis translates into a destabilising demand on the slender margin of rural household resources, the range of crises which rural households are routinely exposed to constitute a set of powerful downward mobility pressures. In such a context, incremental addition to household income on its own may not suffice to address the goal of poverty-alleviation unless at the same time one addresses the issue of downward mobility pressures either in terms of their macro sources or in terms of individual coping capacities. Without such a two-pronged strategy, incremental increases in household income will be overshadowed by cyclical mobility pressures at the poverty margin, thus, posing a major issue of economic graduation for the rural poor.

Personal insecurity as a routine existential predicament within the experience of poverty points towards another critical gap in the poverty debate. Mainstream development thinking does not pose the problem of personal insecurity as an issue in itself but sees it simply as derivative of economic power. There is a failure here to distinguish between security as end-state and insecurity as experiential context. Arising as it does from anomie in the structure of community life on the one hand and the injurious interface of local society and regulatory organs of the state, such as police and courts on the other, insecurity has a far more insidious significance for the poverty debate than simply in defining the quality of life. What mainstream thinking obscures is the whole issue of the opportunity frontier and initiative space which the poor can self-define for themselves in their quest for livelihood and how pervasive insecurity can critically serve to constrain such frontiers and spaces.

Such a perception indicates a whole new arena for poverty-alleviating action, namely, the reform of administrative and regulatory structures which have the social effect of constraining and undermining livelihood initiatives of the poor.

Income and non-income dimensions are not competing foci for the poverty debate. At stake rather is the perception of poverty as a multi-dimensional reality and the importance of cognising it as such. The point of departure for such a perception is not academic invention but closer attention to the reality of routine life of the poor. An additional outcome of positing the poor as human subjects is to bring within the discussion agenda the interface of government, community and individual households as actors in the removal of poverty. None of these levels alone carry the full potential for poverty-alleviating action. Indeed, perceiving it as such may itself be part of the problem, since it has the effect of obscuring the role of the other two levels. Yet, it appears frequently to be the case that the government assumes such an exclusionary jurisdiction and the political centre fosters public expectations of precisely the same. Not only does this serve to delegitimise and obscure the community and the individual as critical domains of initiatives on poverty, there is also no guarantee that the government is actually able to deliver on its assumed jurisdictions. It may, therefore, be worthwhile to reconceptualise the role of the government in poverty-alleviation. Indeed, while macro-management and service-delivery are clear priority areas of government action on poverty, reform or curtailment of regulatory structures of the government which impair or inhibit community or local initiatives can itself be posed as the other critical area for 'action'. Such a perception at once puts the issues of local self-government and social mobilisation squarely onto the poverty agenda.

What has been argued thus far in some ways is a 'reversing' of the usual terms of the debate on poverty. The focus is less on policies and more on actors, structures and processes which have a bearing on poverty. In the same vein, the focus on government bear some further elaboration. Conventional thinking tends to ignore the distinction between the government as a source for policies and the government as a regulatory and implementing machinery. Such a distinction makes it possible to visualise social contexts in which policy intentions may bear no necessary reference to the actual capacities for implementation, thus, making them in effect no more than mere declarative intentions. In such situations, the focus of the debate has to fall not on policies but on governance and the capacities for implementation. Even if the situation is not so extreme as when all policies are only declarative intentions, the pathology of governance and implementation clearly emerges as a priority issue in the analytical consideration of poverty. In the analysis which follows, rural Bangladesh has been taken as a case study for an in-depth 'rethinking' of poverty.

2

Study Coverage and Methodology

HOSSAIN ZILLUR RAHMAN AND MAHABUB HOSSAIN

Introduction

An adequate monitoring of the poverty process has traditionally faltered on the two major grounds of conceptual coverage and data availability. In Bangladesh, the principal data source for poverty analysis to-date is the periodic Household Expenditure Surveys (HES) carried out by the Bureau of Statistics. This data, however, does not permit the drawing of a comprehensive social profile of the population living in poverty. Nor does it address the non-income dimensions which are crucial to a complete understanding of the poverty process, or allow any regional disaggregation of the poverty picture.

This study was initiated within the Bangladesh Institute of Development Studies (BIDS) to address these twin problems of conceptual coverage and data availability and thereby contribute to a more informed policy process and social discourse on the issue. The starting point was to adopt a multi-dimensional understanding of the poverty process in place of the traditional uni-dimensional approach based on the income indicator. By combining income and non-income dimensions, a four-fold conceptual scheme was developed to analyse the poverty process consisting of:

1. Income
2. Living standard
3. Asset access
4. Institutional capability

Such a conceptual scheme permitted the inclusion of a range of quality of life variables, such as nutrition, living environment, security, crisis-coping capacity and participation, in addition to traditional indicator such as income. Furthermore, such an approach underscored the nature of poverty not only as a state but also as a process.

Poverty does not affect all social groups equally. An important objective of the study was to develop a disaggregated picture of the poverty experience with a special emphasis on bringing out *gender differentials*. In addition, emphasis was also on capturing the *regional* and the *seasonal* dimensions of poverty.

For a study on poverty, the timing of the study has crucial bearing on the extent to which the findings can be generalised. The choice of 1989–90 as the base year was particularly appropriate because it was an agriculturally 'normal' year. This would mean that the findings capture poverty in its 'normal' state rather than in any 'exceptional' state as for example in years when there are major natural disasters, such as floods.

Sample Selection

A multi-stage random sampling method was used to select the sample for this study. A list of all unions (a multi-village administrative unit) of the country was prepared from the report of the 1981 Population Census. In order to be nationally representative the survey needed to cover areas from all geographic regions of the country. The sample size of the unions was fixed at 64 as Bangladesh is divided into 64 districts. The samples were drawn from the list of unions using the random sampling number table. Because of the variation of the size of the district, a few smaller districts are not represented in the sample, while for a few larger districts, such as Comilla and Mymensingh the sample contains more than one union. Two unions were later dropped due to the difficulty of administration of the survey. The sample represents 57 out of 64 districts (see Figure 2.1).

FIGURE 2.1
*Map of Bangladesh Showing Sites Under
BIDS 62 Village Survey*

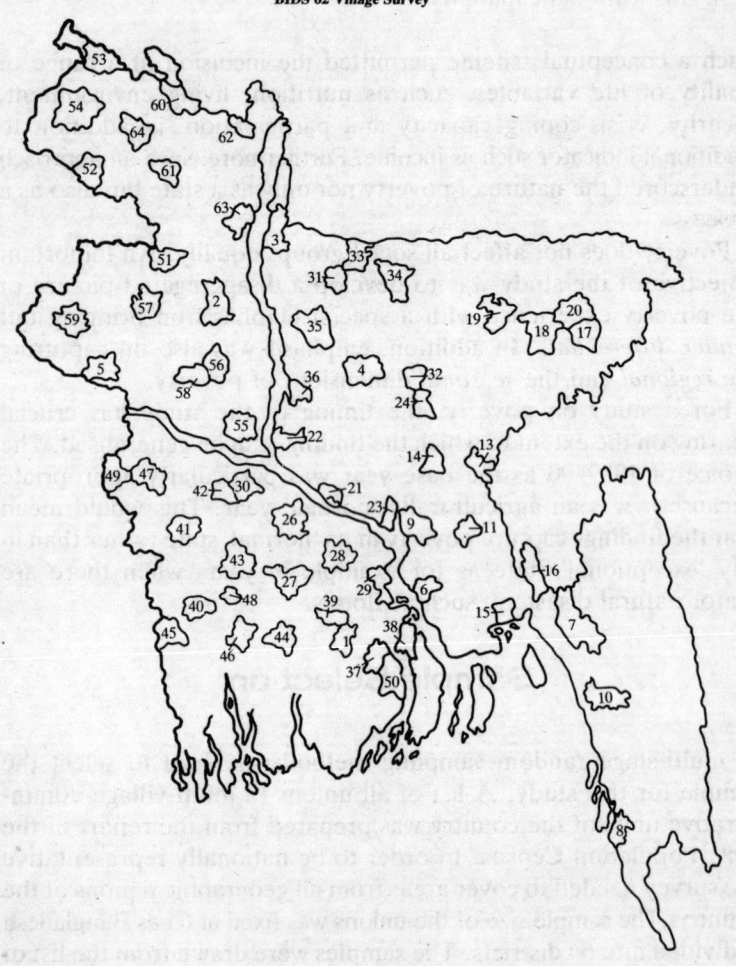

Study Coverage and Methodology • 31

List of 62 Villages

Code	Name of Village	Name of Thana	Name of District
01	Beshainkhan	Jhalakathi Sadar	Jhalakathi
02	Darikamari	Bogra Sadar	Bogra
03	Rampura	Dewanganj	Jamalpur
04	Chandalgaon Nisaiganj	Bhaluka	Mymensingh
05	Teghar	Paba	Rajshahi
06	Shibpur	Raipur	Laxhimpur
07	Shobhanchhari	Fatikchari	Chittagong
08	Nayapara	Cox's Bazar	Cox's Bazar
09	Begumpur	Matlab	Chandpur
10	Sosang	Patiya	Chittagong
11	Bhabanipur	Barura	Comilla
13	Noagaon	Kashba	Brahmanbaria
14	Krishanagar (East)	Bancharampur	Brahmanbaria
15	Karalia	Companiganj	Noakhali
16	Mokamia	Chhagalnaiya	Feni
17	Dakhsin Daspara	Rajnagar	Moulavibazar
18	Bazkasara	Nabiganj	Hobiganj
19	Paschim Kashipur	Sulla	Sunamganj
20	Sirajpur	Balaganj	Sylhet
21	Madhur Khola	Dohar	Dhaka
22	Uttar Basail	Daulatpur	Manikganj
23	Sontoshpar	Serajdikhan	Munshiganj
24	Patardia	Monohardi	Narshindi
26	Shankarpasha	Nagarkanda	Faridpur
27	Bhojergati	Gopalganj	Gopalganj
28	Paschim Bahadurpur	Madaripur	Madaripur
29	Balikuri	Goshairhat	Sariatpur
30	Beradanga	Baliakandi	Rajbari
31	Mojakanda	Nakhla	Sheerpur
32	Mandarkandi	Pakundia	Kishoreganj
33	Konapara	Haluaghat	Mymensingh
34	Panchmarkenda	Purbadhala	Netrokona
35	Sujalkar	Modhupur	Tangail
36	Rashidpur	Tangail	Tangail
37	Patkathi	Bakerganj	Barisal
38	Jamiralata	Bhola	Bhola
39	Dariabad	Banaripara	Barisal
40	Mirzanagar	Keshabpur	Jessore
41	Niamatpur	Kaliganj	Jhenaidah
42	Baraichara	Sreepur	Magura
43	Balarampur	Narail	Narail
44	Katakhali	Bagerhat	Bagerhat
45	Parandaha	Satkhira	Satkhira
46	Mailmara	Batiaghata	Khulna
47	Khudiakhali	Alamdanga	Chuadanga
48	Noapara	Kushtia	Kushtia
49	Maniknagar	Meherpur	Meherpur
50	Dakshin Kabir kati	Bawphal	Patuakhali
51	Hanial Bambu	Joypurhat	Joypurhat
52	Ratnaur	Birol	Dinajpur
53	Ghotbar	Panchagarh	Panchagarh
54	Baikunthapur	Thakurgaon	Thakurgaon
55	Majhgram	Santhia	Pabna
56	Sakaidighi	Tarash	Sirajganj
57	Halghospara	Noagaon	Noagaon
58	Udbaria	Gurudaspur	Natore
59	Uttar Chandipur	Nachoule	Nawabganj
60	Arazi Sekhsundar	Hatibandha	Lalmonirhat
61	Gopinathpur	Badarganj	Rangpur
62	Rasunsimulbari	Fulbari	Kurigram
63	Khidir	Gaibandha	Gaibandha
64	Kanai Kata Gyan Das	Nilphamari	Nilphamari

Information on area of land, number of households, total population and literacy rate was obtained for all villages under the selected unions from the 1981 district census reports. Two villages were then purposively selected on the basis of this information so that (*a*) the selected village is not either too small or too large—the village with less than 100 or more than 250 households were excluded, (*b*) the land–person ratio and the literacy rate of the village are similar to those for the selected union. Thus, 124 villages were selected at this stage. The first choice among the two villages was the one which was more closely representative of the union. A community level survey was carried out in both villages for each of the selected unions through group interviews with local leaders and school teachers (key informants) to find out about the characteristics of the village, such as access to various types of infrastructure, land tenure system, use of new agricultural technology and importance of non-farm activities. The village to be studied for an in-depth household survey was chosen at this stage on the consideration of cooperation from the villagers. In seven out of the 62 cases, the second choice village had to be chosen due to lack of cooperation from key informants in the village of the first choice.

A census of all households was carried out for the 62 sample villages to collect information on ownership of land, major source of income, type of housing and age and education status of the head of the household. The households were then classified into four landownership groups; (*a*) functionally landless (having less than 0.5 acres of land) (*b*) small owner (with 0.5 to 2.49 acres) (*c*) medium owners (2.5 to 4.99 acres) and (*d*) large owners (5.0 acres or more). Each of the land ownership group was further classified into two land tenure groups according to whether the household is engaged in tenancy cultivation or not. From each village 20 households were selected using the stratified random sampling technique, the samples being drawn from each of the 8 strata proportionate to their size as determined from the census. For a few villages the number of samples drawn had to be 21 because of the rounding error. The total size of the sample selected was 1245 households, which was then subjected to the in-depth inquiry. The number of the sample households went on increasing because of the division of the households due to demographic pressure. The sample households were first visited in early 1988 for studying the impact of the new agricultural technology. When the investigators went to administer the survey for this study in early 1990, the number of the sample households had increased to 1300, implying a growth rate of 2.2 per cent per year.

Representativeness of the Sample

Bangladesh has 4401 unions. The selected unions for the study comprise 1.4 per cent of the total unions in the country. The census carried out in the selected villages enumerated 9874 households, i.e., 159 households per village. The enumerated households comprise about 0.068 per cent of the households in the country. The Bangladesh Bureau of Statistics (BBS) uses a sample size of approximately 6,000 households for its periodic household level surveys (Household Expenditure Survey, Labour Force Survey, etc.). Thus, the samples covered in the study is quite large compared to other national-level surveys and widely spread out geographically. (Table 2.1).

The representativeness of the sample is indicated by the similarity of the pattern of distribution of land ownership obtained from the

TABLE 2.1
Representativeness of the BIDS Sample with Regard to the Distribution of Land Ownership in the Country

Size of land owned (acres)	BIDS census of households in sample villages (January 1988)		Bangladesh agricultural census carried out by BBS (1983–84)	
	No. of households (thousand)	Per cent	No. of households	Per cent of households
Less than 0.5 (functionally landless)	4,825	48.9	6,398	46.3
0.5–2.49 (small owner)	3,179	32.2	4,639	33.6
2.5–4.99 (medium owner)	1,088	11.0	1,598	11.6
5.0 and more (large owners)	782	7.9	1,183	8.6
Total	9,874	100.0	13,818	100.0

Source: Analysis of Poverty Trends Project, BIDS: 62 Village Survey.

first survey (1988) to that obtained from the 1983–84 Agricultural Census carried out by the Bangladesh Bureau of Statistics, which was conducted on a full-count basis. The survey estimated the proportions of functionally landless households at 48.9 per cent compared to 46.7 per cent obtained in the Agricultural Census. The proportion of large land owners is estimated at 7.9 per cent by the BIDS survey compared to 8.6 per cent by the Agricultural Census.

The average size of land ownership obtained from the census of all households in the selected villages was 1.61 acres. The estimate obtained from the 1983–84 Agricultural Census was 1.67 acres. The cropping intensity estimated from the sample survey is 175 per cent compared to 179 per cent estimated by the census. The BIDS survey however estimated a some what larger proportion of area under tenancy (23 per cent) compared to the Agricultural Census (19 per cent) (Table 2.2). The BIDS sample, thus, appears to be fairly representative for the country as a whole.

TABLE 2.2
Indicators of Rural Economy Obtained from BIDS Sample Compared with National Level Indicators Published by the BBS

Indicators	BIDS sample (1988)	BBS official statistics (1983/84)
Average size of landholding	1.61	1.67
Per cent of cultivator households	66.1	72.7
Average size of cultivated holding (acres)	2.18	2.27
Proportion of tenant cultivators	43.5	37.4
Cropping intensity	175	179
Per cent of households using irrigation	52	40

Source: Analysis of Poverty Trends Project, BIDS: 62 Village Survey.

Survey Modules

The four-fold conceptual scheme indicated earlier was operationalised into an empirical survey consisting of 10 separate modules. These were:

Study Coverage and Methodology • 35

1. Household Structure
2. Asset Structure and Living Environment
3. Land Tenancy Market
4. Credit Access
5. Income Sources and Labour Market Participation
6. Expenditure-saving Scope
7. Crisis and Crisis-coping
8. Social Sector Expenditure and Institutional Participation
9. Household Income
10. Credit Market Dynamics

All these ten modules were administered over the whole sample in two rounds, December 1989–February 1990 and May 1990–July 1990. In addition to these modules, three more were administered over a smaller sample of 16 villages. These were:

11. Household Expenditure
12. Child Anthropometry
13. Dietary Intake

The expenditure module was administered over the period May–July 1990, while the two nutritional modules were administered in two rounds, the first in the period June–October 1990 (considered a lean period) and the second continuing from February 1991 to May 1991 (considered a normal period). Issues related to the situation of women have been incorporated in each of the modules listed above.

It may be noted here that the application of survey modules have reference to two different sample frames, a large one of 62 villages and a smaller one of 16 villages. Modules administered on the larger sample frame are based on 'stock' type information, such as assets, household structure, income sources, which require monitoring at longer intervals. By contrast, modules administered on the smaller sample frame are based on 'flow' type information, such as expenditure, employment and nutritional status which require monitoring at more frequent intervals.

The previous sections have explained how the larger sample of 62 villages was chosen. An important consideration behind the decision to take this choice was the fact that such a sample had already been identified courtesy an earlier BIDS survey on the differential impact of modern agricultural technology. By adopting this sample once its representativeness had been established, the current exercise was able to avoid an unnecessary and time-consuming exercise in household listing in preparation for the actual survey modules. Our decision was also dictated by the consideration that the choice of a nationally representative sample covering a very wide regional spectrum would help to create the strongest possible base line for long-term monitoring. For continuous monitoring, however, it was unrealistic to retain such a large sample. The choice of a smaller sample was not, however, an arbitrary one. One of the objectives of our initial efforts was to disaggregate the country into representative socioeconomic zones along dimensions having the clearest bearing on the poverty issue. Accordingly the following variables were chosen for a zoning exercise:

1. Agrarian structure, represented by the two variables, extent of landlessness and preponderance of large land owners.
2. Level of agricultural development, represented by per acre cereal productivity.
3. Degree of ecological vulnerability, represented by the proportion of land under flood-risk and drought-risk crops (broadcast aman and broadcast aus respectively)
4. Degree of diversification of the economy, represented by the percentage of population reporting non-farm sources as principal source of income.

Using these analytical variables disaggregated to sub-district level, a cluster technique was applied to derive five representative socio-economic zoning categories. These had the following identifying characteristics:

1. Ecologically Vulnerable
2. Dominated by Large Land Owning Groups
3. Agriculturally Progressive
4. High Landlessness combined with High Economic Diversification
5. Average

Once the country had been stratified into representative socioeconomic zones, a smaller sample of 16 villages out of the larger sample of 62 villages was chosen to accommodate the representative socioeconomic zoning categories in proportion to their respective weights vis-à-vis the national area coverage. In the text, the smaller sample villages will often be referred to as cluster villages.

Disaggregation in Data Presentation

Along what dimensions data is best disaggregated obviously depends on the specific issue being explained. From this standpoint, a number of disaggregation procedures have been utilised:

1. Disaggregation by region; two levels have been used here, i.e., district and the multi-district unit of division.
2. Disaggregation by social groups; again two categories have been used, i.e., land ownership and deficit status.

Non-Sampling Errors

However well a sample is chosen, there remains the actual task of data-generation. Here it is important to anticipate the possibility of various non-sampling errors which may reflect on the reliability of the data. Such non-sampling errors may arise from three major sources: (*a*) faults in research design in terms of conceptual errors or inappropriate questions, (*b*) investigator's failure to communicate with the respondents, and (*c*) respondent's unwillingness or inability to provide information. It is possible to narrow down the margin of non-sampling errors by anticipating likely problems in each of these areas and then trying to overcome them as best as possible. On this consideration, survey preparation focused on three vital anticipatory steps: firstly, a rigorously worked out conceptual framework to guide the survey;[1] secondly, an intensive training of field investigators in the three areas of concepts, questionnaire and field consistency checks,[2] and lastly, the establishment of a rapport with the village population through observing a proper code of conduct and where possible supporting the villages in their community needs.[3] To these was added a fourth ingredient, namely, an effective structure of supervision. It is our expectation that these anticipatory steps may have substantially reduced the scope for non-sampling errors. However, in the final analysis it is only the social validation of the findings which can show how well such anticipatory preparations yielded fruit in terms of data reliability.

Notes

1. See, Hossain Zillur Rahman, 'Monitoring Rural Poverty: Conceptual Framework and Organisational Options', BIDS, 1988 (mimeo.).
2. Apart from the core research team directly involved in the project, a number of other researchers from BIDS as well as other relevant institutions also participated in conducting this training programme.
3. It may be noted that a primary school and a bus shelter were built in two of the study areas selected for the field survey with the direct participation of project members.

3

Rural Poverty Trends, 1963–64 to 1989–90

BINAYAK SEN

Introduction

Should poverty be defined mainly as a uni-dimensional phenomenon or be viewed as a complex multi-dimensional process? The uni-dimensional approach would lead to one set of measurements of poverty usually aimed at estimating income deprivation or nutritional deprivation. By contrast, a multi-dimensional approach would take into account both income and non-income dimensions of poverty. The latter include a range of quality of life variables, such as nutrition, health and sanitation, housing, security, access to state distribution system, participation and institutional capability and crisis-coping capacity. As opposed to the uni-dimensional approach, various dimensions of poverty are by no means reducible to any single indicator of poverty. Instead the phenomenon of poverty is best captured by a set of indicators which focus on the entitlement of the poor to several crucial inputs relating to social security, welfare and the living standard. This has been empirically demonstrated by Jodha (1988) with respect to poverty situation in India, and argued strongly by Kabeer (1989) and Rahman (1988) in their methodological review on monitoring rural poverty in

Bangladesh. However, evidence on poverty in rural Bangladesh is yet to be assembled in a systematic manner and analysed within a holistic framework. Most of the studies on poverty in Bangladesh, by and large, are concerned with a uni-dimensional approach, namely, the income measure of poverty.

Data Sources

Household Income and Expenditure Surveys (HES) periodically carried out by the Bangladesh Bureau of Statistics (BBS) constitute the main source of information for most of the previous studies on rural poverty. Lack of panel data at the household level, lack of a uniform method of recording data flow, shortfall of the memory recall method, etc., are some of the limitations of these surveys. There is also an additional problem of 'missing cases'. As the HES data are focused on current household units, it is possible that these surveys might have excluded those household units which may be lost to the reference population through distress migration. One may also classify under the missing cases those landless households who do not possess even homestead lands. However, there is no disagreement that the quality of these surveys carried out from 1983–84 onwards are more reliable than the earlier years.

There has been considerable controversy centering around the trend in rural poverty in the eighties. A study by Rahman and Haque (1988) based on the BBS data showed that the poverty situation deteriorated till 1981–82 but substantial improvement took place during the period 1981 to 1986. The study raised controversy since the improvement in the poverty situation in the early eighties was incompatible with the trend in macro-indicators as per BBS national accounts data, which showed a deceleration in agricultural and overall economic growth and a declining public sector investment and savings ratio. This does not necessarily mean that the BBS national accounts data are more reliable than the HES. Incomes derived from rural non-farm sector are probably under reported in national accounts. For example, the HES estimate of per capita income in 1988–89 was about 16.5 per cent higher than the estimate from national accounts. The difference was mostly due to an underestimation of non-agricultural income (Task Force

Report, 1991). National Accounts Statistics exclude substantial portion of the informal sector income, especially those derived from rural non-farm activities. Targeted rural non-farm activities supported by various anti-poverty programmes are also not captured by National Accounts. This may explain why the growth in per capita rural income as derived from HES data is substantially higher than the growth estimated from National Accounts data. Thus, between 1973–74 and 1988–89, per capita income grew in real terms at a rate of 2.2 per cent per annum as per HES, while the corresponding figure as per national accounts was 1.6 per cent.[1] The quality of National Accounts data has been subjected to critical appraisal by the National Income Commission as well. The report of the Commission has pointed to significant underestimation of sectoral growth rates in BBS National Accounts vis-à-vis the Planning Commission figures (Table 3.1).

From the available evidence it appears that both HES and

TABLE 3.1
Sector-Wise Growth Rate of GDP, 1984–85 to 1987–88 (at constant 1984–85 market prices) as Prepared by the Bangladesh Bureau of Statistics (BBS) and the Planning Commission (PC)

Sectors (1984–85 to 1987–88)	Data source	Av. growth rate
Agriculture	BBS	0.49
	PC	2.62
Industry	BBS	3.69
	PC	4.88
Electricity	BBS	20.24
	PC	13.34
Construction	BBS	6.94
	PC	6.87
Transport	BBS	5.66
	PC	5.71
Trade	BBS	1.44
	PC	4.18
Housing	BBS	3.19
	PC	4.01
Other (public services)	BBS	6.74
	PC	5.59
GDP at factor cost	BBS	2.73
	PC	3.80

Source: Report of the National Income Commission, BBS, Dhaka, February 1990.

National Accounts data provided by BBS suffer from limitations. It is, however, difficult to judge which set of figures is more reliable. An in-depth study on HES and National Accounts data by sifting available information from various sources is needed to settle this controversy. A comparison between HES data generated through BBS and household-level data collected by BIDS shows yet another source of discrepancy. Referring to Table 3.3, it may be seen that expenditure on protein-rich food as well as vegetables and fruits as percentage of total food expenditure appear to be lower in case of BBS compared to BIDS data. The observed discrepancy may be due to the possible exclusion from the BBS survey (i.e., HES) of certain consumption items which are gathered by rural households directly from the ecological reserves. By contrast, the survey carried out by BIDS collected information on such items. Under the circumstances, the need for developing an alternative data set which would independently capture the recent trend in rural poverty, can hardly be exaggerated. The development of such a data set has been one of the major purposes of the current study.

Methodological Issues

This section presents a consistent time-series estimate of rural poverty based on a uniform methodology since it is difficult to form a definitive idea on such a trend from previous studies. For example, no single study has estimated the head count ratio for each time-point starting from 1973–74 and ending with 1988–89, the last year for which the HES has been carried out by BBS. This obviously necessitates inter-study comparisons—a task rendered difficult due to differences in methodology adopted by these studies in estimating head count ratio.[2]

A methodological point to underscore here is that the calculation of household incomes may be arrived at from two different standpoints, i.e., from the household product account and the household expenditure account. Expenditure data consistently give a higher estimate of household income compared to product account data, the difference being accounted for by expenditure saving activities or simple under-reporting. The current review of poverty trends is with reference to income calculated from the expenditure data.

At this juncture, a few words are in order about the sample design of the current BIDS survey on household expenditure. The income (i.e., product account) module of the survey was executed in all the 62 villages selected for the study, but the expenditure module was implemented in the 16-village cluster sample only on account of the greater time and resources needed in the collection of the data. Expenditure data have been used in the study primarily for comparison with earlier HES carried out by BBS since expenditure data are found to be more sensitive to levels of income and poverty vis-à-vis income data. The reason why this should be so arises from various factors, such as deliberate underreporting of income, underestimation of household-based consumption items as well as non-monetised part of household incomes, etc. To illustrate the point, one may refer to Table 3 2 which compares household income estimates between income and expenditure data. The table shows that the estimated average household income earned from fishery and livestock sectors is 38 per cent higher in case of expenditure data compared to income data. Income from indigenous fuel sector as per income data is just half the amount estimated from the expenditure data. Altogether per capita annual income, according to expenditure data, is about 8 per cent higher than that estimated from income data.

TABLE 3.2
Discrepancy of Annual Household Income Estimates on Account of Certain Consumption Items between Income and Expenditure Data

Broad items/ sectors per income data	Av. income of household as per income data	Av. income of of household as per expenditure data	% difference
Fishery and livestock	1376	1901	38
Fuelwood, indigenous fuel items	656	1312	100
(Per capita annual income, Tk.)	(6415)	(7140)*	8

Source: 16-village survey, Analysis of Poverty Trends Project, BIDS.
* Includes both consumption and investment expenditures.

In order to make expenditure figures of the BIDS survey comparable to earlier HES carried out by BBS, only consumption expenditures have been considered since BBS data exclude information on investment expenditures. Expenditure schedule thus defined includes expenditures on food and non-food basic necessities including clothing, footwear, health, education, recreation and entertainment, transport, etc. Expenditure on food items as a proportion of total consumption expenditure is found to be comparable between the two sources: 70 per cent according to the BIDS survey and 68 per cent as per BBS (See Table 3.3).

TABLE 3.3
Comparison of Estimates between BIDS Household Expenditure Survey and BBS Data

	1989–90 (BIDS)	1988–89 (BBS)
1. Expenditure on food as per cent of total consumption expenditure	69.7	67.6
2. Expenditure on cereals as per cent of total food expenditure	41.8	52.8
3. Expenditure on protein-rich food as per cent of total food expenditure	18.5	14.3
4. Expenditure on pulses as per cent of total food expenditure	3.6	3.6
5. Expenditure on edible oil, fat sugar, etc., as per cent of total food expenditure	6.0	5.3
6. Expenditure on spices and condiments as per cent of total food expenditure	5.6	6.0
7. Expenditure on vegetables and fruits as per cent of total food expenditure	16.4	9.8
8. Expenditure on tobacco, betal leaf, etc., as per cent of total food expenditure	4.9	6.4
9. Miscellaneous food items as per cent of total food expenditure	3.2	1.8
10. Total food expenditure	100	100

A sifting of the studies on rural poverty carried out over the last decade shows substantial discrepancies among the head count estimates recorded for the same year (see Table 3.4). The major source of discrepancy is due to the choice of prices by which the normative food consumple bundle is converted into poverty lines. Most of the previous studies used urban retail prices for the food items in the consumption bundle and then used a discount rate to

TABLE 3.4
Variations in the Rural Head Count Ratios amongst the Previous Studies
(Figures indicate percentage of rural population below poverty)

	Ahmad and Hossain (1984)	Islam and Khan (1986)	Muqtada (1986)	Rahman and Haque (1988)	Hossain (1989)	Official estimates by the BBS (1988)
1973–74	55.7	47.7	55.9	65.27	77.3	82.9
1976–77	61.1	62.3	68.2	–	–	–
1977–78	67.9	–	–	–	–	–
1978–79	–	–	68.7	–	–	–
1981–82	–	–	–	79.12	77.8	73.8
1983–84	–	–	–	49.81	52.1	57.0
1985–86	–	–	–	47.08	49.9	51.0

Notes: 1. All the estimates pertaining to head count measures are carried out on the basis of HES data generated by the Bangladesh Bureau of Statistics.
2. 'Official estimates' of head count ratios have been compiled from the *Report of the Bangladesh Household Expenditure Survey* (Various volumes) published under the auspices of the BBS.

generate rural retail price levels.[3] A movement in urban prices out of line with rural prices may generate unpredictable fluctuations in the trend of the poverty line which may result in conflicting trends in rural poverty. A more important problem of using prices from the source other than the HES relates to the treatment of the generic items, such as fish, meat pulses and vegetables. A poor household may go for an inferior species within the broad generic item[4] in order to reduce the unit cost of calories in its food basket. So its implicit price for a generic item may be lower than for a higher-income household. Use of a standard price for a standard food item to represent the generic group will fail to capture these realities. The main point of methodological departure from the earlier studies is that prices used for costing the minimum diet were derived from the information on consumption of goods in physical quantities and values in HES itself. The estimates give substantially lower prices for fish, meat and pulses than those used by earlier studies in estimating poverty lines. Because of this one may expect that our estimates of poverty line expenditure and head count ratio of poverty would be lower compared to earlier studies.

Trend in Rural Head Count Ratio

A poverty line (expenditure level) has been computed on the basis of a per capita minimum diet of 2112 calories to which was added a 30 per cent allowance of non-food basic needs[5] (see Table 3.5 and 3.6 for details). Persons whose aggregate expenditure falls below the normative poverty line are defined as the absolute poor. Per capita expenditure data are available for six years, namely, 1973–74, 1981–82, 1983–84, 1985–86, 1988–89 and 1989–90. Once the respective poverty lines are specified, the corresponding head count ratios can be calculated. Table 3.7 reports on changes in the level of head count ratio which is the most common measure for capturing trends in absolute poverty. Head count ratios are computed on a per capita basis. It should be noted that, given the aforementioned limitations of the BBS data, one would be more concerned in this section with the *broad directionality of changes* in the level of absolute poverty rather than in explaining the quantitative fluctuations in its *magnitude*.

The estimates presented in Tables 3.7 and 3.8 show that during the two and a half decade, the poverty situation has improved only marginally by 6 percentage points (from 44 per cent in 1963–64 to 38 per cent in 1989–90). There was however, considerable fluctuation in the incidence of poverty around this horizontal trend line. (Figure 3.2). The poverty situation deteriorated sharply in the immediate post-independence period due to the destruction of productive capacity caused by the War of Liberation, dislocation in the economy due to large-scale migration and resettlement of people, and severe droughts and floods in the 1972–74 period. Further aggravation occurred due to the famine and consequent disinvestment of assets by the low income groups during the 1974–76 period.[6] Thereafter, there was a reversal and the head count ratio started declining in the late seventies (since 1978–79) and this trend continued upto the mid-eighties and almost reached the pre-independence level. The situation took a turn for the worse again in 1988–89 which was a bad agricultural year resulting in a rising head count ratio. This deterioration was mainly due to the adverse impact of the 1988 floods, the severest one in living memory. However, the rural economy appears to have recovered fast from the adverse impact of the natural disaster and during the period

TABLE 3.5
Rural Consumer Prices

	Per capita Normative Daily Requirement		Rural Consumer Prices (Tk/Kg)					
	(calorie)	(gm)	1973-74	1981-82	1983-84	1985-86	1988-89	1989-90
Rice	1386	397	2.82	5.29	7.52	8.00	10.01	10.21
Wheat	139	40	1.64	3.77	5.42	6.11	7.63	8.06
Pulses	153	40	3.55	9.48	7.48	13.11	16.12	20.43
Milk (Cow)	39	58	1.72	4.70	6.66	8.92	9.95	10.75
Oil (Mustard)	180	20	16.72	29.20	37.08	41.71	40.30	48.39
Meat (Beef)	14	12	5.88	16.93	23.88	34.97	36.44	43.01
Fish	51	48	5.18	9.88	18.31	22.74	23.21	32.26
Potato	26	27	2.58	2.61	3.27	4.17	6.69	6.45
Other vegetables	36	150	1.11	1.53	3.04	3.34	4.33	3.76
Sugar (Gur)	82	20	3.76	7.23	9.71	11.57	14.73	16.13
Fruits (Banana)	6	20	1.57	3.98	5.42	7.40	9.21	9.68
Total (Calorie/gm)	2112	832	–	–	–	–	–	–
Poverty line expenditure on food (Taka per day)			2.42	4.69	6.64	7.80	9.15	10.09
Basic non-food needs (at 30% of expenditures on food)								
Taka per day			0.73	1.41	1.99	2.34	2.74	3.03
Poverty line (Taka per day)			3.15	6.10	8.63	10.14	11.89	13.12
Poverty line (Taka/year)			1150	2227	3150	3701	4340	4790

Table 3.6
Poverty Line for Rural Areas

(in current prices)

Poverty line expenditure (per month)	1973–74	1981–82	1983–84	1985–86	1988–89	1989–90
Per capita (Tk)	94.50	183.00	258.90	304.20	356.70	399.17
Per household (Tk)	555.66	1076.04	1522.33	1788.70	2097.40	2566.66

Table 3.7
Trends in Rural Absolute Poverty

	Percentage of rural population in poverty						
	1963–64 (HES)	1973–74 (HES)	1981–82 (HES)	1983–84 (HES)	1985–86 (HES)	1988–89 (HES)	1989–90 (BIDS)
Per capita expenditure classification	43.6	71.3	65.4	50.0	41.3	43.8	37.5

Table 3.8
Head Count Ratios for Rural Areas According to 'Per Household' Classification

	Percentage of rural population in poverty						
	1973–74 (HES)	1976–77 (HES)	1977–78 (HES)	1978–79 (HES)	1981–82 (HES)	1983–84 (HES)	1985–86 (HES)
Per household expenditure classification	60.35	78.91	77.45	65.87	55.34	46.29	37.27

Note: Head count ratio based on 'per household' classification is not an accurate measure of incidence of poverty. However, per capita expenditure data are not available for 1976–77, 1977–78 and 1978–79 which necessitates re-estimation of head count ratios for the successive years on a 'per household' basis.

which immediately followed, there has been a resurgence of development activities thanks to the survival efforts of the peoples themselves.[7] Consequently, one observes a gradual improvement in the head count ratio since 1988–89 which stands at 38 per cent by 1989–90 (Figure 3.1).

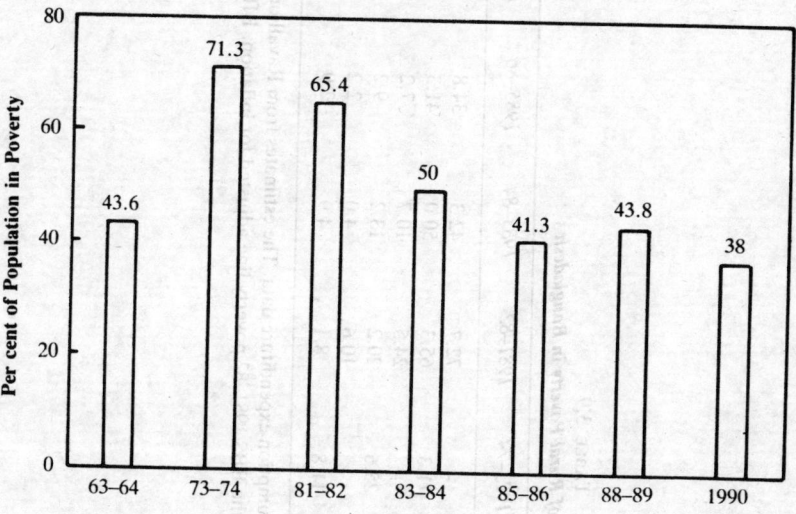

FIGURE 3.1
Trend in Rural Absolute Poverty as per Uniform Method of Calculation
(per capita expenditure classification)

The head count measure is, however, insensitive to changes in the distribution of income among the poor and to the absolute level of income deprivation. The Foster-Greer-Thorbecke (FGT) measures of poverty do not suffer from this deficiency. The FGT estimates are presented in Table 3.9. The trend of the FGT poverty gap as well as distributionally sensitive measure broadly corresponds to the trend of the head count ratios.

The incidence of poverty in Bangladesh, as revealed in the estimated head count ratio for 1989–90, is still alarming. It is much higher compared to not only the fast growing East Asian countries but also other neighbouring countries of South Asia. The recent estimate of the head count ratio is 23 per cent for Pakistan, 27 per cent for Sri Lanka and 35 per cent for India.

TABLE 3.9
FGT Measures of Rural Poverty in Bangladesh

FGT Measures	Source	1973–74	1981–82	1983–84	1985–86	1988–89	1989–90
Head Count, P(O)	Ravallion (1990)	–	72.7	42.3	34.8	–	–
	BIDS	71.3	65.3	50.0	41.3	43.8	37.5
FGT Poverty Gap, P(1)	Ravallion (1990)	–	24.5	10.7	7.2	–	–
	BIDS	25.6	20.2	13.2	9.2	10.8	9.0
Distributionally Sensitive Measure, P(2)	Ravallion (1990)	–	10.6	4.0	2.2	–	–
	BIDS	11.8	8.1	4.9	2.9	3.7	3.2

Sources and Notes: All calculations are based on per capita consumption expenditure data. The estimates from Ravallion (1990) are based on per capita consumption expenditure data using the BBS 1981–82 poverty line adjusted for inflation. BIDS estimates are derived from the present study.

Seasonal Dimension to Rural Poverty

So far the focus of the discussion has been on inter-year fluctuation in rural head count ratios. Besides inter-year fluctuations in poverty ratios between 'good' and 'bad' agricultural years, the issue of intra-year fluctuation in head count ratio between 'peak' and 'slack' agricultural seasons is also an important aspect of poverty monitoring. This aspect of rural poverty has seldom been documented in Bangladesh largely due to lack of seasonal data. Unpublished HES data for 1988–89 provides a unique opportunity to measure the extent of fluctuation in rural head count ratio across different quarters of a year. As may be seen from Table 3.10, the rural head count ratio is at its maximum during the second quarter

TABLE 3.10
Seasonal Variation in Rural Head Count Ratio, 1988–89

First quarter (July–Sept. 1988)	Second quarter (Oct.–Dec. 1988)	Third quarter (Jan.–March 1989)	Fourth quarter (April–June 1989)	All seasons
44.5	51.1	46.6	33.0	43.7

Source: Estimated from unpublished HES for 1988–89 carried out by BBS.

(October–December) which is a 'slack' season and at its lowest in the fourth quarter (April–June) which coincides with the period of the boro harvest (Figure 3.2). The year 1988–89, however, was a flood year and this fact should be kept in mind while analysing the extent of fluctuation between seasons. The first quarter represents the very period when the 1988 floods hit the country. The adverse impact of the floods was particularly severe on rural households not so much during the first quarter as in the immediate post flood months (October–December 1988). The latter coincided with the period which is known as the agricultural slack season even in normal years. Distress sales of land went up to alarming proportions during these months,[8] the health and sanitary situation deteriorated severely with the spread of epidemic diseases, pressures mounted with demand for launching relief and food-for-works type activities on a much more wider scale compared to routine lean season relief

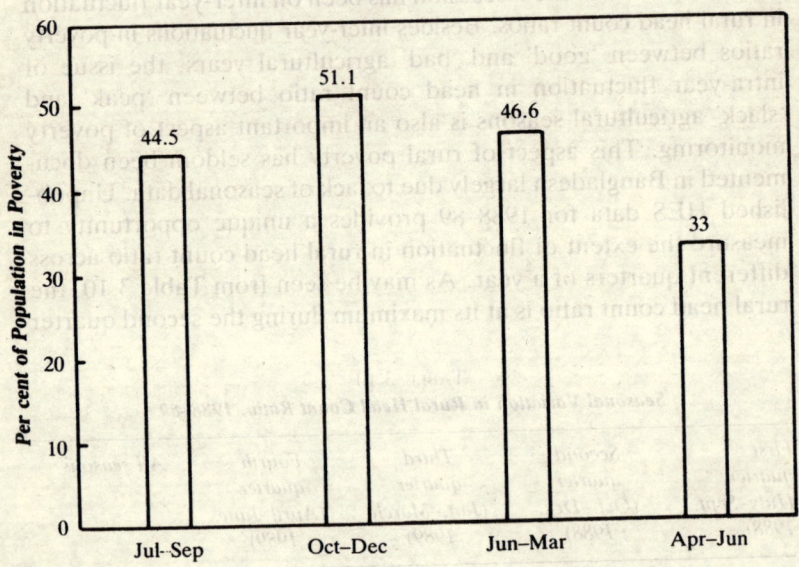

FIGURE 3.2
Seasonal Trend in Rural Head Count Ratio

operations done in 'normal' years. All these processes were associated with decline in purchasing power of the vulnerable segment of rural population as reflected in the rising poverty ratio in the second quarter. There had been a sharp increase (by about 7 percentage points) in absolute poverty: from 44 per cent in the first quarter to 51 per cent in the second quarter. By the end of the third quarter (January–March 1989), there were already clear signs of recovery in the rural economy with a concommitant downward trend in the head count ratio to 47 per cent.[9] The fourth quarter (April–June 1989) witnessed a bumper boro harvest leading to a further drop in the head count to 33 per cent.

Admittedly, it is difficult to form an idea of *routine* seasonal fluctuations in 'normal' years. The fluctuation in seasonal head count ratio during 1988–89 were quite significant due to sudden ecological shocks; the difference between the 'crest' and the 'trough' was as high as 18 per cent within a year which would be lower in case of 'normal' agricultural year. But the lessons may be similar. Seasonal variations in poverty between 'peak' and 'slack' seasons do matter, and specially in the crisis-prone years with strong implications for public action and risk insurance.

Notes

1. Per capita real rural income growth as per HES was estimated to be 1.74 per cent during the aforementioned period. The matched figures is not available from national accounts.
2. These studies can be broadly grouped into two categories: some studies have choosen the 'fixed-bundle' approach while others have preferred the 'graph-fitting' method. If one concentrates on studies based on the 'fixed-bundle' approach only, then it would appear that the set of prices to be used for costing of the 'fixed-bundle' constitutes the major source of discrepancy amongst head count estimates. For a review of approaches in previous studies on rural poverty, 'The Face of Rural Poverty in Bangladesh: Trends and Insights' (mimeo.), BIDS, 1990 (chapter 1).
3. Ahmed and Hossain (1984) assumed that the cost of living in rural areas would be 20 per cent lower than that for urban areas. Muqtada (1986) used prices of the rural low-income groups without mentioning how these prices were derived. Rahman and Haque (1988) used urban retail prices and then deflated it by a margin of 10 per cent to arrive at rural consumer prices.
4. The normative consumption bundle specified the amount of food for broad generic items such as pulses, fish, vegetables, etc. The BBS publishes urban retail prices only for Rohu fish which is an expensive fish item. While deriving poverty line expenditure the earlier studies on poverty used this price since prices for other fish items are not available. Similarly costing for vegetables were carried out by using prices for potato and of pulses by price of *masur* which is of superior quality.
5. Considerable discrepancy exists in the literature regarding the provision of non-food basic needs for estimating the poverty line. Ahmed and Hossain (1984) adds 15 per cent to the cost of food items, while most other studies used 20 per cent. A closer look at the HES data reveals that for an average household the proportion of non-food basic needs in total expenditure steadily increased over time from 25 per cent in 1973–74 to 35 per cent in 1985–86. This, however, includes the imputed value of owner occupied housing. In view of this information we have considered 30 per cent of expenditure on food as reasonable provision for non-food basic needs at poverty level income.
6. For insights into the process leading to disinvestment of assets by the low income group during the post-famine period, see Alamgir (1978).
7. For a review of impact of 1988 flood on the rural economy, see Hossain (1990).

8. By December 1988, the GOB had to respond to sudden increase in the incidence of distress land sales by proclaiming a legal ban on the registration of all land transactions through purchases and sales. This measure, however, was met without much of a success and soon the ban was lifted out.
9. It may be noted that the drop in the head count ratio at the end of the third quarter was less than would have been expected in normal years. Usually the end of the third quarter coincides with the period of harvest of aman crop. However, the aman crop output during 1988–89 was also affected by the flood.

References

Alamgir, M., 1978, *Bangladesh: A Case of Below Poverty Level Equilibrium Trap*, BIDS, Dhaka.

Hossain, M., 1989, 'Recent Development Trends in the Rural Economy of Bangladesh', *The Bangladesh Unnayan Samiksha*, Vol. 6, BIDS, Dhaka.

Islam, I. and **H. Khan**, 1986, 'Income Inequality, Poverty and Socio-economic Development in Bangladesh: An Empirical Investigation', *Bangladesh Development Studies*, Vol. 14, No. 2.

Jodha, N.S., 1988, 'Poverty Debate in India: A Minority View', *Economic and Political Weekly*, November, (Special Number).

Kabeer, N., 1989, *Monitoring Poverty as if Gender Mattered: A Methodology for Rural Bangladesh*, Discussion Paper No. 255, Institute of Development Studies, Sussex.

Muqtada, M., 1986, 'Poverty and Inequality: Trends and Causes', in Islam R. and Muqtada M. (ed.), *Bangladesh—Selected Issues in Employment and Development*, ILO-ARTEP, New Delhi.

Rahman, A. and **T. Haque**, 1988, *Poverty and Inequality in Bangladesh in the Eighties: An Analysis of Some Recent Evidence*, Research Report No. 91, BIDS, Dhaka.

Rahman, H.Z., 1988, *Monitoring Rural Poverty; Conceptual Framework and Organisational Options*, BIDS, Dhaka.

Ravallion, M., 1990, 'The Challenging Arithmetic of Poverty in Bangladesh,' *The Bangladesh Development Studies*, Vol. 18, No. 3.

Report of the Task Forces on Bangladesh Development Strategies for the 1990s, Vol. 1, 1991, University Press Limited, 1991.

Report on the Household Expenditure Survey, 1973/74, 1981/82, 1983/84, 1985/86, Bureau of Statistics, Dhaka.

Statistical Yearbook, 1973/74, 1981/82, 1983/84, 1985/86, 1986/87, Bangladesh Bureau of Statistics, Dhaka.

II

Dimensions of Poverty

4

Structure and Distribution of Household Income and Income Dimensions of Poverty

MAHABUB HOSSAIN

Introduction

It is difficult to estimate rural incomes accurately because most households are self-employed and very few keep records. Many households are also engaged in expenditure-saving activities, such as producing fruits and vegetables in kitchen gardens, rearing poultry and livestock, and manufacturing personal household effects for consumption of members. Respondents often under report incomes from such self-employed activities because they do not consider cost-saving as income. Only detailed recording of consumption and expenditures can capture income from these sources. However, such recording is extremely tedious and time-consuming. In the present survey we have estimated annual income from the production account for the entire sample, while an expenditure account module was additionally applied on a sub-sample of 16 villages to estimate income from the expenditure account. It is found that the income estimate from the product account is substantially lower than the estimate of income obtained from the expenditure account, the difference being substantially accounted for by cost-saving[1] activities. Since the cost-saving activities are undertaken more by the lower income groups, the degree of income inequality and poverty estimated from the income data used here may be biased upwards.

The Structure of Household Income

The estimate of household income and its composition is reported in Table 4.1. The table also shows the sources of income for farm and non-farm households separately. The average income for the sample households for 1989–90 is estimated at Tk 37,000. The average size of the household is found to be 6.19. So the per capita rural income is estimated at Tk 6017, equivalent to about US $172.

Farm households, defined as those who cultivate some land, comprise about 66 per cent of the total sample. The annual income for these households is estimated at about Tk 46,000 (per capita income US $200). The remaining 34 per cent of the households did not cultivate any land, but they owned on average 0.60 acres including the homestead. Among this group, marginal landowners rent out their tiny holding and are engaged in full time non-agricultural activities. Others sell their labour services in the market. The average annual income for this group is estimated at about Tk 21,000 (per capita income, US $110), which is about 55 per cent lower than the income of farm households.

Agricultural sources account for 63 per cent of the total household income (Figure 4.1). Crop cultivation which is dependent on ownership of agricultural land accounts for only 40 per cent of the total income for all rural households, and 46 per cent in case of farm households. An important implication of this finding is that although ownership of land is highly concentrated, land is no longer an overriding determinant of income inequality in rural Bangladesh. Kitchen gardening and non-crop agriculture which are carried out mostly in the homestead, account for about 16 per cent of total income. About 40 per cent of income comes from crop cultivation. As stated earlier, this part of the rural income is under estimated by our survey so the importance of this source may be even higher. For non-farm households who are land-poor, this source accounts for 11.5 per cent of the total income. Nearly

TABLE 4.1
Rural Household Income and its Composition

Sources of income	All households		Farm households		Non-farm households	
	Tk per annum	%	Tk per annum	%	Tk per annum	%
Agriculture:	23,271	62.5	30,736	67.2	8,893	42.4
Crop cultivation	14,821	39.8	20,818	45.5	3,272	15.6
Kitchen garden	2,422	6.5	3,073	6.7	1,169	5.6
Non-crop agriculture	3,688	9.9	4,962	10.9	1,236	5.9
Agricultural wage	2,339	6.3	1,883	4.1	3,216	15.4
Non-agriculture:	11,768	31.5	12,496	27.3	10,363	49.5
Industry	1,809	4.9	1,998	4.4	1,441	6.9
Trade	5,306	14.2	5,923	13.0	4,120	19.7
Services	2,642	7.1	2,812	6.2	2,314	11.0
Transport and construction	929	2.5	864	1.9	1,054	5.0
Non-agricultural wage	1,082	2.9	899	2.0	1,434	6.9
Remittances	2,208	5.9	2,478	5.4	1,695	8.1
Total income	37,247	100.0	45,710	100.0	20,951	100.0

Source: Analysis of Poverty Trends Project, BIDS: 62 Village Survey.

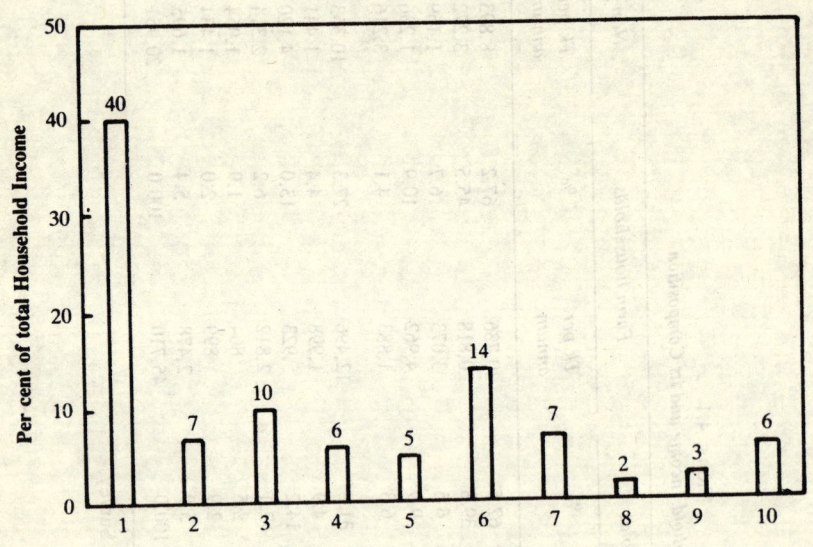

FIGURE 4.1
Composition of Rural Income
(All Households)

Note: 1 = Crop cultivation   6 = Trade
      2 = Kitchen garden   7 = Services
      3 = Non-crop agri.   8 = Transport/Construction
      4 = Agri., wage   9 = Non-agri. wage
      5 = Industry   10 = Remittances

three-fourths of this income is earned by working as agricultural wage labourers. Since land is scarce and the scope for redistribution of land to the poor through land reform is limited, policies and strategies for alleviation of rural poverty should contain elements to improve the productivity and earnings from home based agriculture.

Agricultural wage accounts for 6.3 per cent and non-agricultural wage another 2.9 per cent of the total incomes of rural households. This shows the relative unimportance of the labour market as a source of livelihood for rural households. Even non-farm households earn only 22 per cent of their incomes by selling labour services in the market; 15 per cent from agricultural labour market and 7 per cent from non-agricultural labour market. This suggests that increasing the wage rate may not make a substantial contribution to increasing the income of the land-poor households.

Non-agricultural activities, such as rural processing and manufacturing, trade, transport, construction and community and personal services are important sources of rural incomes. These comprise 38 per cent of total income for the sample households; 33 per cent of the farm households and 58 per cent for the non-farm households. Nearly 6 per cent of the total income is earned from remittances sent by migrant members living in towns and abroad. Rural processing and manufacturing is often regarded as the principal rural non-agricultural activity. This is not found to be the case from our survey. The income from rural industrial activities account for only 5 per cent of the total household income, and only 13 per cent of non-agricultural incomes. Even for non-farm households, rural industry accounts for only 12 per cent of the total income.

The major sources of rural non-agricultural income are trade and services. Trade accounts for 14 per cent of total rural incomes and nearly two-fifths of the non-agricultural incomes. The non-farm households derive nearly 20 per cent of the total income from trade, which is their single most important source of income. Services (excluding domestic service which is included in non-agricultural wage) account for another 7 per cent of rural incomes. The capacity of the household to earn income from trade and services depend on their access to capital and investment on human resource development. Households with ownership of assets (such as land), literate family members and better access to financial institutions have the capacity to earn more from these sources.

Income Inequality

The sample households have been ranked on the basis of per capita income, and the income shares of the successive decile groups have been estimated in order to see the pattern of income distribution for the sample households. A similar exercise has also been done by ranking households with respect to per capita land ownership. The results are used to derive Lorenz curves for total income as well as for agricultural and non-agricultural incomes. These are presented in Figures 4.2 to 4.5. A summary of the findings may be reviewed from Table 4.2 and 4.3.

The income distribution is found fairly unequal. The top 10 per cent of the households in the income scale earn about 32 per cent of the income, while the bottom 40 per cent earn only 15 per cent. The gini concentration ratio of per capita income is estimated at 0.43 (Table 4.2). The distribution of income is however less unequal than the distribution of land. The top 10 per cent of the households in the per capita land ownership scale, control about 45 per cent of the total land while the bottom 40 per cent own only 3 per cent. The gini ratio for land ownership is estimated at 0.65 (Table 4.3).

The inequality of agricultural income is moderated by several factors. In the agricultural sector, some of the income is transferred from the land-rich to the land-poor through the operation of the labour and tenancy markets. The agricultural wage labourers belong mostly to households owning less than 1.5 acres of land. In the tenancy market, land is transferred from large to small and marginal owners. Thus, although the bottom 40 per cent of the households in the land ownership scale own 3 per cent of the total land, they earn 16 per cent of total agricultural incomes (Table 4.2).

The most important factor behind the moderation of rural income inequality is, however the income from non-agricultural sources. The bottom 40 per cent in the land ownership scale earn nearly 32 per cent of the non-agricultural incomes, while the top 10 per cent earns only 15 per cent (Table 4.3). The concentration ratio of non-agricultural income across the land ownership scale is estimated at only 0.16. Thus, non-agricultural incomes is fairly equally distributed across the land ownership group. Land-poor households who manage to participate in non-agricultural activities move up in the per capita income ladder. This is the reason why non-agricultural income is found to be highly unequally distributed when measured in the per capita income scale (Table 4.2). The concentration ratio is estimated at 0.47. Thus, access to non-agricultural employment provides scope for income mobility for the land-poor households. An implication of this finding is that the

Structure and Distribution of Household Income • 63

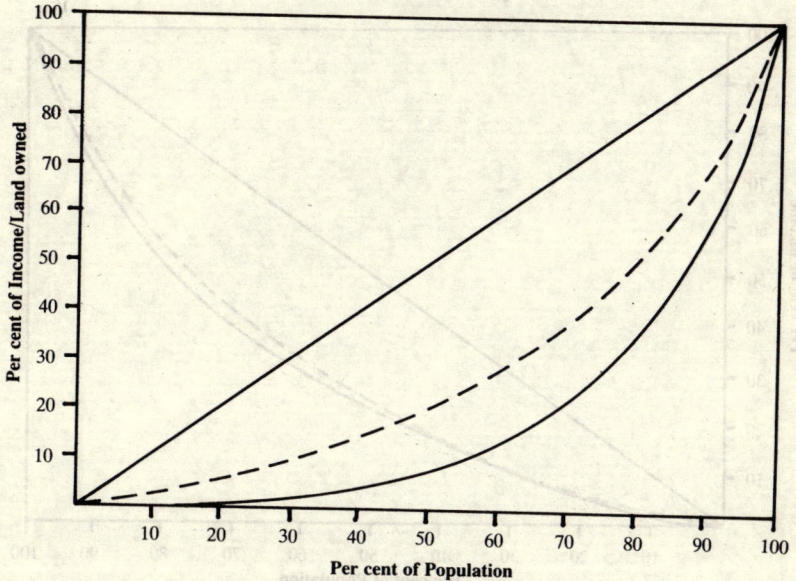

FIGURE 4.2
Concentration of Per Capita Income and Landownership, 1989–90

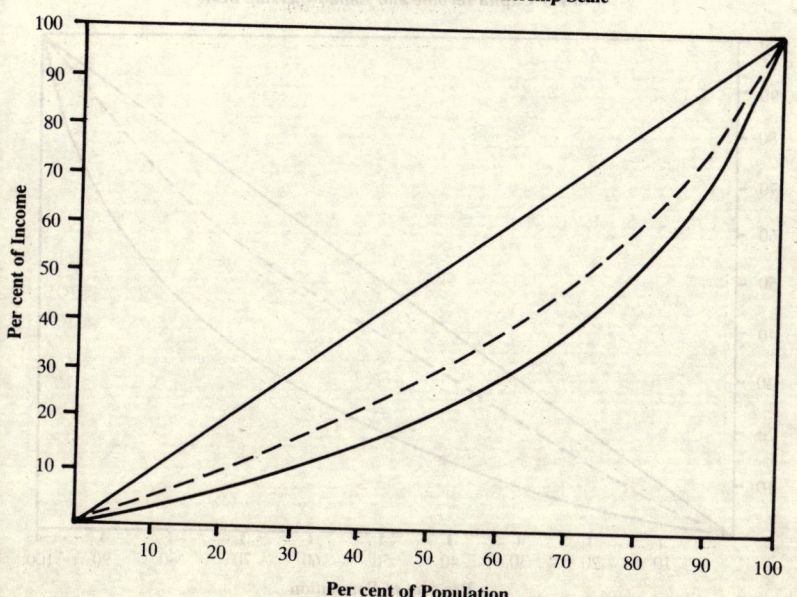

FIGURE 4.3
Concentration of Household Income in Per Capita Income and Landownership Scale

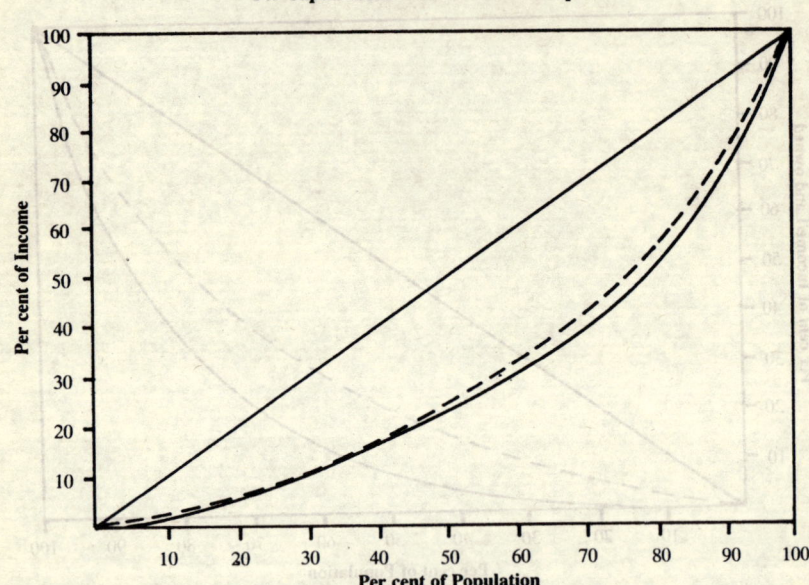

FIGURE 4.4
*Concentration of Agricultural Incomes in
Per Capita Income and Landownership Scale*

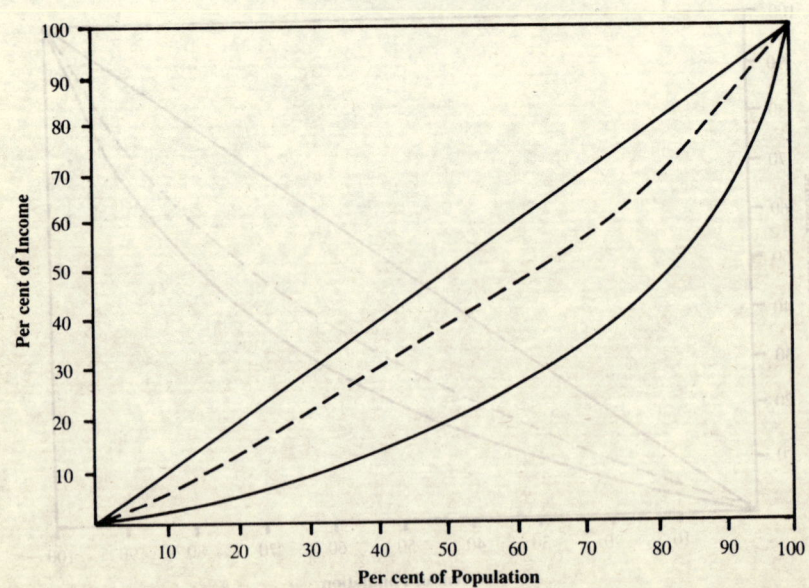

FIGURE 4.5
*Concentration of Non-agricultural Incomes
in Per Capita Income and Landownership Scale*

TABLE 4.2
Degree of Inequality in the Distribution of Income and Land: Per Capita Income Scale, 1989-90

(Figures in % of total)

Income Groups	Household income			Per capita	
	Agriculture	Non-agriculture	Total	Income owned	Land
Bottom 40%	15.9	13.2	14.8	15.2	14.8
Middle 40%	37.3	33.3	35.8	36.3	36.5
Top 10%	30.8	36.1	32.9	32.2	32.4
Top 5%	20.2	25.2	22.1	21.3	20.1
Concentration ratio	0.41	0.47	0.43	0.43	0.43

Source: Analysis of Poverty Trends Project, BIDS: 62 Village Survey.

TABLE 4.3
Degree of Inequality in the Distribution of Income and Land: Per Capita Land Ownership Scale, 1989-90

(Figures in % of total)

Income Groups	Household income			Per capita	
	Agriculture	Non-agriculture	Total	Income owned	Land
Bottom 40%	15.5	31.5	21.9	24.4	2.8
Middle 40%	41.0	36.6	38.6	37.0	31.4
Top 10%	25.3	15.0	21.7	23.0	45.0
Top 5%	15.2	10.2	13.0	14.7	29.7
Concentration ratio	0.36	0.16	0.28	0.26	0.65

Source: Analysis of Poverty Trends Project, BIDS: 62 Village Survey.

anti-poverty strategy and policies should contain elements that empower landless and marginal farmers to participate in the non-agricultural sector.

The Incidence of Poverty

This section analyses the income data collected from 62 villages to measure the incidence of poverty for various socioeconomic groups and to asses the characteristics of the poor vis-à-vis the non-poor households. The limitations of the income data have already been mentioned in earlier sections. The income of the poor households is understated more than that for the non-poor group because of the failure to capture income from expenditure-saving activities. So *not* only the level of poverty measured from this data set would be biased upwards, the income differentials between the poor and non-poor households would also be over stated. Given these limitations, the *direction* of poverty differences suggested by the estimates presented here is more meaningful than the *absolute* differences in poverty levels.

The methodology used in estimating poverty, more specifically the head count ratio, is presented in chapter 3. We have used Tk 4790 per person per annum as the cut-off line of moderate poverty. This provides for a calorie intake of 2112 per capita per day derived from a food intake of 832 grams including consumption of 48 grams of fish, 12 grams of meat, 20 grams of oil and 20 grams of sugar per capita per day (based on a local assessment for Bangladesh made by FAO adjusting for age and sex). It also provides for 30 per cent additional expenditure for meeting non-food basic needs. It is however observed that the rural poor acquire hardly any rich food, such as milk, meat, fish, oil and sugar from the market. If they consume, the consumption is from self-production, such as rearing of poultry and goats or fishing from common property creeks, canals and rivers. These are not captured in the income data. In view of these realities, we have identified another poverty line by taking the expenditure on normative requirement of grains, pulses, potato and vegetables, and adding 30 per cent over it for meeting the non-food basic needs. This provides for an intake of 64 grams of food and 1740 calories per capita per day, which is about 82 per cent of the normative requirement for moderate poverty. The estimated expenditure comes to Tk 2810 per capita per annum, which is termed as the cut-off line of extreme poverty. Households having per capita income below this level may be considered the 'hard core' poor.

The estimates of the head count ratio obtained by using the above methodology is presented in Table 4.4. The table also presents the estimates of poverty obtained from another BIDS survey carried out on the same sample in 1987–88, when the rural economy was ravaged by a disastrous flood. It will be seen that

TABLE 4.4
Poverty Lines and Head-Count Ratio: Estimates from Income Data, 1987–88 and 1989–90

Indicator	Extreme Poverty		Extreme and Moderate Poverty	
	1987–88	1989–90	1987–88	1989–90
Poverty line expenditure (Tk per capita per annum)	2460	2810	4300	4790
Head count ratio (per cent of population)	25.8	27.5	60.1	55.4

Source: Analysis of Poverty Trends Project, BIDS: 62 Village Survey.

households containing about 55 per cent of the population had inadequate income to meet the poverty line expenditure. This may be contrasted with 38 per cent poor households estimated from direct information on household consumption expenditure. This suggests that expenditure-saving activities carried out around the homestead using surplus family labour and drawing on ecological common property reserves are quite important in the alleviation of poverty. Households with per capita income below the line of extreme poverty contain nearly 26 per cent of the total population. This group may be termed as the 'hard core' poor.

During the course of the survey, we tried to ascertain the self-evaluation of the respondents regarding poverty status. Households containing 21 per cent of the population evaluated themselves as those suffering from chronic food deficit (Table 4.5). According to our objective estimate, 55 per cent of these households in 1989–90 could be termed as poor and 28 per cent 'hard core' poor. Households evaluating themselves as self-sufficient or solvent contain nearly 30 per cent of the total population. A strong correlation is found between the objective estimate of poverty obtained from survey data and the self-evaluation done by the respondents themselves.

The incidence of poverty at the disaggregated regional level may be reviewed from Table 4.6 (Figure 4.6). There is not much variation in poverty levels across divisions. The proportion of poor population is found to be about 53 per cent in Khulna and Rajshahi

TABLE 4.5
Incidence of Poverty by Self-Evaluation Indicator

Self-evaluation	Per cent of category	Extreme poverty population 1989–90	Extreme and moderate poverty 1989–90
Chronic deficit	20.8	51.4	81.4
Occasional deficit	49.6	27.3	59.6
Self-sufficient	19.1	15.2	40.3
Surplus	10.4	3.4	10.8
Total	100.0	60.1	55.4

Source: Analysis of Poverty Trends Project, BIDS: 62 Village Survey.

TABLE 4.6
Incidence of Poverty by Geographical Division, 1989–90

Divisions	Extreme poverty	Moderate poverty	Extreme and moderate Poverty	Amount of land owned (acre)
Chittagong	30.2	27.2	57.4	1.43
Dhaka	27.0	30.4	57.4	1.30
Rajshahi	28.3	25.2	53.5	1.76
Khulna	24.5	28.4	52.9	1.83

Source: Analysis of Poverty Trends Project, BIDS: 62 Village Survey.

divisions and at 57 per cent in Dhaka and Chittagong divisions. The incidence of 'hard core' poverty is the least in Khulna division (25 per cent) and the highest in Chittagong division (30 per cent). It appears from the estimate that poverty is related to land endowments. Khulna division has the highest average size of land holding and the Chittagong division the lowest.

The sample villages have also been classified into environmental groups and the incidence of poverty have been estimated for them. The results may be seen from Table 4.7 (Figure 4.7). The incidence of poverty is found highest in flood-prone villages (63 per cent). This group includes villages where more than 50 per cent of the land is flooded at a depth of 30 cm during the peak monsoon season. The major portion of the land in these villages is not suitable for growing the dwarf modern varieties of rice during the

Structure and Distribution of Household Income • 69

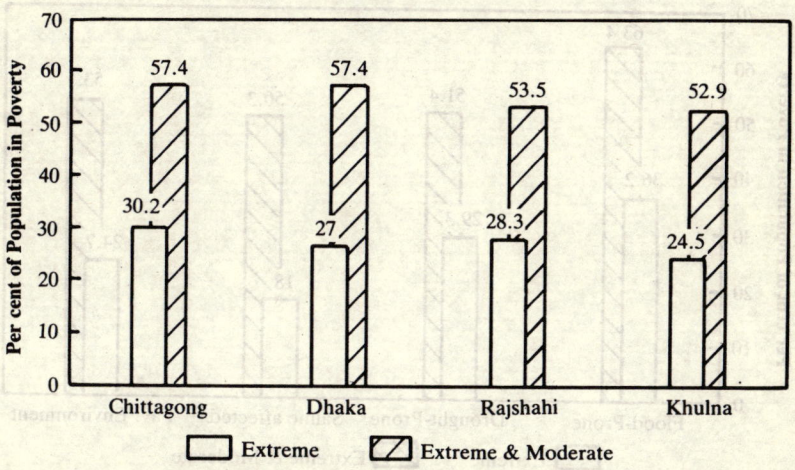

FIGURE 4.6
Regional Variation in Moderate and Extreme Poverty (Division-wise)

TABLE 4.7
Incidence of Poverty by Production Environments, 1989–90

Production environments	Extreme poverty	Moderate poverty	Extreme and moderate poverty	Amount of land owned (acre)
Unfavourable				
Flood-prone	35.2	28.2	63.4	1.61
Drought-prone	29.3	24.7	54.0	1.76
Saline affected	18.0	32.3	50.3	1.71
Favourable environments	24.7	28.4	53.1	1.39

Source: Analysis of Poverty Trends Project, BIDS: 62 Village Survey.

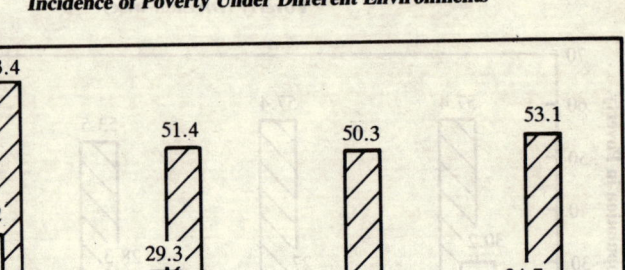

FIGURE 4.7
Incidence of Poverty Under Different Environments

monsoon season. Even traditional rice varieties may suffer from being temporarily submerged during high rain and abnormal floods. The highest incidence of poverty in these villages is because the production environment constraints diffusion of the modern agricultural technology. The drought-prone and the saline affected villages also have unfavourable production environments but the incidence of poverty is almost similar to villages with favourable production environments. In fact the saline affected coastal villages have the lowest incidence of 'hard core' poor. The main reason behind this is that the saline affected and the drought-prone villages have higher land endowments than the other two groups.

Changes in Poverty Situation during the Period 1987-90

The overall poverty situation seems to have improved somewhat in 1989-90 compared to 1987-88, when (according to the income estimate) nearly 60 per cent of the population lived below the poverty line (Table 4.4). The improvement however occurred mostly for the moderate poor whose number fell from 34 to 27 per cent. The proportion of the 'hard core' poor did not decline. Rather it increased marginally. The deterioration in extreme poverty is found highly pronounced for the landless and marginal landowners, agricultural and non-agricultural wage labourers. The deterioration was also experienced by households who evaluated themselves as those suffering from chronic food deficit. The improvement in the poverty situation was noted mostly for the medium and large cultivator households.

This change in the poverty situation may be explained by the abnormal economic situation prevailing in 1987-88. The loss in crop production due to the disastrous floods reduced the income of the farm households. The larger landowners were obviously more seriously affected. So the extent of poverty was above the normal level for cultivator households. With normalcy restored in the 1989-90 production year, the cultivator households have improved their economic position.

The situation for the poor households was quite the opposite. In response to the floods, the government increased allocation of resources for the targetted employment generation programmes, such as Vulnerable Group Development (VGD) and Food For Works (FFW) in order to provide relief to the poor. The allocation of food aid under these programme was around 700,000 tons of foodgrains in 1985 and 1986. The allocation was raised to 1.05 million tons in 1987-88 and further to 1.42 million tons in 1988-89 (Table 4.8). This should have generated additional employment and income for workers selling manual labour. At the same time the prices were kept low through additional imports of foodgrains through commercial channels and maintaining large foodgrain stocks. Since the poor spend a larger proportion of their income on food compared to the non-poor households, the low prices have had a positive effect on easing 'hard core' poverty. The allocation

TABLE 4.8
Allocation of Food for Work and Targetted Employment Generation Programme
(Figures in 000' MT)

Year	Food for work	Vulnerable group development programme	Total
1984–85	572	231	803
1985–86	500	154	654
1986–87	534	177	711
1987–88	743	310	1053
1988–89	917	507	1424
1989–90	600	186	786

Source: World Food Programme, *Bangladesh Foodgrain Forecast*, Dhaka, March 1991.

TABLE 4.9
Trends in Real Wage Rate, 1973–74 to 1990

Year	Money wages (Tk/person/day)	Prices of coarse rice (Tk/Kg)	Coarse rice equivalent wage (Kg)
1973–74	6.69	2.83	2.36
1981–82	15.48	6.64	2.33
1983–84	19.58	6.69	2.93
1985–86	29.83	7.25	4.09
1986–87	32.56	8.54	3.81
1987	31.10	9.19	3.50
1988	32.75	9.39	3.48
January 1991	36.05	10.97 (10.11)	3.29 (3.56)

Source: Bangladesh Bureau of Statistics upto 1986–87 and BIDS field survey for 1987, 1989 and 1991.
Note: The figures within brackets are averages for July 1989 to March 1991.

to the targeted employment generation programme was restored to normal levels in 1989–90 (786,000 tons). The prices of foodgrains started increasing which had an adverse effect on real wages. The trend in real wages shows that it increased rapidly during the 1981–87 period. After that real wages had a downward trend (Table 4.9).

Note

1. For details on cost-saving activities, see, chapter 13.

References

Alamgir, M., 1978, *Bangladesh: A Case of Below Poverty Level Equilibrium Trap*, BIDS.
Sen, Binayak et al. 1990. *The Face of Rural Poverty in Bangladesh*, 1990, Analysis of Poverty Trends Project, BIDS.
Hossain, M., 1990, 'Natural Calamities, Instability in Production and Food Policy in Bangladesh', *The Bangladesh Development Studies*, Vol. XVIII, No. 4, December 1990.
Rahman, A. and **T. Haque**, 1988, *Poverty and Inequality in Bangladesh in the Eighties: An Analysis of Some Recent Evidence*, Research Report No. 91, BIDS.

5

Nutritional Dimensions of Poverty

OMAR HAIDER CHOWDHURY

Introduction

Poverty rears its ugliest face in terms of hunger and malnourishment. To be free of hunger and malnourishment is the most basic human need. But unfortunately protein-energy malnutrition (PEM) remains the most important public health problem afflicting a large proportion of people in under developed countries, such as Bangladesh. Poverty means the absolute minimum level of living below which the very maintenance of physical health is impaired. We can think of an exogenously defined biologically determined minimum nutritional requirement for the maintenance of physical health to be such a definition of abject poverty. Below this level of living, physical manifestation of hunger and starvation become evident. Thus, poverty defined in terms of nutritional risk is adopted not on the grounds of superiority of this concept but because of its unambiguous characterisation of poverty as well as direct relevance as a policy objective. However, poverty is a multi-dimensional concept. Our definition is intended to complement rather than substitute other concepts used in this study to provide a more realistic and overall picture of poverty in Bangladesh.

Recent studies[1] on poverty situation in Bangladesh seem to have generated more heat than light. These studies raised controversies not only regarding the magnitude of poverty prevailing in the country but also about the changes in its direction during the eighties. In fact, Paul Streeten (1990) has likened the measurement of poverty to the removal of six veils, in which one starts with the outer veil, money income, and arrives via real income, direct measures, and impact indicators to the distribution of the benefits within the household. Our indicators of poverty in terms of nutritional norms falls within the category of direct impact measures. In this, the present study has sought to avoid some of the conceptual and methodological problems that vitiated recent debates on poverty and its intertemporal change in Bangladesh.

Identifying the poor is an important aspect of poverty study concerned with formulation of policies. It should be remembered that the poor are not a homogenous group of people. One group differs from the other in terms of occupation, geographic location, age-sex structure, etc. The interests of different groups in poverty need not necessarily coincide. Therefore, information for measuring poverty will have to be generated for each of these identifiable interest groups. But the unit for generating information for any socioeconomic study is the household. Hence, a very important aspect of poverty problem in poor developing countries, namely, the gender bias in distribution of resources within the household remain unaddressed. But it is increasingly becoming clearer that the weight of poverty falls differentially not only among various socioeconomic classes but also on different age-sex groups within the household. Information on nutritional status is by nature collected on individuals and as such is suitably geared to identifying not only the regional, seasonal and socioeconomic dimensions of poverty, but also the very important age-sex composition of it as well.

Nutritional Indicators of Poverty

Malnutrition describes a wide range of physical conditions starting from deficiency in a single nutrient in an otherwise balanced and adequate diet to inadequate dietary intake in general. Inadequate dietary intake and/or poor absorption or decreased biological utilisation of the intake, triggers off a chain reaction of nutritional deficiencies which cause depletion of body tissues and fluids resulting in loss of body weight and impairment of physical growth, especially among children.

Nutritional status is a complex phenomena for which no single measure is sufficient. Measurement of nutritional status relies on several indicators which are suggestive of the whole. One set of measures compares nutrient intakes against some requirement standards to assess nutritional status. These indicators may be classified as input-based indicators, such as those dependent on dietary intakes. Another set of indicators based on physical manifestation of malnutrition, such as anthropometry, clinical or biochemical symptoms, may be considered as outcome-based indicators. Appropriateness of the measure depends on the purpose of enquiry. In this study our focus is not on malnutrition per se, but to the extent it reflects on poverty. Inadequate food intake as a consequence of poverty leads to protein-energy malnutrition (PEM). PEM also hinders physical growth especially among children. Hence, nutritional short fall (calorie and protein) as well as anthropometric measures will be used as our indicators of poverty.

Data

Nutrition module of the study was conducted on a smaller sample of 16 villages chosen out of the larger sample of 62 villages. Details on the methodology adopted for sample selection is provided in chapter 2. Information for this component of the study was generated by carrying out two rounds of surveys: the first, during July to October of 1990 and the second, from February to April 1991, reflecting respectively lean and peak periods of agricultural activities in rural Bangladesh. Two of the 16 villages in the first round could not be surveyed. One due to hostility of conservative local people who would not allow even female investigators to interview family members of their households. The other village was too remote and backward for female investigators to work satisfactorily. Four of the remaining 14 villages were severely shattered by the devastating cyclone of April 1991 and had to be abandoned for the second round survey. Hence, we were left with 10 of the original 16 villages where both the two rounds of surveys were conducted. It may be noted further that the three highest consuming villages in terms of per capita food intake were among the four that were abandoned in the second round out of the 14 covered in the first round survey. Thus, it may be argued that ultimately we were left with a sample which was not representative of the sample surveyed in the first round, since the richest three villages were dropped in the second round compared to those covered in the first round.

The survey was carried out on 20 carefully selected households in each of the 10 villages. Information was collected at an individual level on anthropometric measures, deitary intake, health status, water supply and sanitation as well as on the socioeconomic backgrounds of the households. Trained male and female investigators took the anthropometric measurements, i.e., weight, height and mid-arm circumference of all members of the household. Age and weaning status, which are necessary for the interpretation of both anthropometric and dietary information, were recorded. Dietary intake of each individual was measured using a one-day weighment plus recall method. Both lifetime episodes of serious diseases for each member of the household and a three-month history of their duration were recorded.

Food Consumption

It is argued that food intake and disease are the immediate determinants of malnutrition. Disease, again depends on physical environment within which people live. Therefore, food as well as non-food physical environment (drinking water, sanitation, medicare facility, etc.) contribute towards the maintenance of a healthy body. An adverse environmental condition in terms of hygiene and sanitation would lead to various diseases in a body and lower the absorptive capacity requiring more food compared to a healthy body to retain the same amount of nutrient. Hence, there seems to be a trade-off between increasing food intake and improving non-food environmental conditions to maintain a healthy body. But such complementarity may disappear altogether when the food intake is below the requirement and the problem is compounded if the physical environment is also not congenial. Therefore, ensuring adequate food is a precondition for physical well-being of an individual.

Dietary Intake

Table 5.1 reports per capita food intake per day in the periods 1962–64, 1975–76, 1981–82 as per country wide nutrition surveys carried out respectively by the Department of Biochemistry, University of Dhaka and published by the US Department of Health, Education and Welfare (DHEW, 1966), the Institute of Nutrition and Food Science (INFS), University of Dhaka in 1982–83[2] and 1990–91[3] and BIDS. According to the table, food intake in 1981–82 has dropped by about 5 per cent since 1975–76 and by around 14 per cent since 1962–64. But Chowdhury (1988), on the basis of a review of various studies on food production, food availability and consumption in Bangladesh for the relevant period, concludes that food intake on a per capita basis fluctuated widely in individual years but on an average stagnated between the early sixties and the early eighties. The food intake figure for 1990–91 shows that it was higher by about 6 per cent compared to that in 1981–82 and lower by around 9 per cent compared to that in 1962–64. If we accept the earlier argument that there is wide yearly fluctuation in food intake in Bangladesh then we may conclude from the evidence provided in Table 5.1 that per capita food intake in general stagnated between the early sixties and the early nineties in rural Bangladesh.

TABLE 5.1
Per Capita Food Intake in Rural Areas

(gm/person/day)

1962–64 (1)	1975–76 (2)	1981–82 (3)	1982–83 (4)	1990–91 (5)
886.0	807.3	764.5	746.3	810.7

Source: Cols 1, 2, 3 from Chowdhury, O.H. (1989) and the rest from BIDS Surveys.

Nutritional Dimensions of Poverty • 79

TABLE 5.2
Regional Variation in Per Capita Food Intake (gm/person/day)

District	Village	Total
Bogra	Darikamari	751.49
Comilla	Bhabanipur	812.62
Munshiganj	Sontoshpara	701.29
Sherpur	Majakanda	929.19
Barisal	Pathathi	806.71
Magura	Baraichara	682.44
Kushtia	Noapara	1123.59
Joypurhat	Hanailbamboo	828.01
Panchagar	Ghatbor	770.12
Natore	Udbaria	750.45

Source: BIDS Survey 1990–91.

TABLE 5.3
Seasonal Variation in Food Intake

	(gm/person/day)
Peak period (January–March)	884.60
Lean period (August–October)	736.90

Source: BIDS Survey 1990–91.

TABLE 5.4
Age-Sex Composition of Food Intake

Age Group Age (in year)	Male (in calories)	Female
1–3 years	433.01	416.30
4–6 years	562.99	491.53
7–9 years	632.66	572.33
10–12 years	756.04	660.80
13–15 years	848.25	760.16
16–19 years	1012.48	831.11
20–39 years	1109.04	836.12
40–49 years	1143.18	772.07
50–59 years	957.19	701.01
60–69 years	967.14	745.91
70+	764.51	581.60

Source: BIDS Survey 1990–91.

Seasonal and Regional Variations in Food Intake

Agricultural activity in general and food production in particular, in rural Bangladesh revolves around three main seasons of rice production, namely, the Aus, Amon and the Boro seasons. If there is any relationship between food consumption and domestic food production as suggested earlier then one would expect seasonal variation in food consumption to coincide with the cycle of food production. Moreover, the level of food consumption between regions may also vary according to the productivity of land. Amon is the major crop accounting for about half of the total rice production. It is harvested between mid-November and January. Pulses are available early in the year being harvested from February through March. Boro is also a winter crop being harvested between April and May. Aus is grown in March and April and harvested from June to August. One would, thus, expect that the level of food intake would be highest after the harvesting of the major crop, Amon. In general, the peaks and troughs of food consumption would be expected to match the crop cycle of different regions. Thus, a close relationship between food consumption and domestic food production would mean that there would be seasonal as well as regional variation in food consumption in rural Bangladesh matching crop cycle and agro-climatic zones respectively.

Table 5.2 shows that the highest per capita food intake in Noapara village of Kushtia district (1123.59 gm) is about 65 per cent higher than that in Baraichara village of Magura district (682.44 gm) which is the lowest per capita food intake in 1990–91.

Seasonal variation in food intake reported in Table 5.3 shows that the peak period food intake of 884.6 gm per day is higher by only 20 per cent from the lean period food intake of 736.9 gm/day in 1990–91. Hence, it is clear that regional variation in food consumption in rural Bangladesh is equally, if not more, important than seasonal variation.

Gender Bias in Food Intake

Table 5.4 shows that food intake of female members in all the age-groups without exception are lower than those for their female counterparts. (Also see Figure 5.1 based on information from first round of the survey.)

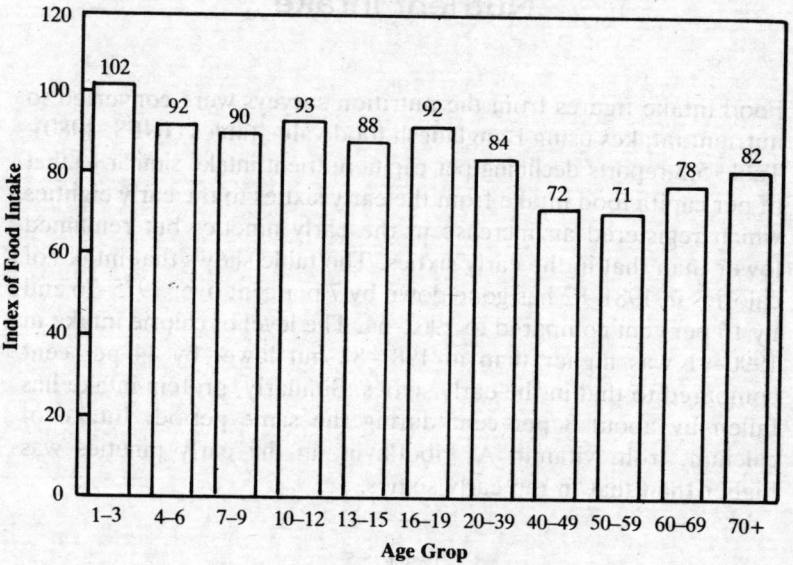

FIGURE 5.1
Female Food Intake as Per cent of Male Intake

Food Intake: Conclusions

In sum, evidence for rural Bangladesh strongly suggests that food intake at an aggregate level stagnated over the eighties upto the early nineties with wide yearly, seasonal and regional variations. Such regional and seasonal variations imply that food consumption is primarily determined by food production in the locality which in its turn follows the crop cycle in the area. Hence, overall food consumption at the national level is also largely determined by domestic food production. Therefore, infrequent point estimates on dietary intake in rural Bangladesh cannot be used for drawing conclusions regarding trends in food consumption during the intervening periods, since the intervals are marked by wide yearly, seasonal and regional variation in food production. Further, there is a strong gender bias in food intake showing female members of all age-groups to be worse off compared to their male counterparts.

Nutrient Intake

Food intake figures from the nutrition surveys were converted to nutrient intakes using Bangladesh food value tables (INFS, 1980). Table 5.5 reports declining per capita nutrient intake similar to that of per capita food intake from the early sixties to the early eighties which registered an increase in the early nineties but remained lower than that in the early sixties. The table shows that intake of calories in 1981–82 has gone down by 7 per cent over 1975–76 and by 16 per cent compared to 1962–64. The level of calorie intake in 1990–91 was higher than in 1981–82 but lower by 14 per cent compared to that in the early sixties. Similarly, protein intake has fallen by about 8 per cent during the same period. Intake of calcium, iron, vitamin A, riboflavin, in the early nineties was higher than that in the early sixties.

TABLE 5.5
Per Capita Nutrient Intake 1962–64 to 1990–91

Nutrients (1)	1981–82 (2)	1975–76 (3)	1962–64 (4)	1990–91 (5)	Requirement (6)
Energy (cal)	1943	2094	2301	1989	2273
(kg)	8129.71	8761.51	9627.62	–	9510.46
Protein (g)	48.4	58.5	57.9	47.4	45.3
Fat (g)	9.8	12.2	15.8	14.2	–
Carbohydrate (g)	412	439	482	417	–
Calcium (mg)	260	305	273	335	450
Iron (mg)	23.4	22.2	10.3	25.9	7.6
Vitamin A (iu)	763	730	1870	2087	2013
Thiamine (mg)	1.38	1.65	1.50	1.34	0.90
Riboflavin (mg)	0.68	0.87	0.50	0.73	1.35
Niacin (mg)	13.15	22.21	23.20	–	14.84
Vitamin C (mg)	13.26	9.51	48.00	39.84	26.00
No. of families	597	674	1052	400	–

Source: Cols 2, 3, 4 and 6 from Chowdhury (1989) and col 5 from BIDS Survey 1990–91.

Inter-Household Distribution of Nutrient Intake

It can be noted from Table 5.5 that the problem of calorie-protein malnutrition in rural Bangladesh is not alarming in terms of the average intake. But the situation changes dramatically when the distribution among the households is taken into consideration. Table 5.6 shows that only 41 per cent, 24 per cent and 21.2 per cent households met calorie requirement in 1975–76, 1981–82 and 1990–91 respectively. In other words, poverty according to nutritional norm (meeting calorie requirement) increased substantially between 1975–76 and 1990–91. Percentage of households meeting less than 80 per cent of calorie requirements ('hard core' poor) for the relevant periods were 35 per cent, 49 per cent and 39.6 per cent respectively. Hence, it seems that 'hard core' poverty had declined substantially between the early eighties and the early nineties.

TABLE 5.6
Percentage Distribution of Rural Households Meeting Different Proportions of Calorie and Protein Requirement

Per cent of requirement	Calorie			Protein		
	(INFS) 1975–76 (1)	(INFS) 1981–82 (2)	(BIDS) 1990–91 (3)	(INFS) 1975–76 (4)	(INFS) 1981–82 (5)	(BIDS) 1990–91 (6)
Less than 50	9	8	4.2	4	5	0.5
50–59	6	10	4.2	2	5	2.1
60–69	8	14	13.2	3	9	5.8
70–79	12	17	18.0	7	12	12.2
80–89	11	15	18.0	6	12	16.4
90–99	13	12	21.2	7	9	12.7
100 and above	41	24	21.2	71	48	50.3

Source: Cols 1, 2, 4, 5 from C. Chowdhury, O.H. (1993) and cols 3 and 6 from BIDS 1990–91 Survey.

Intra-family Distribution of Nutrient Intake

It was earlier pointed out that there is evidence of acute maldistribution of calorie and protein among households in rural Bangladesh. Table 5.7 provide information on distribution of nutrient intake as a percentage of requirement within the family according to the

TABLE 5.7
Age-Sex Structure of Malnutrition

(Percentage of nutritional requirements met)

Age group Age (in year)	Calorie		Protein		Calcium		Iron		Carotin (Vit-A)		Vitamin 'C'	
	Male	Female	Male	Female	Male	Female	Male	Female	Male	Female	Male	Female
1–3 years	52.0	48.3	69.9	66.0	36.4	39.3	78.1	78.1	120.1	319.2	59.3	89.3
4–6 years	67.7	58.9	95.2	87.8	58.9	47.0	148.4	143.4	354.1	501.9	101.4	134.8
7–9 years	68.1	60.9	93.9	83.9	57.3	55.4	194.0	169.8	360.7	409.6	144.6	161.4
10–12 years	70.9	71.1	92.3	81.9	53.5	37.3	229.7	176.8	347.2	219.5	181.0	130.5
13–15 years	76.4	85.6	83.9	93.8	53.3	46.1	155.3	115.1	265.9	304.1	143.3	149.3
16–19 years	84.5	96.2	103.9	98.8	65.7	67.7	329.8	110.0	377.3	274.1	188.1	142.5
20–39 years	90.4	97.8	121.8	102.7	95.0	62.6	387.9	101.5	327.3	247.0	165.2	136.4
40–49 years	95.9	96.9	130.2	109.9	95.2	75.5	420.9	87.7	411.5	362.7	175.8	134.0
50–59 years	88.0	98.6	110.0	104.1	103.3	59.1	347.2	259.5	308.6	233.7	147.8	131.7
60–69 years	95.9	107.0	104.4	96.3	82.6	69.1	363.3	246.7	436.7	337.0	160.6	119.7
70 years and above	105.1	114.6	96.9	83.6	91.3	46.2	288.1	198.4	223.9	47.5	125.4	53.2

Source: BIDS (1990–91) Survey.

age-sex composition in 1990–91. It shows that none of the boys and girls under the age of 20 years meet the calorie requirement. Further, the younger they were the higher was the deficiency. In general, girls were worse off compared to boys. There is, thus, an acute maldistribution of food intake within the household with children and mothers being particularly vulnerable. The picture is similar for other nutrients as well.

Anthropometry

The etiology of the nutrition problems in Bangladesh, as in most developing countries, is very complex. But it is generally agreed that the immediate factors determining nutritional status are food intake and diseases. Anthropometric measures are based on the physical manifestation of malnutrition. They may be considered outcome-based indicators which not only reflect malnutrition due to inadequate food intake but also poor absorption or decreased biological utilisation of nutrient intake due to presence of various infectious diseases. Hence, anthropometric measures reflect the impact of both food and non-food factors in explaining nutritional status.

Height and Weight

The average height and weight of the under 5 year age group in 1981–82 was higher than those reported in the preceeding two surveys conducted in 1975–76 and 1962–64 respectively (INPS, 1983). The heights and weights of children above 5 years, however, registered a declining trend. BIDS surveys carried out in 1982–83 and 1990–91 (reported in appendix tables A.1 and A.2) show that the average height and weight of male as well as female children of all age groups in 1990–91 in general was higher than those in 1982–83. Thus, it seems that there has been some improvement in the nutritional status of children under all age groups during the eighties in rural Bangladesh. However, Tables A.3 and A.4 (in the appendix) also show that heights and weights of children of all age groups were lower in 1990–91 compared to median heights and weights of the reference population.

Child Anthropometry

All parts of the body are not equally responsive and do not respond at the same time to nutritional well-being or insult. Earlier, weight-for-age based on the Gomez classification (Gomez et al., 1955) was the primary indicator used to assess nutritional status. Later, three different categories or types of malnutrition using age, weight and height were suggested (Scoane and Lathum, 1971). The suggested categories were (*i*) acute, current, short duration malnutrition where weight-for-height is low, but height-for-age is normal; (*ii*) past, chronic malnutrition, where weight-for-age and height-for-age are low but weight-for-height is normal; and (*iii*) acute or chronic long duration malnutrition where weight-for-age, height-for-age and weight-for-height are all low. Waterlow (1977) in a paper suggested that acute malnutrition be termed 'wasting', that chronic malnutrition be termed 'stunting', and that the combined condition of acute and chronic malnutrition be labelled 'wasting cum stunting'. Although the nutritionists have not reached firm agreement either on the terms to be adopted or on the cut-off points for low weight and low height, this classification is now widely used in anthropometric measures of nutritional status.

Table 5.8 reports the changes in the nutritional status of children in rural Bangladesh over the period 1975–76 to 1990–91. It may be pointed out that two reference standards, namely Harvard for the period 1975–76 to 1982–83, and the USA National Center for Health Statistics (UNCH) Standard for 1982–83 to 1990–91 have been used by different agencies for measuring nutritional status. To make the findings comparable between these two periods we reported the BIDS 1982–83 results both according to Harvard as well as the UNCH standards.

The table shows that the proportion of normal children (according to the Harvard Standard) rose from around a fifth in 1975–76 to more than a third by the early eighties (INFS 1981–82 and BIDS 1982–83). The percentage of normal children reported by INFS 1981–82, i.e., 36 per cent is comparable with the BIDS 1982–83 estimate of 35.7 per cent. But it is difficult to reconcile the findings of the HKI for 1982–83 with that of the findings of the INFS 1981–82 and the BIDS 1982–83 surveys. HKI reported 54.6 per cent of the children to be normal according to the UNCH standard in 1982–83 while the BIDS findings converted to the UNCH Standard turned out to be 41.58 per cent for the same year. In the

TABLE 5.8
Changes in Nutritional Status of Rural Children Under Five Year Age Group in Rural Bangladesh

Indicator Agency	Year	Normal	Stunting	Wasting	Stunting and wasting	Sample size	Reference standard
1. INFS	1975–76	20.47	57.91	5.81	15.81	430	Harvard
2. INFS	1981–82	36.08	43.92	7.06	12.94	510	Harvard
3. BIDS	1982–83	35.70	47.70	5.60	11.00	1003	Harvard
4. BIDS	1982–83	41.58	43.97	6.18	8.28	1003	UNCHS
5. HKI	1982–83	54.60	37.00	3.40	5.00	4443	UNCHS
6. BIDS	1990–91	51.76	35.68	5.53	7.04	398	UNCHS

Source: Row 1, 2 and 5 from Chowdhury, O.H. (1989) Table 4.1 pp. 29, cols 3 and 4 from unpublished BIDS survey data from *Developmental Impact of Food-for-work Study* and row 6 from present study.

absence of an objective criteria to choose between the two findings we are tempted to accept the BIDS findings since it tallies with the result of another independent agency, namely, the INFS for 1981–82. Reasons for discarding the results of the HKI findings will be clearer when we discuss other findings. The latest BIDS survey shows that the proportion of normal children has gone up to 47.8 per cent in 1990–91 compared to 41.58 per cent reported in the 1982–83 BIDS survey. Hence, it is clear that there has been substantial improvement in the nutritional status of rural children under 5 years of age between the mid-seventies and the early nineties. During this period, the proportion of children categorised as normal increased from 20.47 per cent in 1975–76 to as high as 47.8 per cent in 1990–91.

Table 5.9 shows that the stunting rate has declined from around 74 per cent in 1975–76 to around 57.3 per cent in 1981–82 according to the INFS and to 58.7 per cent in 1982–83 according to the BIDS using the Harvard Standard. Here again we see that the findings by the INFS and the BIDS are similar for the early eighties. But the HKI results show that the rate of stunting according to the UNCH Standard was 42 per cent in 1982–83 which is substantially less than the BIDS findings of 52.25 per cent when converted to the UNCH Standard. Furthermore, the BBS reports a stunting rate of 55.9 per cent in 1985–86. Such a dramatic increase in stunting rate from around 42 per cent in 1982–83 according to HKI to around 56 per cent by 1985–86 according to

TABLE 5.9
Intertemporal Comparison of Nutritional Status of Children under Five Year Age Group in Rural Bangladesh

Agency Year	INFS 1975–76	INFS 1981–82	BIDS 1982–83	BIDS 1982–83	HKI 1982–83	BBS 1985–86 (Rural)	BBS 1989–90	BIDS 1990–91
Indicator	(1)	(2)	(3)	(4)	(5)	(6)	(7)	(8)
Stunting	73.7%	57.3%	58.7%	52.25%	42.0%	55.9%	52.2%	42.7%
Wasting	21.6%	20.0%	16.6%	14.46%	8.4%	9.1%	8.8%	12.6%
Age	0–59M.	0–59M.	0.59M.	0.59M.	3–59M.	6–59M.	6–71M.	0–59M.
Reference Standard	Harvard	Harvard	Harvard	NCHS	NCHS	NCHS	NCHS	NCHS
Sample Size	430	510	1003	1003	4443	1500	1513	398

Source: Cols 1, 2, 5 and 6 from Chowdhury, O.H. (1989 Table 4.2 pp. 31), Col 7 from BBS, Child Nutritional Status Survey (1989–90). Table 6, pp. 24, Col. 8 from present study.

the BBS, is very unlikely because the stunting rate or height-for-age is an indicator of the long-term nutritional status of children. Linear retardation in growth does not occur during short-term episodes of nutritional deficiency or illness. Hence, such sharp changes in the rate of stunting between 1981–82 and 1982–83 or between 1982–83 and 1985–86 is very difficult to explain. Therefore, it is reasonable to accept the BIDS 1982–83 stunting rate which is similar to that of the INFS for 1981–82. The table further shows that the rate of stunting declined from 52.2 per cent in 1989–90 according to BBS to 42.7 per cent by 1990–91 according to BIDS. Here again it is difficult to explain such dramatic change in stunting rate in one year. But it is clear that the stunting rate has declined substantially between the early eighties and the early nineties.

Severity of Malnutrition

Weight-for-age is one of the most widely used nutritional status indicators. It combines both the short-term as well as the long-term consequences of undernutrition. The severity of malnutrition may be indicated by using different cut-off points in terms of percentage short fall from the reference median weight-for-age.

Table 5.10 reports that rural children under 5 years of age were suffering from various degrees of malnutrition according to the Gomez classification. It can be seen from the table that the proportion of children suffering from severe malnutrition declined from around 26 per cent in 1975–76 to around 9 per cent in 1982–83 (Harvard Standard) and then increased from 7.4 per cent in 1982–83 to around 10 per cent in 1985–86, and fell to around 7.4 per cent in 1989–90 and rose again to 10 per cent in 1990–91. It seems that the severity of malnutrition fluctuated during the eighties though it fell appreciably compared to the mid-seventies and early eighties.

Sex Bias in Nutrition Status

It was earlier pointed out that food intake of girls in general is less than that of boys. It was further shown that even when requirements are taken into account girls fare worse than boys. Table 5.11

TABLE 5.10
Nutritional Status by Gomez Classification

(Per cent)

Indicator agency	Year	Normal	Mild (1st degree)	Moderate (2nd degree)	Severe (3rd degree)	Reference standard	Sample size
1. INFS	1975–76	3.49	17.68	53.02	25.81	Harvard	430
2. INFS	1981–82	10.00	28.82	46.08	15.1	Harvard	510
3. BIDS	1982–83	6.7	31.8	52.6	8.8	Harvard	1035
4. BIDS	1982–83	7.3	34.0	51.2	7.4	NCHS	1003
5. BBS	1985–86	5.3	33.1	52.0	9.6	NCHS	1003
6. BIDS	1990–91	10.6	44.95	36.36	8.08	NCHS	398

Source: Cols 1, 2, and 5 from Chowdhury, O.H. (1989) Table 4.3 pp. 33. cols 3 and 4 from unpublished BIDS survey data from *Developmental Impact of Food-for-work Study* and row 6 from present study.

TABLE 5.11
Nutritional Status of under Five Year Group Boys and Girls

	Normal	Stunting	Wasting	Stunting and wasting	Sample size
Boys	62.35	27.06	7.06	3.53	85
Girls	43.86	42.11	4.39	9.65	114

Source: *Analysis of Poverty Trends Project*, BIDS: Nutrition Survey.

reveals that higher proportion of boys (62.4 per cent) are categorised as normal compared to girls (43.9 per cent). Prevalence of stunting as well as wasting is higher for girls (10 per cent) compared to boys (4 per cent). Hence, the boys are better off both in terms of input- and output-based indicators of nutritional status.

Conclusion

Some broad conclusions emerge from the analysis of dietary intake and child anthropometry carried out in this study. It was found that per capita food consumption per day declined continuously from 885.9 gm in 1962–64 to 764.5 gm in 1981–82 and then increased to 810 gm by 1991–92. But a review of literature on domestic food production, food availability and consumption in rural Bangladesh reveals that there is wide yearly, regional and seasonal fluctuation. Further, there is a close relationship between regional food production and local food intake. Hence, it is suggested that under these circumstances infrequent national nutrition surveys on food intake cannot solely be relied upon to draw conclusions regarding the trends in food consumption during the intervening period. In fact, it is argued on the basis of literature review on food production, availability and consumption in Bangladesh that food production and intake at an aggregate level stagnated between the mid-sixties and the early nineties. This study shows that food intake is not equally distributed between seasons, among regions and within the household.

It was found that nutrient intakes at an aggregate level fell between the sixties and the eighties and then increased substantially in the nineties reflecting the change in food consumption during the corresponding period. It was further noted that the problem of protein-calorie malnutrition, that is, when intake is compared with requirement, is not alarming in per capita terms. A look at the distribution of nutrient intake among the households provide a different picture compared to that at the aggregate level. It was observed that only 71 per cent, 48 per cent and 50.3 per cent of the households had adequate protein intake in 1975–76, 1981–82 and 1991–92 respectively even though there was no protein shortage at the aggregate level. Similarly, only 41 per cent, 24 per cent and 21.2 per cent of the households met calorie requirements in the corresponding periods. Energy deficiency affects protein utilisation, and hence, a reduction in energy intake impairs utilisation of protein added in the diet. Thus, the households which are not meeting calorie needs will also be protein deficient. As a result the proportion of households which are effectively protein deficient may rise due to deficiency in calorie intake even though they are not purely protein deficient. Hence, it is clear that a large number of households in rural Bangladesh suffer from inadequate as well as unbalanced food intake. As a consequence, protein-calorie malnutrition is quite high in present day rural Bangladesh which is not apparent from aggregate data reported in per capita terms.

Intra-family distribution shows that food and nutrient intake are unequally distributed among the members within the family. Female members in general and mothers and children in particular are adversely affected as a consequence of such maldistribution of food within the family. In fact, the findings show that the weight of poverty falls differentially between seasons, among regions and on different members within the family.

Conclusions in terms of child anthropometry are similar to those revealed in terms of food and nutrient intake. It was found that average weight and height of children in each age group (upto 11 years) in 1990–91 were higher than those in 1982–83. Proportion of children categorised as normal according to child anthropometry improved from around 20 per cent in 1975–76 to around 52 per cent by 1990–91. Children categorised as both stunted and wasted also declined from around 16 per cent to around 7 per cent during the same period. Hence, it seems that the nutritional status of children has improved substantially since the mid-seventies. But it should be remembered that around 50 per cent of the children are still suffering from malnutrition. Furthermore, though the average heights and weights of children in each age group increased in 1990–91, compared to that in 1982–83, they were still lower than the corresponding median figures for the reference population. Sex bias in nutritional status according to anthropometric measures confirms the earlier conclusions regarding sex bias in food intake and nutrient intake. Table 5.11 reports that girls were worse off than the boys according to all the indicators of nutritional status (except wasting).

In sum we can conclude that there seems to have been some improvement in the poverty situation since the early seventies though a large proportion of the population continue to suffer from malnutrition. Severity of malnutrition varies between seasons, regions, and different age-sex groups within the household. Women and children are particularly vulnerable as it was found that about 50 per cent of all children under 5 years of age suffer from malnutrition and female members in each age group fare worse than their male counterparts.

Intra-family maldistribution of resources point to a special kind of problem regarding eradication of poverty. Increasing income or food at the household level cannot address the problem of bias against female members within the family. But a recent study (Chowdhury, Omar H., 1990) compared the outcome-based (weight-for-age) and input-based (calorie requirement) indicators of under 5 year old children in rural Bangladesh and found that while 11.7 per cent of children had adequate calorie intake, only 6.7 per cent of them showed up as normal according to the outcome-based indicator. Thus, it was pointed out that about 50 per cent of the under 5 age group who had adequate calorie intake ended up with poor physical growth performance. This gap between the input-based indicator (calorie intake) and the outcome-based (anthropometric) measure according to the author account for the importance of such non-food factors as pure drinking water, proper sanitation and medicare facility, nutrition, education, etc. It clearly indicates that improving these facilities is as important as providing extra food at the household level. Access to these facilities which improve the physical environment can be ensured to all members of the household if they are provided by the government at the community level. Hence, appropriate public expenditure policy by diverting resources to these activities can address the overall nutritional problem as well as the relatively intractable gender issue involved in the poverty-alleviation objective of the country.

It may be pointed out that recognition of food as an important factor in determining poverty and nutritional status has led the government to attach the highest priority to food production and achievement of self-sufficiency in food among the development objectives of Bangladesh. It is high time that importance of non-food factors in alleviating poverty and malnutrition be acknowledged as well appropriate national policies on health, education, etc., be formulated.

Our study has shown that the only asset a poor man has is his labour power. He is unemployed most of the time because he is unskilled and/or sick. Access to health care and education can turn this poor unemployed labourer into a healthy productive labour force. Thus, the twin objectives of growth and equity can be achieved by increasing expenditure in human capital formation.

The nutritional problem is a complex one involving not only specific health intervention measures but broader development issues, such as income, wealth, employment, etc. Differences in nutritional levels between regions, seasons and age-sex groups are determined not only by differential access to food and non-food physical environment, but also by variations in socioeconomic status and such family characteristics as education, housing condition, health practice among members, etc. Bangladesh's experience seems to suggest that the nutritionally most vulnerable groups are the children and mothers. Improving their nutritional status can have spectacular impact on the health status of the population in general. Prevalence of widespread malnutrition among mothers and children under 5 years of age should point to the fact that a distinction should be made between economic effects of survival at older age and demographic effects of survival of the mother after child birth and of infants and children under five. Increased survival at older ages will not only reduce the national wasted consumption burden but will contribute to economic efficiency and increase in productivity. Hence, expenditure to improve the conditions of mothers and children in rural Bangladesh can be justified both from the point of view of saving cost and increasing productivity. Indeed the expenditure to alleviate their health status should really be considered as an investment. In fact, it will be hard to find any alternative investment opportunity that can match a realistic estimate of return in terms of cost saving and increased productivity than that due to improved nutritional status of mothers and children in rural Bangladesh. Directing resources towards primary health care and womens' education that includes nutrition education can dramatically lower overall mortality rates and increase life expectancy at birth, and put Bangladesh in the League of Nations hailed as high health achievers even at low levels of income, such as Sri Lanka, Costa Rica and the state of Kerala in India.

It is generally argued that a poor country cannot afford to spend large share of its total income on such social overheads as education, health, medicare, etc. But we have pointed out that such expenditures should be treated as an investment where returns are possibly higher than the alternative opportunities available to the country. It was shown that investment in social overheads not only promotes growth but also reduces inequality. Hence, we are arguing that the poorer a country higher should be the share of expenditure in social overheads. In truth a poor country cannot afford not to spend a higher proportion of its total income on social expenditure compared to a richer country.

Notes

1. See, among others, Rahman and Haque (1988), Khan (1990), Osmani (1990), etc.
2. See Kumar, S.K., and Omar Haider Chowdhury (1985) for details.
3. As reported in this study.

References

BBS (1991), 'Report of the Child Nutrition Status Survey', 1989–90, Dhaka.
Chowdhury, Omar Haider, 1989, *Analytical Bibliography on Rural Development. A Critical Review of Studies, Nutrition in Rural Bangladesh*, BIDS.
———, 1990, *Nature of Poverty in Bangladesh*, unpublished.
———, 1993, Review of Literature on Nutrition Studies in Bangladesh, Bangladesh Institute of Development Studies.
Department of Health, Education and Welfare, 1966, *Nutrition Survey of East Pakistan 1962–64*. Office of International Research, National Institute of Health, Bethesde, Maryland.
Gomez, F. et al., 1956, 'Mortality in Second and Third Degree Malnutrition', *Journal of Tropical Pediatrics*, 2: 77–83.
———, 1955, 'Malnutrition in Infancy and Childhood with Special Reference to Kwashiorkor', *Advances in Pediatrics*, 7: 131–64.
Helen Keller International (HKL), 1985, *Bangladesh Nutritional Blindness Study 1982–83*.
Institute of Nutrition and Food Science (INFS), 1983, *Nutrition Survey of Rural Bangladesh 1981–82*, Dhaka University.
———, 1980, *Nutrition Values of Local Food Stuffs*. Dhaka, INFS.
———, 1977, *Nutrition Survey of Rural Bangladesh 1975–76*, Dhaka University, December.
Khan, A.R. (1990), 'Poverty in Bangladesh: A Consequence of and a Constraint on Growth', *The Bangladesh Development Studies* Vol. XVIII, No. 3.
Kumar, S.K. and **Omar Haider Chowdhury** (1985), 'The Effect on Nutritional Status' in *Development Impact of the Food-for-work Programme in Bangladesh*, The Bangladesh Institute of Development Studies, Dhaka, and the International Food Policy Research Institute, Washington, D.C.
Osmani, S.R., 1980, *Poverty, Inequality and the Problem of Nutrition in Bangladesh*, BIDS.
———, 1990, 'Structural Change and Poverty in Bangladesh: The Case of a False Turning Point', *The Bangladesh Development Studies*, Vol. XVIII, No. 3.
Rahman, A. and **Trina Haq**, 1988, 'Poverty and Inequality in Bangladesh in the Eighties: An Analysis of some Recent Evidence', Research Report No. 91, BIDS.
Scoane, N. and **M.C. Iathen**, 1971, 'Nutritional Anthropometry in the Identification of Malnutrition in Childhood', *Journal of Tropical Pediatrics* 17: pp. 98–104.

Streeten, P., 1990, 'Poverty: Concepts and Measurement', *The Bangladesh Development Studies*, Vol. XVIII, No. 2.

Waterlow, J.C. et al., (1977), The Presentation and use of Height and Weight Data for Comparing the Nutritional Status of Groups of children under the Age of 10 years, *Bulletin of the WHO*, 55, 1977: 489–98.

APPENDIX TABLE 5.1
Comparing Average Weight between 1982–83 and 1990–91

Age group	Sex	BIDS 1982–83 (Kg)	BIDS 1990–91 (Kg)
0–11 Months	Male	6.2	6.2
	Female	5.3	6.6
12–23 Months	Male	8.4	9.0
	Female	7.8	7.8
24–35 Months	Male	9.7	10.8
	Female	9.2	9.6
36–47 Months	Male	11.4	11.9
	Female	10.8	10.8
48–59 Months	Male	12.7	13.3
	Female	12.1	13.5
5 Years	Male	14.1	14.7
	Female	13.3	13.6
6 Years	Male	15.3	15.6
	Female	14.7	15.6
7 Years	Male	17.2	18.2
	Female	16.8	17.2
8 Years	Male	19.2	19.3
	Female	18.6	19.2
9 Years	Male	20.1	21.8
	Female	20.2	20.5
10 Years	Male	22.1	22.8
	Female	21.8	25.3
11 Years	Male	24.5	24.1
	Female	24.5	25.9

Source: 1982–83 Data from BIDS Survey on *Developmental Impact of Food-for Work Study* and 1990–91 data from present study.

APPENDIX TABLE 5.2
Comparing Average Height between 1982–83 and 1990–91

Age group	Sex	BIDS 1982–83 (CM)	BIDS 1990–91 (CM)
0–11 Months	Male	62.8	64.0
	Female	59.5	64.0
12–23 Months	Male	74.0	77.6
	Female	71.4	72.1
24–35 Months	Male	80.9	82.5
	Female	78.5	82.0
36–47 Months	Male	88.3	87.6
	Female	86.1	86.1
48–59 Months	Male	93.4	95.2
	Female	93.5	97.4
5 Years	Male	99.9	97.1
	Female	98.9	101.5
6 Years	Male	104.6	105.1
	Female	104.2	104.5
7 Years	Male	111.9	115.9
	Female	111.2	111.8
8 Years	Male	116.9	119.1
	Female	116.4	117.5
9 Years	Male	120.0	123.8
	Female	119.9	119.4
10 Years	Male	123.8	128.5
	Female	123.0	126.4
11 Years	Male	128.7	129.1
	Female	129.2	130.2

Source: 1982–83 Data from BIDS Survey on *Developmental Impact of Food-for-Work Study* and 1990–91 data from present study.

Appendix Table 5.3
Average Weight as a Percentage of Reference Weight

Age group	Male	Female
0–11 Months	94.55	95.65
12–23 Months	77.86	72.91
24–35 Months	80.88	73.30
36–47 Months	76.54	75.17
48–59 Months	75.60	80.06
5 Years	75.03	73.92
6 Years	71.90	76.32
7 Years	76.25	72.98
8 Years	73.01	73.66
9 Years	74.43	69.38
10 Years	69.37	74.05
11 Years	64.43	68.78

Source: 1982–83 Data from BIDS Survey on *Developmental Impact of Food-for Work Study* and 1990–91 data from present study.

Appendix Table 5.4
Average Height as a Percentage of Reference Height

Age group	Male	Female
0–11 Months	94.55	95.65
12–23 Months	94.34	89.42
24–35 Months	91.54	91.50
36–47 Months	88.70	90.19
48–59 Months	84.48	92.52
5 Years	86.24	91.23
6 Years	88.50	89.14
7 Years	93.61	87.94
8 Years	92.23	91.62
9 Years	92.34	89.23
10 Years	92.04	89.92
11 Years	88.01	88.30

Source: 1982–83 Data from BIDS Survey on *Developmental Impact of Food-for Work Study* and 1990–91 data from present study.

6

Selected Living Standard Indicators

BINAYAK SEN

Introduction

A complete assessment of trends in rural poverty should take account of several dimensions of poverty, of which income or consumption levels per head is only one. Equally relevant are factors, such as access to adequate clothing and shelter, longevity, access to health and education facilities and security of consumption levels from extreme shocks. However, time-series data on these dimensions are not available. The HES data provided by the BBS do not adequately address these 'non-income' dimensions of poverty. With a view to achieving a more informed analysis in this regard, information were collected in course of the BIDS survey on several living standard indicators. (Figure 6.1).

Clothing

Clothing is usually mentioned right after food in any listing of basic needs. Some indication of the inequality in the distribution of cloth availability may be obtained from Table 6.1[1] Information were

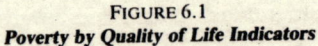

FIGURE 6.1
Poverty by Quality of Life Indicators

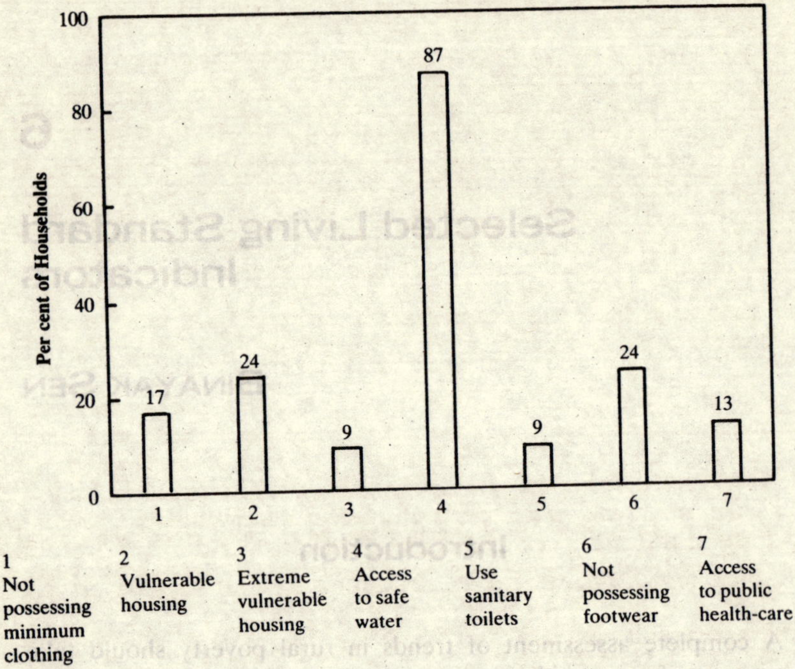

100
80
60
40
20
0
Per cent of Households
87
24
17
9
9
24
13
1
2
3
4
5
6
7
1 Not possessing minimum clothing
2 Vulnerable housing
3 Extreme vulnerable housing
4 Access to safe water
5 Use sanitary toilets
6 Not possessing footwear
7 Access to public health-care

sought on two items. Firstly, whether each adult household member owned a minimum of 2 pieces of clothing, i.e., lungi or saree. Secondly, whether each household member owned a piece of winter clothing. The table shows that, as of November 1989–February 1990, 17 per cent of the adult rural population did not own a minimum of two pieces of the most common apparel (lungi for men and saree for women). This average figure conceals significant variation amongst different land owning groups. The table shows that 26 per cent to 30 per cent of adult rural population in the landless and functionally landless categories did not have a minimum of two pieces of clothing compared to only 2 per cent to 4 per cent in the medium and large land owning groups. This aspect of deprivation is more starkly seen when one considers access of rural household members to winter clothing. The average percentage not having access to winter clothing was 22 per cent. The corresponding figures for the landless and the functionally landless groups

TABLE 6.1
Selected Living Standard Indicators, 1989–90

Land Ownership Category (in acres)	% of households in each land category having access to:		% of adult household members in each land owning category not having:		
	Safe drinking water facilities*	Sanitary toilet**	Minimum of two pieces (lungi/saree)	Winter clothing	Footwear
Landless (less than 0.05)	85	4	30	40	44
Functionally landless (0.05–0.49)	86	1	26	34	39
Marginal owner (0.50–1.49)	87	7	10	18	20
Small owner (1.50–2.49)	91	15	6	10	11
Medium owner (2.50–4.99)	90	21	4	6	8
Large owner (5.00 +)	94	36	2	2	5
All households	87	9	17	22	24

Source: Analysis of Poverty Trends Project, BIDS: 62 Village Survey.
* Access to tubewell water.
** Access to toilet types of 'pucca' and 'slab' categories.

are 40 per cent and 34 per cent, respectively. In comparison, medium land owning groups show a figure of 6 per cent without winter clothing, while it is only 2 per cent in case of large land owning group. Striking differences have been observed between the land-poor and larger land owning groups in respect of access to footwear as well. Table 6.1 shows 44 per cent of adult members in the landless group as not having any footwear vis-à-vis 5 per cent in the large land owning category.

Health and Sanitation

As regards health and sanitation, the situation appears to be precarious across the board. The BBS figure for 1982 previously indicated that 54 per cent of the rural households did not have access to any toilet facilities and had to use open nature (BBS, 1990). The situation seems to have improved only marginally by 1989–90, the corresponding figure having slightly declined to 44 per cent.[2] However, if one considers access to sanitary toilets only (i.e., *pucca* and *slab* categories), a much more depressing picture emerges. Only 9 per cent of rural households appear to have access to sanitary toilets which have strong adverse implications for primary health security. The corresponding figure for the landless and functionally landless category is restricted to 4 per cent. Even within the large land owning group, only 36 per cent have maintained sanitary toilet facilities, thus, reflecting a problem of sanitary awareness over and above the problem of an inadequate resource-base.

One health and hygiene indicator which has registered a significant improvement over time is the access to safe drinking facilities. This has positively impacted on health and morbidity status of the poor. As Table 6.1 shows, 87 per cent of rural households have reported access to safe, i.e., tubewell water compared to 53 per cent in 1981 as per BBS data. Additional data reveal little variation amongst different land owning groups; the percentage of households having access to safe water is uniformly in excess of 80 per cent for all household categories on the poverty scale.[3]

Table 6.2 provides information on types of medicare enjoyed by the rural population in 1989–90. Only 13 per cent of the rural patients are treated by government health centres. The BIDS survey on primary health care carried out in 1987–88 put the figure at 12 per cent[4] which shows practically negligible improvement over the late eighties. Furthermore, this indicator reveals little variation across the surplus/deficit categories, thereby indicating limited access of the rural sector as a whole to the existing network of public health facilities. The 'self-sufficient' and 'surplus' categories, however, have the resources to pay for the medical services available from qualified private doctors. The proportion of the rural patients receiving medical assistance from the qualified private doctors monotonically increases from about 18 per cent in case of 'chronic deficit' households to 41 per cent recorded for the 'surplus' households.

On the whole, the primary health care facilities needs to be improved. In the absence of viable risk-insurance mechanisms,

TABLE 6.2
Distribution of Rural Patients by Type of Medicare, 1989–90

Self-categorisation of respondents according to surplus/deficit status	Type of medicare received:				
	Govt. clinic/ hospital	Private clinic	Qualified private doctor	Indigenous	Total
Chronic deficit	49	7	61	225	342
	(14.33)	(2.04)	(17.84)	(65.79)	(100.0)
Occasional deficit	91	39	166	422	718
	(12.67)	(5.43)	(23.12)	(58.77)	(100.0)
Self-sufficient	25	7	86	109	227
	(11.01)	(3.09)	(37.88)	(48.02)	(100.0)
Surplus	12	7	49	51	119
	(10.08)	(5.88)	(41.18)	(42.86)	(100.0)
All	177	60	362	807	1346
	(13.15)	(4.46)	(26.89)	(55.50)	

Source: Analysis of Poverty Trends Project, BIDS: 62 Village Survey.
Note: Figures indicate number of patients who received medical treatment during the last month preceding the survey.

sudden deterioration in health status of poor household members often leads to a crisis-situation for the household as a whole in terms of a steep decline in income and welfare.[5] As revealed by the 1989–90 survey, incidence of 'crisis' relating to health hazards represents about 35 per cent of the various types of crises experienced by rural households over the last three years and ranks right after 'ecological vulnerability'. The aggregate impact of the primary health situation prevailing in the rural areas is reflected in the high proportion of households reporting sickness and disease (Table 6.3). Thus, one finds that the share of sickness prone households is about 54 per cent at the lowest end of the land ownership groups compared to 46 per cent with respect to the large land owning groups. Incidence of sickness and diseases would be still higher for the land-poor groups than recorded in course of the survey if one accounts for the under reporting of such cases by the 'hard core' poor due to their low level of health awareness.

If one concentrates on the disease pattern on the basis of reported cases, the following picture emerges (Table 6.4). First, influenza/ common cold represent about 48 per cent of rural sickness. It is

TABLE 6.3
Morbidity Status by Land Ownership Groups (1989–90)

Land Ownership categories	No. of HH in the group (1)	No. of HH Reporting sickness/ disease (2)	(2) as % of (1)
Landless and functionally landless households	600	324	54.0
Marginal	262	145	55.3
Small	136	85	62.5
Medium	146	76	52.0
Large	81	37	45.6
All	1225	667	54.4

Source: Analysis of Poverty Trends Project, BIDS: 62 Village Survey.

possible that a variety of diseases which are classified under the category of influeza/common cold are actually symptomatic of some 'chronic' or 'infectious' diseases of which the respondents did not have the faintest notion. Second, gastro-intestinal diseases figure prominently amongst the reported sickness (about 28 per cent of the total) indicating the adverse consequences of under-nutrition and deplorable conditions of primary health care. Third, an alarming proportion of rural sickness falls under the category of infectious/chronic type of diseases (about 35 per cent if the so-called 'others' type is taken into account). However, a relatively low proportion of reported 'infectious' diseases shows that there might have been some improvement over time in the eradication of epidemic type fatal diseases, like small pox, yellow fever, DPT, TT, Polio, BCG and Measles. The introduction of the Expanded Immunisation Programmes (EPI) in the mid-eighties and their subsequent rapid expansion in the recent years may have positively impacted on this particular aspect of the health situation. Fourth, the revealed disease pattern shows some variation across the land ownership groups. Incidence of gastro-intestinal and influenza/ common cold type diseases is higher for the landless and functionally landless households compared to the large land owning group (79 per cent vis-à-vis 65 per cent).

TABLE 6.4
Disease Pattern by Land Ownership Categories in Rural Bangladesh (1989-90)

Type of Disease	Land ownership categories:					
	Landless and functionally landless (upto 0.49 ac.)	Marginal (0.50– 1.49 ac.)	Small (1.50– 2.49 ac.)	Medium (2.50– 4.49 ac.)	Large (5.00) ac. +)	Total
Gastro-intestinal	162 (28.3)	70 (29.3)	38 (29.9)	36 (26.8)	16 (24.2)	332 (28.3)
Influenza/common cold	290 (50.7)	115 (48.1)	53 (41.7)	56 (41.8)	27 (40.9)	541 (47.5)
Infections	53 (9.3)	21 (8.8)	12 (9.4)	11 (8.2)	11 (16.6)	108 (9.5)
Chronic	32 (5.6)	18 (7.5)	15 (11.8)	16 (11.9)	5 (7.6)	86 (7.5)
Others	35 (6.1)	15 (6.3)	9 (7.2)	15 (11.3)	7 (10.7)	81 (7.2)
Total	572 (100.0)	239 (100.0)	127 (100.0)	134 (100.0)	66 (100.0)	1138 (100.0)

Source: Analysis of Poverty Trends Project, BIDS: 62 Village Survey.
Note: Figures relate to incidence of diseases reported by respondent households over the last one month, figures in parentheses represent percentages of column total.

Education

Available data also suggest limited access of the rural population to education. Currently, there is on the average one primary school per 3.2 sq. km. The expansion of primary education facilities has been extremely slow in the eighties: the number of primary schools has increased by only 1.2 per cent during the Third Plan period over the benchmark set by the Second Plan. According to current official statistics, the enrollment ratio (i.e., enrollment as a percentage of age cohort) in primary education has gone up to 78 per cent from 52 per cent in 1985. The quality of official statistics on primary education however remains suspect. There is also the problem of a very high drop-out in the system (believed to be about 80 per cent). The BIDS survey collected some information on primary school enrollment rates differentiated by sex and by land-ownership groups (Table 6.5). The enrollment ratio for boys varies from 53 per cent in case of the landless group to about 80 per cent in case of large land owning groups. The corresponding figures for girls of school-going age are 49 and 72 per cent respectively.

TABLE 6.5
Primary School Enrollment Rate

Land Ownership Groups	Primary school of enrollment rate*	
	Boys	Girls
Landless	53	49
Functionally landless	67	62
Marginal	79	73
Small	80	75
Medium and Large	79	72
All	65	60

Source: Analysis of Poverty Trends Project, BIDS: 62 Village Survey.
* Enrollment rate is expressed as enrollment in primary school as a percentage of age cohort (i.e., 6–14 years).

In view of these findings the issue of raising the financial allocation for primary health care and education facilities can hardly be exaggerated. Indeed what the provision of adequate resources can do even within the existing institutional constraints is strikingly exemplified by the recent progress of the Expanded Programme of Immunisation (EPI). The proportion of rural infants (upto 1 year of age) immunised against DPT, measles and polio has reportedly increased within a span of just five years from 1 to 2 per cent to 50 to 70 per cent. Even after applying the usual discount, this is a most impressive performance by any standards. There is, however, a need to strike a balance between the 'soft-ware' and 'hard-ware' elements in social sector expenditures. Both health and education expenditures display a strong bias towards hard-ware, eg., buildings over soft-ware elements, such as curricula and teacher training. As a result, performance statistics on these sectors overplay the role of narrowly quantitative performance at the expense of qualitative performance.

Housing

The housing status is another living standard indicator which is sensitive to the poverty scale. Table 6.6 provides the distribution of rural households disaggregated by 5 housing categories: (*i*) 'jhupri', i.e., matchbox-type houses made of leaves, (*ii*) 'single structure' houses, (*iii*) houses with one plus structures with 'thatch' roofs, (*iv*) 'semi-durable' house-structure with one plus rooms and (*v*) 'durable' house-structure with one plus rooms. If one combines together the three categories at the lower end of the housing scale (i.e., 'jhupri', 'single structure' and 'thatch and 1 + structure'), the share of the vulnerable segment of the rural population would constitute about 60 per cent of the rural households.

TABLE 6.6
Housing Condition by Land Ownership Categories, 1989–90

Land Ownership Category (in acres)	Intra-group per cent distribution of housing categories					
	Jhupri	Single structure	Thatch and 1 + structure	Semi-durable	Durable	Total
Landless (less than 0.05)	15	48	24	9	4	100
Functionally landless (0.05–0.49)	13	33	29	18	7	100
Marginal owner (0.50–1.49)	8	15	30	38	9	100
Small owner (1.50–2.49)	6	11	26	39	18	100
Medium owner (2.50–4.99)	3	4	17	37	39	100
Large owner (5.00 +)	–	–	7	36	57	100
All Households	9	24	25	27	15	100

Source: Analysis of Poverty Trends Project, BIDS: 62 Village Survey.

In addition to this, the housing indicator identifies two further levels of differentiation. 'Jhupri' and 'single structure' categories together constitute 32 per cent of the rural households which compares with the 24 per cent of the 'chronic deficit' households by the self-evaluation criterion and possibly constitutes the 'hard core' poor (or 'ultra poor') group within the broader ranks of the absolute poor households. If one concentrates on the 'jhupri' category only, one can identify a even more extreme level of distress: about one-tenth of the households possibly represent a floating rural under class beyond the pale of regular society.

Significant differentiation exists amongst different land owning groups with respect to housing status. The proportion of households with durable and semi-durable houses varies from 13 to 25 per cent in case of landless and functionally landless groups, compared to 76 to 93 per cent for medium and large landowning categories (Table 6.6). With regard to change in housing status over time, two sets of inter-temporal data are available: (*i*) housing status by land ownership available from HES 1988–89 carried out by BBS against which the 1989–90 BIDS survey data on housing status can be broadly measured (Table 6.7); and (*ii*) change in housing condition over 1987–90 as perceived by the respondents of the BIDS survey (Table 6.8).

Table 6.7 indicates clear sign of improvement in housing condition across the broad over 1988–90. However, it may be argued that the extent of improvement would be over reported if a flood year is used as a benchmark for comparison. Indeed many of the house-structures that were badly affected by the flood had to be rebuilt in the immediate post-flood periods which show up in Table 6.7 as 'improvement' in housing condition over 1988–90.[6]

Data presented in Table 6.8 confirms the sign of improvement recorded in Table 6.7. About 13 per cent of rural households reported improvement in housing condition which is comparable to 18 per cent cited by BBS for 1988–89. Table 6.8 further shows significant intra-village variation in this regard. The proportion of households reporting improvement is only 6 per cent in case of landless and functionally landless households; for another 29 per cent the housing condition has deteriorated over time. This may be contrasted to the change indicator recorded for the large land owning group (36 per cent reported 'improvement' while only 7 per cent reported 'deterioration').

TABLE 6.7
Change in Housing Status by Land Ownership Categories: Comparison of BBS and BIDS Data (1988–90)

Land Ownership Category (in acres).	1988–89 (BBS)				1989–90 (BIDS)			
	Rank 1	Rank 2	Rank 3	Rank 4	Rank 1	Rank 2	Rank 3	Rank 4
Less than 0.05	6	5	21	68	4	9	24	63
0.05–0.49	6	8	35	51	7	18	29	46
0.50–1.49	11	12	42	35	9	38	30	23
1.50–2.49	18	15	40	27	18	39	26	17
2.50 +	33	17	33	17	41	38	15	6
All groups	13	11	36	40	15	27	25	33

Source: Computed from unpublished HES data of BBS and BIDS Survey.

Note: For comparison purposes, housing types have been ranked into the following order:

Rank 1: (1988–89) Wall = brick/cement, roof = Cement;
Wall = c.i. sheet/brick/cement, roof = c.i. sheet/wood;
(1989–90) Durable and 1 + structure;

Rank 2: (1988–89) Wall = mud/mud brick, roof = tile/c.i. sheet/wood;
(1989–90) semi-durable and 1 + structure;

Rank 3: (1988–89) all other housing types;
(1989–90) thatch and 1 + structure;

Rank 4: (1988–89) Wall = thatch, roof = thatch;
(1989–90) 'jhupri' and single structure house.

TABLE 6.8
Change in Housing Condition: 1987–90

Land Ownership Category (in acres)	Improved	As before	Worsened	Total
	% of group total	% of group total	% of group total	
Landless and functionally landless	6	65	29	100
Marginal owner	11	70	19	100
Small owner	23	65	12	100
Medium owner	17	66	17	100
Large owner	36	57	7	100
All households	13	65	22	100

Source: Analysis of Poverty Trends Project, BIDS: 62 Village Survey.

Access to Prestige Items

Some of the consumer items which are traditionally regarded as prestige items may be included in the category of secondary living standard indicators. These items include almirahs, radio/cassette player, television, watch/clock, bicycle, motorbike, ornaments, etc. As evident from Table 6.9, the living standard of the land-poor households is quite low by any standard. For example, proportion of households owning radio/cassette players and watch/clock is only 11 to 16 per cent in case of landless and functionally landless households compared to 41 to 80 per cent in medium and large land owning groups. Only 7 to 9 per cent of landless and functionally landless households own bicycle, while the corresponding figure for the large land owning group is as high as 69 per cent. Valuable ornaments such as those made of gold and silver are important liquid assets with considerable potentials for risk-insurance in times of crisis, but they are also widely regarded as socially prestigious items. Table 6.9 shows only 11 to 13 per cent of landless and functionally landless households as possessing ornaments as against 57 to 79 per cent in medium and large land owning groups. The extremely limited access to liquid assets in the land-poor group intensifies the likelihood of their vulnerability in

TABLE 6.9
Ownership of Durable Consumer and Socially Prestigious Items by Land Ownership Categories

Land Ownership Category (in acres)	Percentage of households in each land category owning						
	Almirahs	Radio/Cassette Player	Television	Watch/clock	Ornaments (gold/silver)	Motorbike	Bicycle
Landless (less than 0.05)	28	11	—	12	11	—	7
Functionally landless (0.05–0.49)	41	13	2	16	13	—	9
Marginal owner (0.50–1.49)	56	19	2	24	24	1	14
Small owner (1.50–2.49)	74	28	4	49	38	—	24
Medium owner (2.50–4.99)	79	41	4	66	57	—	33
Large owner (5.00 +)	88	57	14	80	79	12	69
All households	53	22	3	31	27	1	17

Source: Analysis of Poverty Trends Project, BIDS: 62 Village Survey.

the face of sudden and unanticipated crisis vis-à-vis larger land owning groups of rural society.

Notes

1. Annual per capita availability of cloth supply per head of population appears to have been broadly stagnant since liberation. The annual per capita cloth availability on a national scale, including non-cotton and second-hand clothes was about 9.96 yards in 1986–87 (see Latif, 1990). The corresponding figure for the rural areas, however, is not available.
2. Distribution of rural households according to toilet type appears as follows (per cent): pucca-7; slab-2; katcha-47; bush/field-44.
3. Promoting safe drinking facilities through expansion of hand-tubewells provides one of the best instances of targeting of aid in kind in the provision of an item in which the poor were particularly poor.
4. The BIDS study on primary health care reported that, in 1987–88, only 12 per cent of rural sick were treated by government health centres (Khan, 1988).
5. For a review of crisis-aspects of household existence, see chapter 7.
6. Several surveys carried out just after the floods were over, recorded high level of private investment in housing.

References

Bangladesh Bureau of Statistics, 1990, *Statistical Pocket Book of Bangladesh*.
Khan, M.R. (ed.), 1988, *Evaluation of Primary Health Care and Family Planning Facilities and Their Limitations Specially in the Rural Areas of Bangladesh*, Research Monograph No. 7, BIDS.
Latif, M.A., 1989, 'Towards an Estimation of Cloth Supply in Bangladesh: 1955–56 to 1986–87', *The Bangladesh Development Studies*, Vol. XVII, Nos. 1 & 2, March–June.

7

Crisis and Insecurity: The 'Other' Face of Poverty

HOSSAIN ZILLUR RAHMAN

Introduction

Poverty is not only a state of deprivation. It is equally a state of vulnerability. For the female half of the rural population in particular, vulnerability without doubt constitutes a core element of the poverty experience. Mainstream development thinking tends to treat this dimension of poverty as simply derivative of economic weakness and consequently fails to address such dimensions. This seriously ignores the fact that over and above individual economic weaknesses, the sources of vulnerability may lie in the specific nature of the social and institutional environment in which households and individuals live and hence have to be cognised as such.

There are at least two major areas in which the issue of vulnerability is germane to the current discussion on poverty. Firstly, vulnerability defines the quality of the social and institutional environment from the standpoint of the security of the person and property of individuals and household members. Insecurity emerges here as a key individual and group concern. Its most stark manifestation is in the incidence of actual exposure to violence of one category or another. Equally telling in this regard is a social environment vitiated by an endemic threat of violence or misuse of power and a perceived defencelessness against such eventualities in terms of the possibility of effective redress.[1] Insecurity in this latter sense has a particularly insidious significance in its effect on the state of confidence with which individuals and households define for themselves the opportunity frontier within which to deploy their livelihood initiatives. Even if resources exist, insecurity constrains here the space for entrepreneurial action and livelihood initiatives, such constraints operating both concretely as external limitations and internally as self-restriction.

The second major bearing which the issue of vulnerability has on the discussion on poverty is with regard to the stability of household welfare. Rural households in Bangladesh are routinely subject to a variety of crisis which significantly affect the household's ability to sustain current welfare levels let alone sustain any welfare increases. Such threats to the stability of household and individual welfare are sufficiently routine and widespread in rural Bangladesh to constitute a general characteristic of the poverty experience. Two important indicators of poverty which emerge here are crisis-proneness and coping capacities.

The definition of crisis needs some elaboration. An important distinction here is that between anticipated and unanticipated threats. Anticipated threats are part of the normal cycle of household existence which may allow for some compensatory strategies by the household. An example of anticipated threat is slack season unemployment. As distinct from this, there is another category of crisis which represents unanticipated threat to household welfare, i.e., unanticipated from the standpoint of the individual household but not for society as a whole. Unanticipated crisis permits little compensatory preparation on an individual basis for households living at the threshold of poverty. To an important extent the margin of vulnerability here is determined less by the household's individual capacities and more by the remedial capacities of social and state domains. The subsequent discussion on crisis will look at both these categories of anticipated and unanticipated threats to household welfare stability.

Anticipated Crisis: Seasonal Deficit

The Extent of Deficit-Proneness

Table 7.1 describes the incidence and duration of seasonal deficits faced by rural households within the annual cycle: 68 per cent of

TABLE 7.1
Intensity of Seasonal Deficits for Rural Households

A: By Land Ownership Category

Land ownership category	Percentage of rural households prone to at least:					
	1 crisis month	2 crisis month	3 crisis month	4 crisis month	5 crisis month	Year-round deficit
Landless	78	76	64	46	11	10
Functionally Landless	78	78	64	47	16	10
Marginal Owner	72	71	56	38	13	2
Small Owner	62	62	43	31	9	1
Medium Owner	42	41	29	16	2	1
Large Owner	25	25	13	9	—	—
All Groups	68	67	53	37	11	6

B: By Occupational Category

Occupational Category	Percentage of rural households prone to at least:					
	1 crisis month	2 crisis month	3 crisis month	4 crisis month	5 crisis month	Year-round deficit
Farmer	61	60	44	28	7	1
Agricultural Labour	88	88	76	59	21	11
Non-Agricultural Labour	80	80	68	48	16	9
Non-Farm Self-employed	66	64	46	33	11	8
Service	46	46	38	24	4	6
All Groups	68	67	53	37	11	6

Source: Analysis of Poverty Trends Project, BIDS: 62 Village Survey, 1989–90.

all rural households face some seasonal deficits and the minimum duration appears to be of two months; 6 per cent of all households are deficit-prone throughout the year. Among land ownership categories, deficit-proneness is the highest for the landless categories and the percentage declines as one goes up the land ownership scale. However, it is only with the transition from small to medium land ownership categories that deficit-proneness marks any noticeable decline. There is some differentiation within the land-poor categories mainly in terms of the duration of deficits. Nearly half the landless and functionally landless households face a minimum of four deficit months a year while a similar percentage of marginal and small owners face a minimum of three deficit months (Figure 7.1).

FIGURE 7.1
Seasonal Deficits in Rural Bangladesh

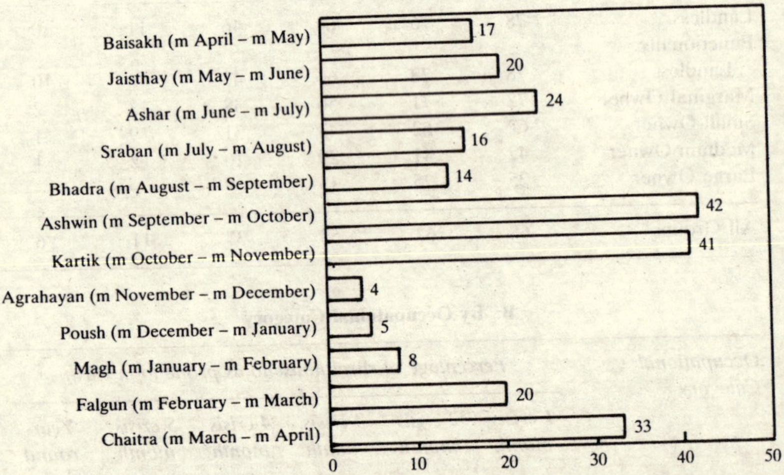

Month	Value
Baisakh (m April – m May)	17
Jaisthay (m May – m June)	20
Ashar (m June – m July)	24
Sraban (m July – m August)	16
Bhadra (m August – m September)	14
Ashwin (m September – m October)	42
Kartik (m October – m November)	41
Agrahayan (m November – m December)	4
Poush (m December – m January)	5
Magh (m January – m February)	8
Falgun (m February – m March)	20
Chaitra (m March – m April)	33

In terms of occupational categories, the most deficit-prone households belong to labouring households (80 per cent to 88 per cent) while 61 per cent and 66 per cent of farmer and non-farm self-employed categories face a minimum of two deficit months a

A: By Land Ownership Category

Division	Percentage of households reporting as most deficit-prone					No change in Deficit Month
	Ashar 16 June–16 July	Sraban 17 July–16 Aug	Ashwin 17 Sept–16 Oct	Kartik 17 Oct–15 Nov	Falgun 16 Feb–15 March	Chaitra 16 March–14 April	
Landless	19	12	40	40	6	14	89
Functionally Landless	17	13	35	31	12	17	83
Marginal Owner	14	8	22	20	18	24	85
Small Owner	11	10	24	30	22	13	82
Medium Owner	8	5	19	17	6	8	76
Large Owner	–	–	9	14	–	–	54
All Groups	14	10	29	23	11	16	83

B: By Region

Division	Percentage of households reporting as most deficit-prone					No change in Deficit Month
	Ashar 16 June–16 July	Sraban 17 July–16 Aug	Ashwin 17 Sept–16 Oct	Kartik 17 Oct–15 Nov	Falgun 16 Feb–15 March	Chaitra 16 March–14 April	
Chittagong	14	5	21	21	15	20	77
Khulna	21	17	27	26	4	8	85
Dhaka	14	13	28	29	17	22	89
Rajshahi	9	6	38	37	10	15	79
All Divisions	14	10	29	23	11	16	83

Source: Analysis of Poverty Trends Project, BIDS: 62 Village Survey, 1989–90.

year. It is the 'service' category which appear to enjoy the least relative vulnerability in this regard. The plight of labouring households is also underscored by the fact that nearly 10 per cent of such households face deficits throughout the year.

The Seasonality of Deficits

Table 7.2 describes the exact location of deficit months on the annual calendar. Overall, there appears to be one distinct lean season on the annual calendar covering a period the mid-September to mid-November and two subsidiary lean months covering the periods mid-June to mid-July and mid-March to mid-April. This pattern of lean seasons has not registered any major change in the recent past. 83 per cent of all households report no change. The inter-group picture follows the overall pattern with predictably smaller percentages for land-rich households in each lean period.

Coming to the regional pattern, the sequence of lean period broadly corresponds to the national pattern. However, some variation to note are the absence of a spring lean season in the Khulna division and the absence of a summer lean season in Rajshahi division. Chittagong division as a whole reports the least intensity of lean periods.

Response to Anticipated Crisis

Anticipated crisis allow for some margin of compensatory preparation though for those at the threshold of poverty such preparation may be as much a mark of their resilience as of their despair (Figure 7.2).The following provide a typology of such response:

1. Creation of buffers or stocks
2. Adjusting living conditions as in times of floods as, for example, by temporary relocation of housing
3. Curtailing consumption or more intensive recourse to expenditure-saving activities
4. Dispersal of household members to be re-united at a more favourable time
5. Recourse to targeted employment programmes as in food-for-work or VGD programmes
6. Temporary migration

Crisis and Insecurity: The 'Other' Face of Poverty • 119

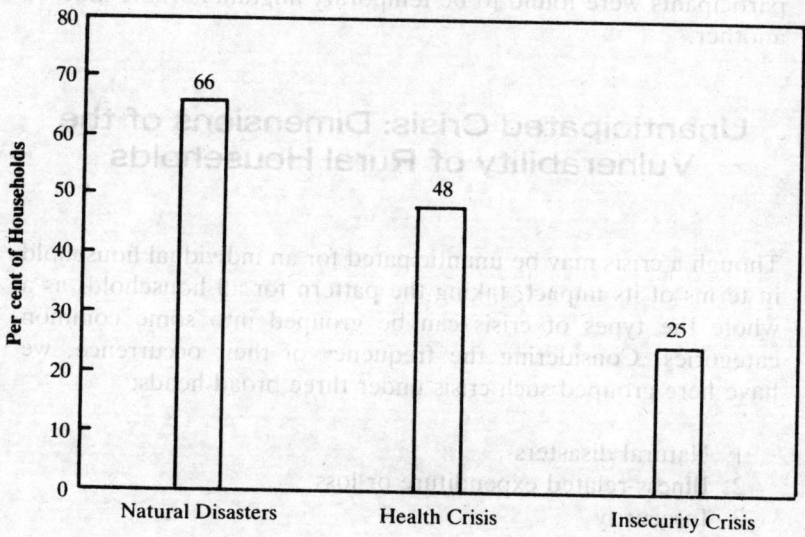

FIGURE 7.2
*A Typology of Crisis Routinely Faced
by Rural Households*

An illustration of some of the above is provided by the following case study from the district of Khulna:

Case Study: Ananta and Lakshmi Mondol (Village: Mailmara, Thana: Batiaghata)

Ananta and Lakshmi Mondol form a stable marital unit with a son (7) and a daughter (11). They have no land of their own and live on Ananta's father's land. Both Ananta and Lakshmi work as seasonal agricultural labourers. During the study period, they were found to have temporarily migrated to a neighbouring village to work as seasonal labourers on a contract of five months. During this period, their son stayed in the house of Lakshmi's brother and their daughter stayed in the house of Ananta's father.

The migration process as reported above and the dispersal of dependents to the homes of kin members indicate the variety of coping responses which the rural poor initiate to keep anticipated deficits at bay. Data from the overall national sample showed 7 per cent of all households to be sheltering kin members at the time of the survey while nearly a quarter (21 per cent) of labour force participants were found to be temporary migrants of one kind or another.

Unanticipated Crisis: Dimensions of the Vulnerability of Rural Households

Though a crisis may be unanticipated for an individual household in terms of its impact, taking the pattern for all households as a whole the types of crisis can be grouped into some common categories. Considering the frequency of their occurrence, we have here grouped such crisis under three broad heads:

1. Natural disasters
2. Illness-related expenditure or loss
3. Insecurity

It should be underscored here that all of the above categories appear as a crisis for the rural household precisely because they involve a tangible loss of one kind or another. Furthermore, such losses either directly threaten household survival or impair household capacity to graduate from the poverty status. The category of crisis expenditure here, is thus, distinguished from household expenditures, as for example on education, whose objective are to ensure economic mobility for the household.

While the category of natural disasters is fairly self-explanatory, the other two bear some elaboration. Illness or death become a crisis when they represent the loss or incapacity of the principal earners in the family. More frequently, illness appear as a household crisis in terms of sudden demands for large expenditures which are quite beyond the routine expenditure margins of the household. Such lumpy expenditures are necessitated because of the very poor state of public health-care in rural Bangladesh. For the context of rural Bangladesh, illness-related crisis also covers the death of cattle property.

Crisis and Insecurity: The 'Other' Face of Poverty • 121

The issue of insecurity-related crisis perhaps require the most elaboration because despite being a crucial dimension of the poverty experience, it has figured so little in academic or policy concerns on the issue. The principal male and the principal female of each surveyed household were asked about their perception of what categories of injustices they were most likely to encounter in their everyday social and economic life. The answers, summarised in table 7.3, illuminate the importance of insecurity as a household and individual concern. Of the eight types of injustices deemed to be of pressing concern, three, i.e., physical insecurity, threat of extortion and violence against women, were directly related to issues of insecurity. Indeed, physical insecurity was found to be the most pressing male concern (49 per cent of responses) and only slightly less so as a female concern (36 per cent responses). The female concern with immorality (42 per cent of responses) has also to be read as an insecurity concern because most often it is they who become direct victims of this immorality. The concern with village politics (24 per cent for both male and female responses) must also be seen as an insecurity concern because such politics frequently revolve around forcible or manipulative threats against persons and property. Interestingly, corruption was not perceived to be a priority concern, a finding on which we may have more to say later.

TABLE 7.3
Perceptions on Injustice

Type of Injustice	Percentage of response	
	Male perception	Female perception
1. Physical insecurity	49	36
2. Extortion	19	13
3. Violence against women	8	5
4. Corruption	7	4
5. Matabbar* dominance	23	12
6. Immorality	22	42
7. Wage discrimination	2	2
8. Village politics	24	24

Source: Analysis of Poverty Trends Project, BIDS: 62 Village Survey, 1989–90.
Note: Each person was asked to list three priority perceptions on types of injustice.
 * Village Influentials.

The concern of villagers with insecurity has of course an objective basis. As noted earlier, one of the three major categories of crisis faced by rural households relate to various forms of insecurity. These cover threats against or loss of property, threats of extortion, entanglement in injurious police and court proceedings and subjection to physical violence. In all such cases, the loss to the individual or the household is a tangible one, involving either a physical loss or the necessity to incur lumpy expenditures.

Table 7.4 reports the frequency of crisis faced by rural households in the annual cycle of their life. 76 per cent of all households faced

TABLE 7.4
Crisis-Proneness of Rural Households

A: By Land Ownership Status

Land Ownership Category	Percentage of households in each category subject in last one year to:		
	1 crisis	2 crisis	3 crisis
Landless	67	26	8
Functionally Landless	74	39	15
Marginal Owners	80	50	25
Small Owners	83	51	25
Middle Owners	81	55	26
Large Owners	70	43	33
All Groups	76	43	19

B: By Occupational Status

Occupational Category	Percentage of households in each category subject in last one year to:		
	1 crisis	2 crisis	3 crisis
Farmer	81	55	28
Agricultural Labour	71	31	9
Non-Agricultural Labour	76	34	12
Non-farm Self-employed	70	37	12
Service	76	35	19
Other	50	33	16
All Groups	76	43	19

Source: Analysis of Poverty Trends Project, BIDS: 62 Village Survey, 1989–90.

Crisis and Insecurity: The 'Other' Face of Poverty • 123

at least one crisis while 43 per cent faced two crisis and 19 per cent faced as many as three crisis within a year. There is little inter-class variation in the percentage facing a minimum of one crisis. Vulnerability in terms of having to face two or more crisis appears to be relatively less pronounced for the very asset less households. However, such households are much more vulnerable in terms of seasonal deficits.

Table 7.5 reports the relative importance of various categories of crisis faced by rural households. Predictably, the highest incidence

TABLE 7.5
Major Types of Crisis Faced by Rural Households

A: By Land Ownership Status

Land ownership category	Percentage of households in each category subject to:		
	Natural disasters	Illness crisis	Insecurity crisis
Landless	36	43	22
Functionally Landless	60	47	21
Marginal Owners	81	63	23
Small Owners	83	45	31
Middle Owners	75	55	29
Large Owners	64	52	20
All Groups	66	48	25

B: By Occupational Status

Occupational Category	Percentage of households in each category subject to:		
	Natural disasters	Illness crisis	Insecurity crisis
Farmer	83	49	31
Agricultural Labour	50	46	16
Non-Agricultural Labour	55	46	21
Non-farm Self-employed	54	46	20
Service	55	50	25
All Groups	66	48	25

Source: Analysis of Poverty Trends Project, BIDS: 62 Village Survey, 1989–90.

of crisis is in the category of natural disasters (66 per cent for the total sample). These include crop failures, damage to land and other assets by flood or cyclone and land loss due to river erosion. The farmer category is most vulnerable to such crisis.

What is noteworthy in the present context are the percentages for the two other categories of crisis, namely illness and insecurity. Nearly half the total population (48 per cent) appear to be vulnerable to illness-related crisis of one sort or another. Illness crises include death of principal earner of the family, large illness-related expenditures and illness or death of household cattle. Such healthcare related crises significantly destabilise the household resource-base and survival calculations and constitute a major barrier to the prospects of economic graduation of the rural poor.

To an extent, the significance of illness-related crisis may already be within analytical cognisance. What is certainly something new is the appreciation that a quarter (25 per cent) of rural households also face various insecurity-related crisis. Such crises include eviction or threats of eviction from property, injurious legal entanglements, theft, robbery or physical harassment, implication in false police cases, large expenditures on court or police proceedings and theft of cattle. A percentage figure as high as 25 per cent underscore if anything that such crises are no isolated incidents but are sufficiently routine to be a crucial feature of rural household existence.

What is of further interest is that both these categories of crisis more or less uniformly affect all social groups with of course relatively greater adverse consequences for resource-poor households. Nevertheless, the fact that such crises bear on all economic groups points to a crucial conclusion, namely, that they are not simply derivative of individual economic capacities. It is rather the institutional environment of rural life and the social and administrative factors which shape it which has the greater bearing on these crises, and hence, on their solutions.

Coping Capacities

Rural households are not mere passive actors in the daily drama of crisis and survival. Their resilience is particularly remarkable and evident in crisis situations which befall whole communities as in the case of the devastating cyclone of April 1991.² However, crisis which befall individual households in the routine cycle of rural life in present-day Bangladesh present a much more complex and difficult challenge for the coping capacities of the rural poor. Table 7.6 summarises the major types of mechanisms by which various categories of rural households attempt to cope with the crisis which routinely threaten their stability and survival.

TABLE 7.6
Coping with Crisis

Type of coping mechanisms	Percentage of various categories of households:				
	Deficit	Occasionally deficit	Break-even	Surplus	All
Dissave	31	46	63	72	48
Distress Sale	31	41	29	3	6
Distress Loan	36	33	18	11	29
Credit Facility	47	48	44	39	46
Commodity Credit	1	1	1	–	1
Legal Redress	–	1	1	–	1
Patron Support	3	2	2	3	2
Network Support	8	6	7	10	7
Others	17	16	17	18	17

Source: Analysis of Poverty Trends Project, BIDS: 62 Village Survey, 1989–90.
Note: Each household could take recourse to more than one mechanisms. A maximum of three mechanisms were considered for each case taking preceding three years as the reference period.

To a lesser or greater extent, all households try to create a buffer against possible contingencies. Thus, not surprisingly, dissaving is seen to be the most frequent crisis-coping mechanism with 48 per cent of all affected households reporting such a response. The capacity to rely on buffers is predictably greater for resource-rich households relative to deficit households of whom only 31 per cent reported dissaving as a coping mechanism compared to 72 per cent in the case of surplus households.

As distinct from buffers, rural households also take recourse to a variety of other coping mechanism. Discounting legal redress which only 1 per cent of households report as a coping mechanism and the residual category of 'others', these fall into two major types. Credit facility, commodity credit, patron support and network support are coping mechanisms which share the characteristic of being a positive aid for the affected household. In this sense, these mechanisms indicate the presence of an informal support system which operates within the rural society and imparts a measure of resilience to rural households. The importance of such a support system is hardly insignificant as the respective percentages in Table 7.6 shows. What is also noteworthy is that the poor as much as the rich are able to take recourse to such mechanisms with little inter-class variation over the respective percentages. Thus, 47 per cent of deficit households avail of non-injurious credit facilities as compared to 44 per cent for break-even households and 39 per cent for surplus households. Similarly, 8 per cent of deficit households report network support to cope with crisis vis-à-vis 7 per cent and 10 per cent for break-even and surplus households respectively.

As distinct from the above more positive type of coping, distress sale of household assets and distress loans i.e., loans at very high rates of interest, are mechanisms which only further dramatise the crisis situation for the household. These represent coping only in the very short run but in effect impair the long-term survival capacity of the household. The relative importance of these injurious coping mechanisms is quite high with 36 per cent of all households reporting distress sale and 29 per cent reporting distress loans. However, there are distinct inter-class variations here with 36 per cent of deficit households reporting distress loans vis-à-vis 11 per cent for surplus households and 41 per cent of occasionally deficit households reporting distress sale vis-à-vis 29 per cent for surplus households.

Conclusions: Crisis and Downward Mobility Pressures

Crisis and insecurity are not merely general characteristics of the social situation, they have a direct bearing on the poverty process. Impairing as they do the survival capacities of rural households, they have an equally insidious significance in constraining the space for entrepreneurial action and livelihood initiatives by the rural poor. The concern with poverty is not only about preventing further decline in welfare, it is also about breaking out of the vicious grip of poverty and making definitive graduation from the vulnerable status. It is precisely from these dynamic perspectives that the issues of crisis and insecurity demand urgent attention within development thinking. To illustrate these points, some indicative data is presented.

Table 7.7 describes the pattern of change in household economic status according to the perception indicator of self-evaluation and the objective indicator of change in land ownership status. The two indicators point towards a broadly similar pattern of economic mobility in rural Bangladesh. Between 35 per cent and 42 per cent of households report no net mobility over the reference period while 36 to 37 per cent report a decline in economic status. A somewhat lesser percentage of 21 to 29 per cent report an upward economic mobility. The inter-class variations in this pattern highlight the greater vulnerability of the rural poor with 42 to 53 per

TABLE 7.7
Change in Household Economic Status in the Eighties

A: By Self-Evaluation

Household categories	Evaluation of change (%)		
	Unchanged	Improved	Worsened
Deficit households	36	22	42
Occasionally deficit households	34	32	34
Break-even households	33	39	28
Surplus households	41	39	20
All Categories	35	29	36

B: By Land Ownership Status

Household categories	Nature of change (%)		
	Unchanged	Improved	Worsened
Deficit households	39	9	53
Occasionally deficit households	42	19	39
Break-even households	48	28	24
Surplus households	32	55	13
All Categories	42	21	37

Source: Analysis of Poverty Trends Project, BIDS: 62 Village Survey, 1989–90.

cent of deficit households reporting a decline as against 13 to 20 per cent for the surplus households. However, if the category of surplus households is disregarded, the difference in the mobility pattern is much less pronounced as between deficit, occasionally deficit and break-even households indicating a possible commonality of cyclical mobility pressures within each category over and above the advantage or disadvantage of initial conditions. Such a mobility pattern is also evident from a different set of data presented in chapter 10 (Table 10.2 and Figure 10.1). Cyclical mobility pressures underscore, if anything, the problem of economic graduation for each of these household categories and bring to the fore vulnerability as a crucial dimension of the poverty issue. Some pointer to the nature of such cyclical mobility pressures is provided in Table 7.8 which lists the factors noted by surveyed households as principally explaining their downward mobility.

TABLE 7.8
Factors Explaining Downward Mobility

Explanation	Percentage of responses:				
	Deficit household	Occasionally deficit household	Break-even household	Surplus household	All households
Life-cycle Factors (More dependents, less earners)	56	40	29	15	46
Structural Factors	17	14	12	–	17
Low Opportunities	10	5	8	–	9
Bad initial conditions	2	2	–	–	2
Inflation	5	7	4	–	6
Crisis Factors	24	36	59	85	37
Natural disasters	9	30	37	57	20
Illness expenditure	3	3	2	14	3
Property loss	7	8	8	14	8
Ceremonial expense	3	2	6	–	3
Litigation	2	3	6	–	3
Others	3	–	–	–	–
	100	100	100	100	100

Source: Analysis of Poverty Trends Project, BIDS: 62 Village Survey, 1989–90.

Crisis and Insecurity: The 'Other' Face of Poverty • 129

Several features are worth noting. In the aggregate, factors seen as explaining downward mobility are life-cycle, crisis and structural in nature. In 46 per cent of cases, downward mobility is occasioned by life-cycle factors, such as loss of earning members or increase in the number of dependents. The importance of life-cycle factors is almost evenly balanced by the negative impact of various crisis factors which together explain downward mobility in 37 per cent of cases. Various structural factors explain the remainder 17 per cent of cases.

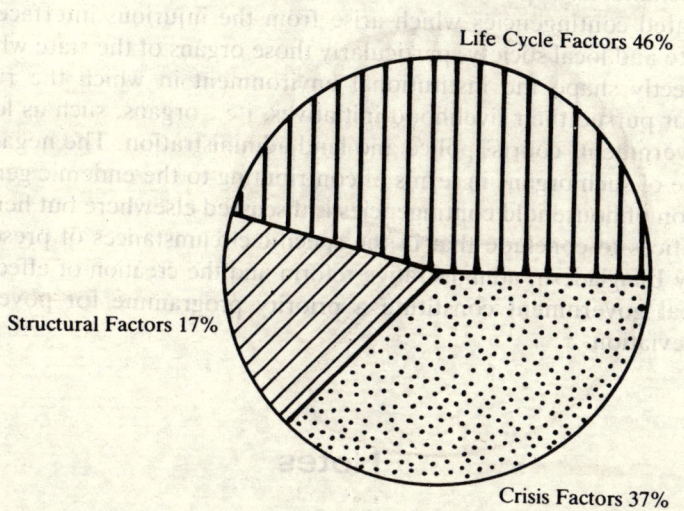

FIGURE 7.3
Factors Explaining Downward Household Mobility

What is particularly noteworthy here is the relative importance of crisis factors which at 37 per cent underscore, all that has been argued about crisis and insecurity as critical dimensions of the vulnerability of rural households. The economic significance of natural disasters is, of course, less important for asset less deficit households but conceding this, the relative significance of crisis factors noted on the aggregate also holds true for poorer households. The vulnerability of the category of break-even households to crisis factors which at 59 per cent illustrate the major constraint on economic graduation for households just above the threshold of poverty, should also be noted.

To conclude, the concern with crisis factors in the discussion on poverty has several aspects to it. One concern is with the buffer capacity of poor households or their capacity of self-provisioning for insurance against contingencies. As distinct from this question of buffers or self-provisioning, there is another major perspective on the issue where the concern is with reducing the very needs for insurance by addressing the sources of vulnerabilities in terms of a more conducive macro institutional environment. A ready example is a better health-care system which substantially reduces household contingencies to meet sudden demands for illness-related lumpy expenditures. Equally important concerns are related to insecurity-related contingencies which arise from the injurious interface of state and local society, particularly those organs of the state which directly shape the institutional environment in which the rural poor pursue their livelihood initiatives, i.e., organs, such as local government, courts, police and land administration. The negative role of such organs in terms of contributing to the endemic generation of household contingencies is discussed elsewhere but here it suffices to conclude that in the specific circumstances of present-day Bangladesh, administrative reform and the creation of effective local government constitute a priority programme for poverty-alleviation.

Notes

1. "You will not understand how utterly problem-ridden we poor women are. How much injustice and exploitation! We feel so defenceless with our honour and our body! Constantly struggling to save our honour! And any women or girl with a pretty face—her life is simply a hell. "Mastans" (local toughs) and even the local police are a constant menace. One night I got delayed in my return to my village from the nearby town of Khulna. Night had fallen. On the way a police patrol caught me. Why are you out at dark? I said I got delayed in my return. But why alone they asked? You have to go to our camp. So they started pulling me

towards their camp despite my protests. This was only a mile and a half from our house. Someone informed my house and two of my cousins rushed to the spot. But the patrol cleverly took everyone to their camp and then they tied up my cousins and charged them with being immoral with me. Imagine! What was I to do? This is how we have to live everyday . . . ." (*Voices from the Villages*, BIDS, forthcoming).

2. See Hossain Zillur Rahman, 1991 *Field Notes from Relief Work*, BIDS.

8

Gender Dimensions of Poverty

SHAMIM HAMID

Introduction

Although several measures of inequality have been developed over time (Sen index, Kakwani index, T-index, Kuznet's index, Gini Coefficient, Head count ratio and Poverty gap ratio), little investigation has been made into the gender dimensions of poverty. It was only much later that the insistence on seeing the deprivation of entire families as the right focus for studying misery and for seeking remedies was openly questioned. It was found that the importance of gender as a crucial parameter in social and economic analysis was complementary to, rather than competitive with, the variables of class, ownership, occupations, incomes and family status. Sen argued that 'to concentrate on family poverty irrespective of gender can be misleading in terms of both causation and consequences' (Sen, 1987). Another argument has been that poverty segregates lives both in space and in task and therefore limits perceptions to personal experience (Jain, 1985). If this is so, then men and women of poor households have less opportunity to plan and live cooperatively than those in households which are better off. Thus, the segmentation of household members' experience is one reason why poverty is likely to intensify age- and gender-based inequalities. Further, the economic condition of male and female within the same household should be one of the many fault lines along which social changes should be monitored (Dwyer and Bruce eds, 1988).

While no gender-based inequality measure has yet been devised, a Human Development Index (HDI) for male-female gap was estimated using the indicators of adult literacy rates, life expectancy and income (UNDP, 1990). Among the low ranking countries, Bangladesh by this index occupied 23rd position out of a total of 130 countries with female HDI as percentage of male HDI being 77 per cent. This was the same as India which was ranked 37th. Again Niger which has been estimated to have the lowest HDI amongst all countries has a female-male HDI ratio of 107, higher even than Japan which occupied the highest position in the HDI ranking. As the report comments, these comparisons 'show that national averages may conceal distressingly large gender disparities [and] professional work needs to be done to bring out clearly the state of the human condition separately for men and women'.

The objective of this chapter is, thus, to provide a clear picture of the poverty-related gender disparities in rural areas using socio-economic indicators which can be monitored over time to record the increase or decrease in the male/female gaps. Besides providing an outline of the basic situation, this chapter gives a gender-based analysis of the rural labour force and analyses the male/female gaps in the rural life-cycle pattern.

Base-Line Gender Disparities

The sample population of the BIDS survey consisted of 7760 persons of which 47 per cent were female giving a sex ratio of 1.13 males to every female. This is marginally higher than the national ratio of 1.06 (BBS Pocket Book, 1989).

Ninety per cent of the male population compared to 97 per cent of the female were regular household members, while 6 per cent of the male population compared to only 1 per cent of the female members were absent from the household most of the time visiting only at irregular intervals. This indicated the higher mobility of males in the rural areas compared to females. A marginally higher proportion of females (76 per cent) belonged to the poor households compared to males (74.5 per cent) (Table 8.1). Households which faced food shortage also reported a higher proportion of female members (71 per cent) compared to male (68 per cent) (Table 8.2). The occupational pattern of the households showed that while there were more men (48 per cent) than women (45.5 per cent) in farming households, those with their principal source of income coming from wage labour had a higher proportion of women (28 per cent) compared to men (25 per cent) (Table 8.3). Thus, more women than men were poor in rural Bangladesh.

TABLE 8.1
Percentage Distribution of Household Members by Poverty Level

Type of household	Male %	Female %	Total %
Poor	74.5	76.0	75.0
Moderately Poor	20.0	18.8	19.7
Non-poor	5.5	5.2	5.3

TABLE 8.2
Distribution of Members by Deficit Status of Household

Food Availability of household	Male %	Female %	Total %
1. Deficit	19.6	22.0	21.0
2. Occasionally Deficit	49.7	49.3	49.5
3. Stable	20.1	18.9	19.5
4. Surplus	10.6	9.8	10.2

Source: Analysis of Poverty Trends Project, BIDS: 62 Village Survey, 1989–90.

Illiteracy rate for the total population (5 years and above) was 63 per cent, with male illiteracy being 55 per cent compared to 71 per cent for females. There has been an overall increase in literacy rates since 1981 from 23.8 per cent to 37 per cent, with male literacy increasing from 31 per cent to 45 per cent and female literacy from 16 per cent to 29 per cent in the period 1981 to 1989. Female literacy grew at nearly the same rate as male literacy in this period, so that the male/female gap remained static.

There was no significant change in the marital status of the population since 1981 (Table 8.4), the widowed and divorced/separated/abandoned women out numbering the men by 7 per cent.

TABLE 8.3
Distribution of Members by Principal Source of Income of Household

Principal source of income of household	Male %	Female %	Total %
Farm	48.0	45.5	46.9
Agricultural Labour	14.9	16.8	15.8
Non-agricultural Labour	10.3	11.2	10.7
Home-based Self-employment	2.0	2.3	2.1
Non-home-based Self-employment	13.2	12.9	13.1
Service	11.2	10.9	11.1
Financially Aided	0.2	0.4	0.3

Source: Analysis of Poverty Trends Project, BIDS: 62 Village Survey, 1989–90.

TABLE 8.4
Marital Status of Household Members by Sex

Marital status	BIDS 1989 (%)		Population Census 1981 (%)	
	Male	Female	Male	Female
Not Married	62.0	49.0	62.0	49.6
Married	37.0	42.0	38.0	41.9
Widowed	1.0	7.0	0.8	7.8
Divorced	0.1	1.0	0.04	1.0
Separated/Abandoned	0.04	0.20	–	–

Source: Analysis of Poverty Trends Project, BIDS: 62 Village Survey, 1989–90.

The standard of living indicators showed that 53 to 55 per cent of the men compared to 45 to 47 per cent of the women owned basic clothing, such as a change of clothes, a pair of shoes or some winter clothing, such as shawl or sweater. This disparity was evident even when the woman was an earning member of the household. 55 to 60 per cent of earning women owning basic clothing compared to 82 to 86 per cent of the earning men (Table 8.5). Thus, being an earning member in the household did not necessarily allocate more resources to the woman. In the case of public media exposure, 62 per cent of men compared to 40 per cent of women listened to the radio while 30 per cent of the men compared to only 13 per cent of the women had access to television. Thus, taking all the above evidence into consideration more women than men were faced with the multi-dimensional aspects of poverty (Figure 8.1).

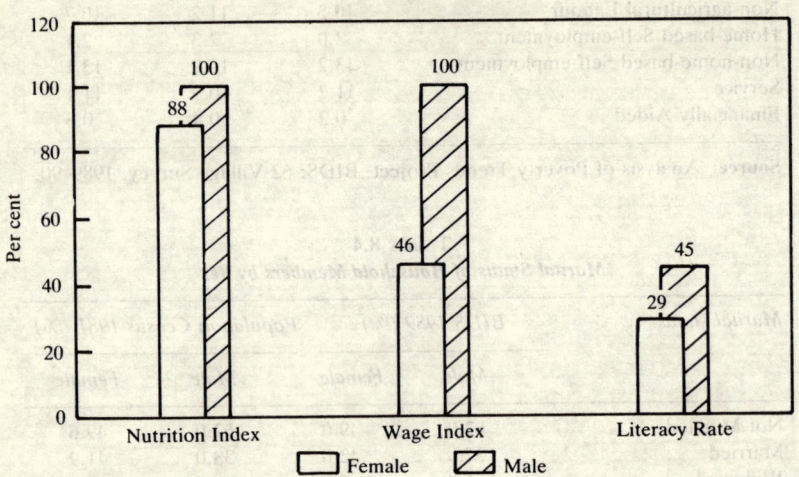

FIGURE 8.1
Male–Female Disparities

TABLE 8.5
Intra-Household Distribution of Minimum Assets of Earning Members by Sex

Sex	Percentage of earning members owning:		
	Minimum set of two clothes	Winter clothes	Footwear
Male	85.6	83.5	82.1
Female	68.5	58.8	55.1

Source: Analysis of Poverty Trends Project, BIDS: 62 Village Survey, 1989–90.

Gender Disparities in the Labour Force

There were 2189 earning members aged 10 years and above in the population of which 12 per cent were female. The economic dependency ratio was 2.54 which showed a 10 per cent increase over the Labour Force Survey (LFS) (Bureau of Statistics, 1985–86) estimate of 2.30. The age specific participation rates showed that while for males the highest participation was between the ages 40–49, for females the highest was between the ages 30–34. Again while the male labour force declined steadily from 50 years onwards the female labour force showed an upward trend from the age of 60 and above. This was evident from BIDS estimates as well as those of LFS 1985–86 (Table 8.6, Figures 8.2 and 8.3). The higher participation in the labour market of elderly females reflected the situation of widows who were without any social network support system, such as sons or other relatives and who had to remain in the labour force to support themselves even in their old age.

TABLE 8.6
Age-Specific Participation Rates

Age Group	Male	Female	LFS 1985–86 Rural Female
10–14	10.2	2.3	7.5
15–19	41.1	5.5	6.9
20–24	68.6	12.3	8.0
25–29	89.4	14.9	8.4
30–34	95.0	21.5	12.3
35–39	97.2	13.4	9.4
40–44	98.7	14.0	8.0
45–49	97.7	19.1	9.6
50–54	94.9	8.3	9.5
55–59	95.7	6.9	9.4
60–64	89.6	1.3	9.0
65 +	67.9	2.5	11.6

Source: Analysis of Poverty Trends Project, BIDS: 62 Village Survey, 1989–90.

Nearly 88 per cent of the female labour force came from poor households compared to 76 per cent of the male, while 5 per cent of the male labour force was from the non-poor households compared to 2.7 per cent females. Again while nearly 48 per cent of

138 • Shamim Hamid

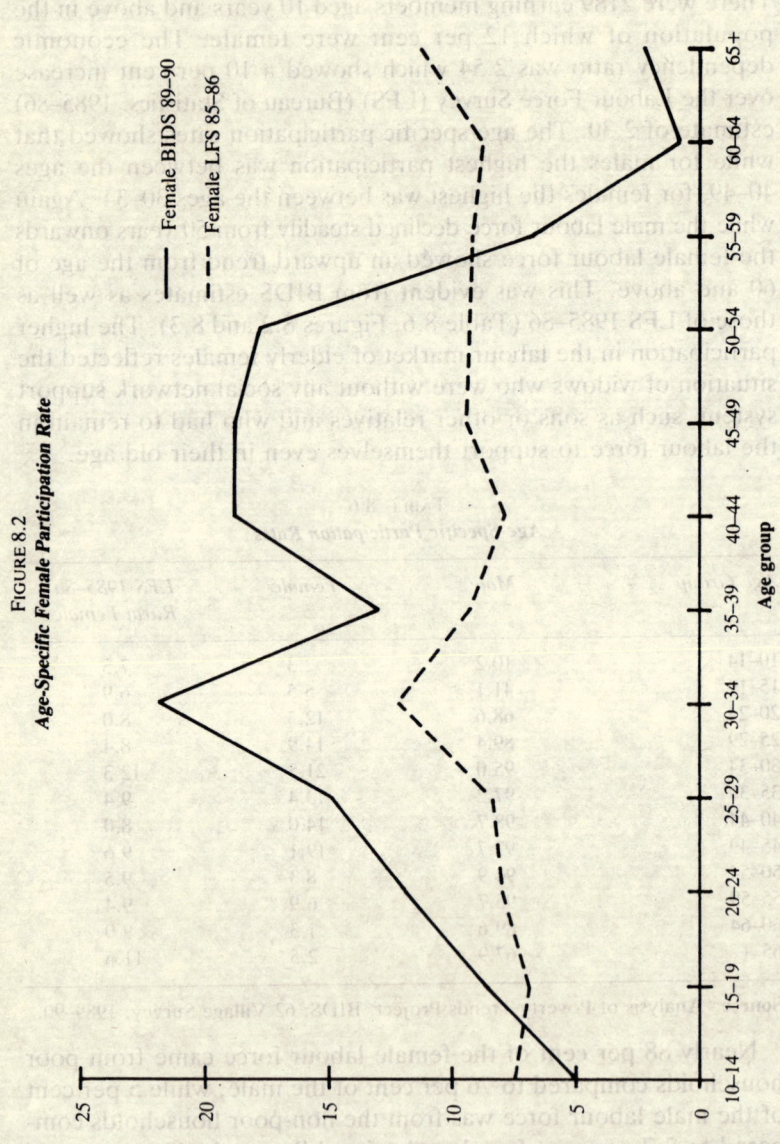

FIGURE 8.2
Age-Specific Female Participation Rate

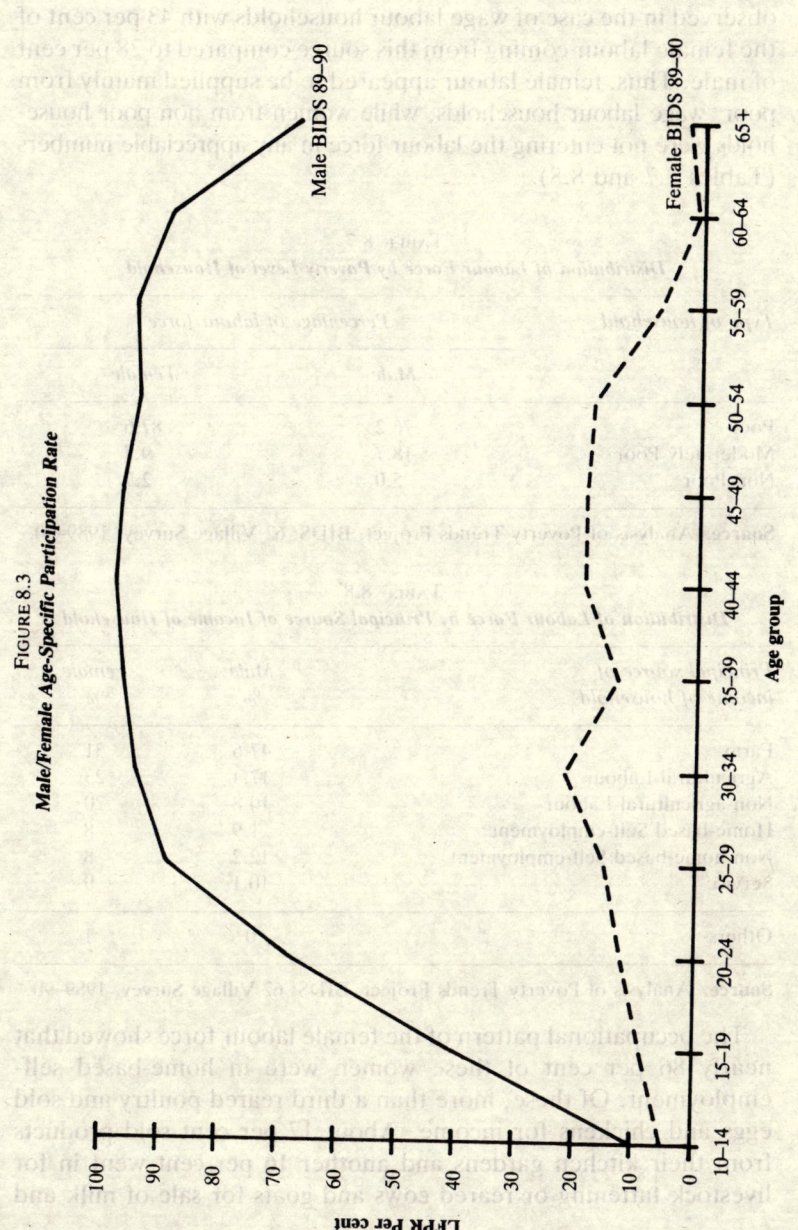

FIGURE 8.3
Male/Female Age-Specific Participation Rate

the male labour came from farming households, only 31 per cent of female labour came from this source. The reverse trend was observed in the case of wage labour households with 43 per cent of the female labour coming from this source compared to 28 per cent of male. Thus, female labour appeared to be supplied mainly from poor, wage labour households, while women from non-poor households were not entering the labour force in any appreciable numbers (Tables 8.7 and 8.8).

TABLE 8.7
Distribution of Labour Force by Poverty Level of Household

Type of household	Percentage of labour force	
	Male	Female
Poor	76.2	87.6
Moderately Poor	18.7	9.7
Non-Poor	5.0	2.7

Source: Analysis of Poverty Trends Project, BIDS: 62 Village Survey, 1989–90.

TABLE 8.8
Distribution of Labour Force by Principal Source of Income of Household

Principal source of income of household	Male %	Female %
Farm	47.6	31
Agricultural Labour	17.4	23
Non-agricultural Labour	10.8	20
Home-based Self-employment	1.9	8
Non-home-based Self-employment	12.2	8
Service	10.1	9
Others	0	1

Source: Analysis of Poverty Trends Project, BIDS: 62 Village Survey, 1989–90.

The occupational pattern of the female labour force showed that nearly 86 per cent of these women were in home-based self-employment. Of these, more than a third reared poultry and sold eggs and chickens for income. About 17 per cent sold products from their kitchen gardens and another 16 per cent went in for livestock fattening or reared cows and goats for sale of milk and the young. Other activities included share raising of livestock, buying paddy for husking and selling it for profit, husking paddy for others, sewing and embroidering for sale, basket weaving, net weaving, weaving jute hanging bags, storing paddy at harvest time for selling later at higher price, sale of betelnut, sale of seedlings, making rice products for sale, and operating a banana plantation.

About 14 per cent were in non-agricultural wage labour of which earth cutting was the most frequent activity. Other employment included day labour, working as domestic help, brick breaking and separating jute fibres. A marginal number were in non-home based self-employment, such as petty trading, running a grocery shop, collecting fuel from the forest for sale or surviving on charity (begging). Five of the earning women were in service which included working for the local family planning project office, for the social welfare office, or working for the village defence groups.

It may be noted that the majority of the women had multiple occupations. Amongst the daily wage labourers, male labourers came from both poor and non-poor households but the female wage labourers came exclusively from poor households (Table 8.9). Daily wages were paid in a combination of cash, commodity and meals. Here the cash wages received by females was between 40 to 50 per cent that of males and the number of meals or commodities received were on an average half that received by males. It may be noted that male labourers from non-poor households received higher wages than those from poor households. Thus, wage discrimination existed between male labourers from poor and non-poor households as well as between male and female labourers.

TABLE 8.9
Minimum Labour Wages (Aman Season)

Type of household	Daily Cash Wage (Tk)		No. of Meals		Commodity (Kg)	
	Male	Female	Male	Female	Male	Female
Poor	17.54	7.0 (9.7)	2.4	1.03	0.97	0.34
Moderately Poor	17.90	–	1.44	–	0.46	–
Non-Poor	21.25	–	2.75	–	0	–
Average	18.17	7.0 (9.7)	2.18	1.03	0.68	0.34

Source: Analysis of Poverty Trends Project, BIDS: 62 Village Survey, 1989–90.
Note: Figures in brackets are averages taken over only non-zero values.

For both male and female labourers the major proportion (about 85 per cent) of the labour was fixed on a daily basis and the majority (55 per cent) of the female wage labourers expressed preference for this type of arrangement. For female labourers contractual labour answered for another 14 per cent while the remaining one per cent was on a seasonal basis. For male labourers, however, 10 per cent was on contractual basis and another 4 per cent seasonal (Table 8.10). They did not express any strong preference between arrangements on daily basis and contractual arrangements. Only 36 per cent of the female wage labourers received the prevalent market price while for 64 per cent the terms of labour was fixed wholly by the employers. In the latter case, this usually worked out to be less than the market wage since the women were required to do both agricultural and domestic work at the time and convenience of the employers. On the other hand, 79 per cent of the male labourers received market wages and only 21 per cent worked entirely on employer's terms (Table 8.11). Female labourers, thus, had less bargaining power than their male counterparts in fixing their terms of labour.

TABLE 8.10
Types of Labour Arrangements

Type of household	Male labourer			Female labourer		
	Daily basis	Seasonal	Contract	Daily basis	Seasonal	Contract
Poor	85.25	5.5	9.25	84.10	1.40	14.50
Moderately Poor	75.00	7.0	18.00	–	–	–
Non-Poor	94.00	0.0	6.00	–	–	–
Average	85.00	5.0	10.00	84.10	1.40	14.50

Source: Analysis of Poverty Trends Project, BIDS: 62 Village Survey, 1989–90.

Disparities in Life-Cycle Patterns of Males and Females

An analysis of the life-cycle pattern of the men and women in the population gave the following picture: A male aged 15 to 24 years is unmarried and living with his parents. His economic condition is

TABLE 8.11
Terms of Wage Labour by Sex

Mode of wage fixation	Percentage of labour days of	
	Male	Female
1. Market Price	78.8	35.7
2. Employer's Terms	21.0	64.3
3. Combination of 1 & 2	0.2	0

Source: Analysis of Poverty Trends Project, BIDS: 62 Village Survey, 1989–90.

a reflection of his parental home which is more than 15 years old. In general the older the household the more stable is its economic condition as can be seen from the Table 8.12 which indicates that older households tend to be less poor than new households. By the time the young man reaches 25 to 39 years he moves downwards

TABLE 8.12
Relationship between Age and Poverty Level of Household

Type of household	Mean age of household (Years)
Poor	16.5
Non-poor	22.0
Average	18.00

from being a member of an economically stable household to a deficit or at best an occasionally deficit household. This would be the time when he marries and either sets up his new household[1] or continues as a joint family in the existing household structure. In either case he has little or no assets, being at best a potential land owner through inheritance. His situation will continue to worsen until the age of 49 after which his economic condition begins to improve and reaches an overall high from 60 years onward. This would be the period when he has either inherited his father's property and/or purchased his own and his life-cycle, therefore, indicates an upward mobility in land ownership (Figures 8.4, 8.5 and 8.6).

The majority of 15 to 24 years old women belong to poor, food deficit households (Figures 8.2 and 8.3). A woman in this age

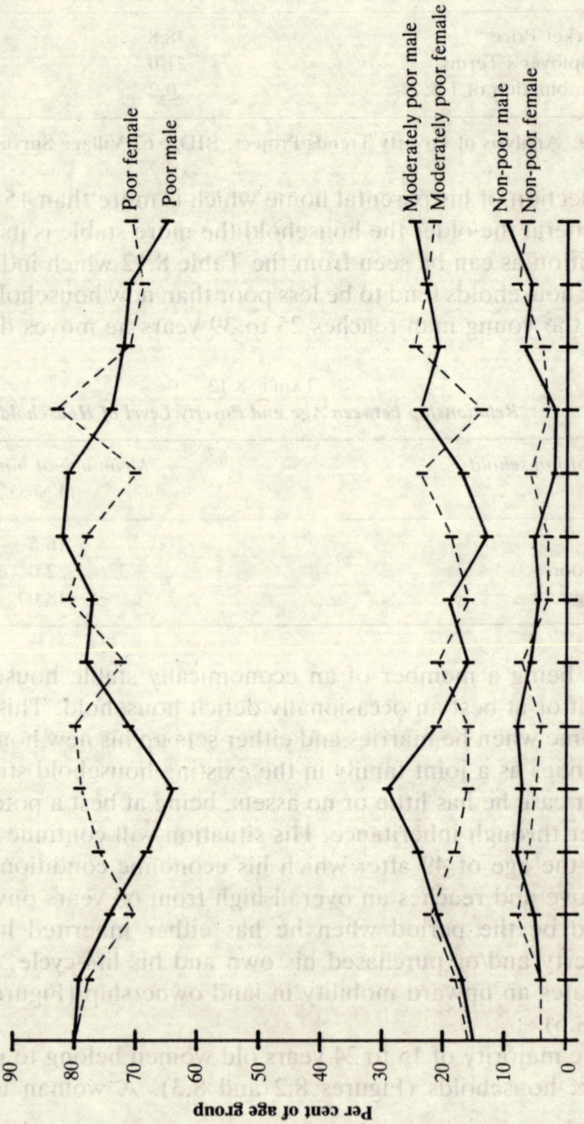

144 • Shamim Hamid

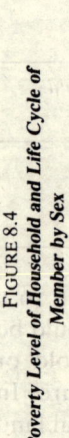

FIGURE 8.4
Poverty Level of Household and Life Cycle of Member by Sex

Gender Dimensions of Poverty • 145

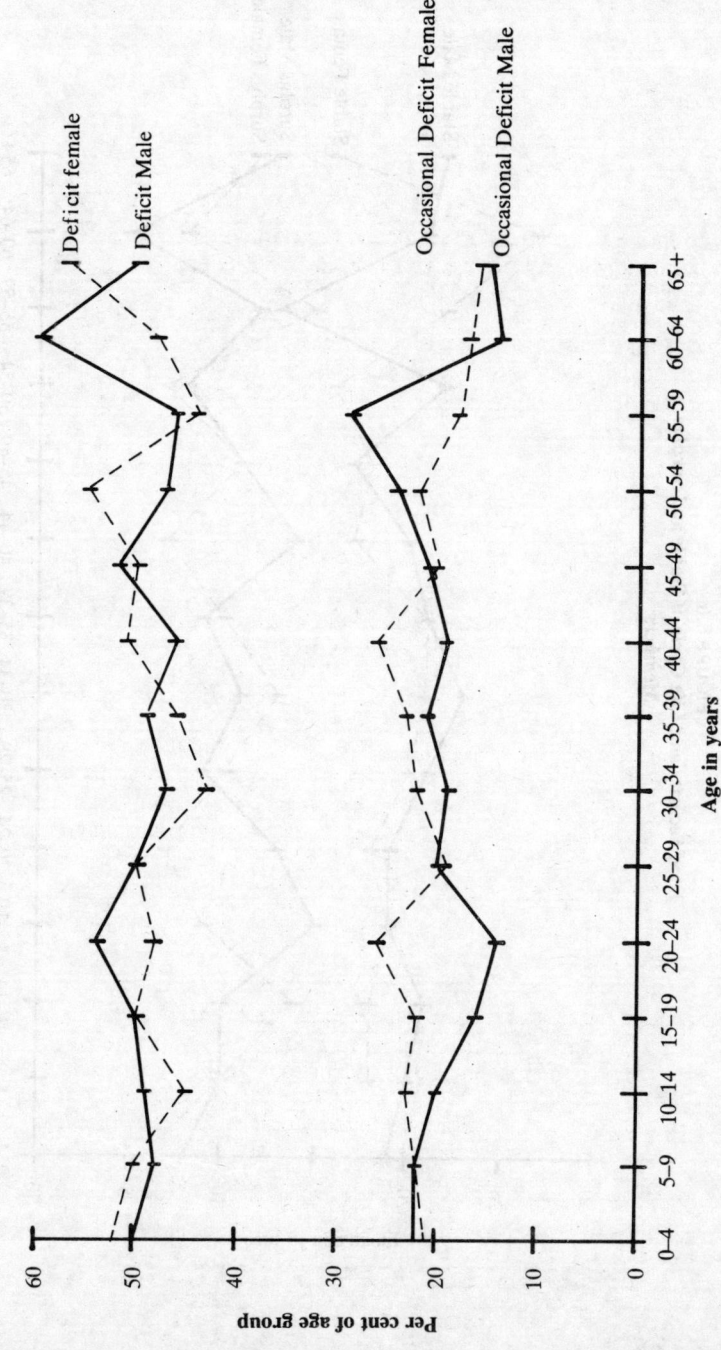

FIGURE 8.5
Food Security of Household and Life Cycle of Members

146 • Shamim Hamid

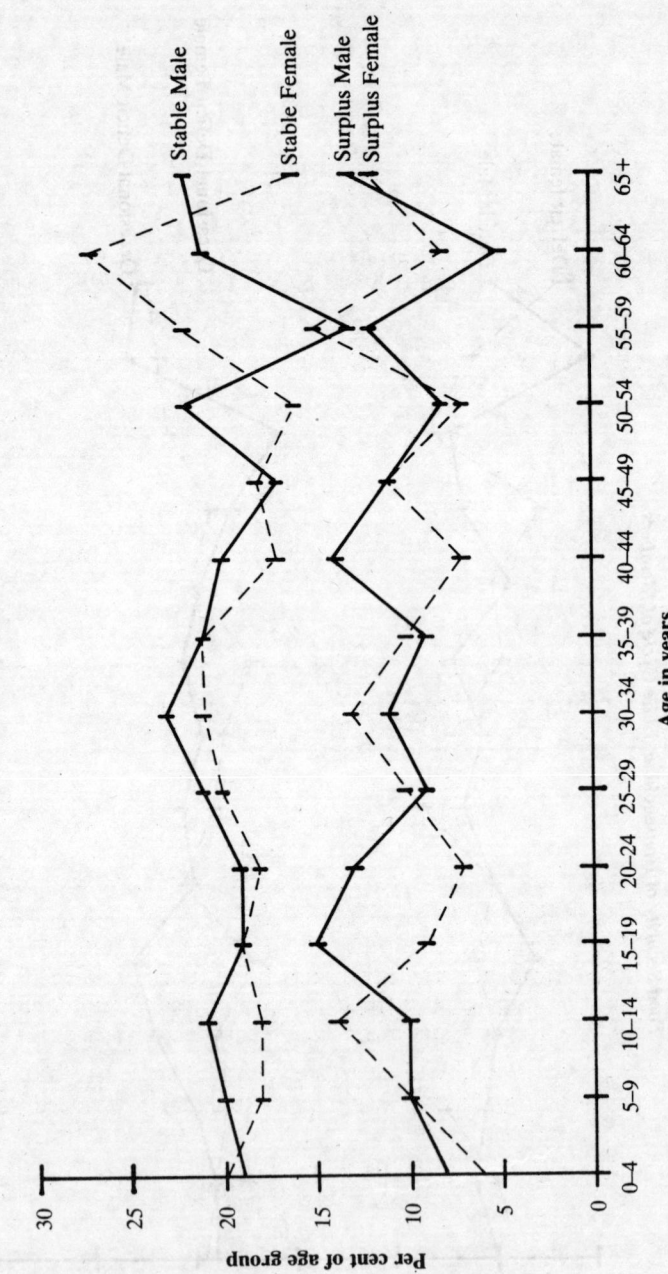

FIGURE 8.6
Food Security and Life Cycle of Stable and Surplus Members

group, therefore, stands in stark contrast to her male counterpart. This is the time when she is newly married (age at marriage for females being 17.6 years [BBS, 1990]) and starting a new family. Her situation at best remains static until she is 40 years old when she moves from a high poverty bracket to a less poor bracket. Women at this period are the least poor and a relatively high proportion come from stable or surplus households. This ties in with the life-cycle period of their husbands (men 50 years and over) when they are most stable/affluent, the average age difference between married couples in the survey being 10 years.

However, where the economic condition of the 65 + male at worst remains stable, that of the 65 + female shows a tendency to deteriorate. This is mainly because at this age the proportion of widows far outnumbers widowers. Seventy three per cent of women over 65 years of age were widows while only 47 per cent of men of this age group were widowers (Table 8.13). The high differential is mainly due to the age gap between married couples and also partially due to the fact that widowers of all ages tend to remarry while social indoctrination prevents older widows (over 50 years of age) from seeking remarriage. As can be seen from Table 8.13 the percentage of widows increases dramatically from the age of 50 onwards. The fact that women over 65 years are worse off is further reinforced by the fact that while the economic participation rate of the elderly male (50 years and above) continues to decrease, that of females shows a sudden upward trend for those over 65 years.

Conclusions

Women in Bangladesh live a life of cultural and economic contradictions. Where on one hand children are taught that heaven lies beneath a mother's feet, that same mother is denied equal inheritance rights from her father's or her husband's property. On one hand the Islamic marriage contract provides a powerful tool whereby a woman can secure a measure of security in case of divorce or widowhood, on the other her bargaining position is so weak that she is seldom able to realise any benefit from it. The life of an average Bangladeshi woman in the rural areas therefore evokes anything but envy.

TABLE 8.13
Distribution of Widowed by Age and Sex

Age group	Percentage of group totals	
	Male	Female
20–24	–	0.6
25–29	–	1.5
30–34	2.9	4.9
35–39	2.9	4.5
40–44	8.8	12.0
45–49	8.8	19.0
50–54	2.9	35.0
55–59	14.7	46.0
60–64	11.8	53.0
65+	47.1	73.0

Source: Analysis of Poverty Trends Project, BIDS: 62 Village Survey, 1989–90.

Although at birth she has at least equal chance at survival as a man, by the time she is four years old she has already forfeited her rights mainly due to social discrimination.[2] Her struggle for survival begins early between the ages 15–24 when she gets married to a man ten years older than her and starts a new home with limited resources. Her economic condition continues to deteriorate until she reaches 40. A man on the other hand is relatively well off until the age of 24 and his struggle for survival begins only from the age of 25 when he gets married and sets up a new home. By the time he is 50 his situation stablises, i.e., if his economic condition, whatever it may be, does not improve it does not worsen either. If he is amongst the fortunate he has generated some surplus by this time and his economic condition continues to improve even after he is 60 years old. By the time a man reaches his peak his wife is 40 years old and shares in the well being of the household. However her years of relative well being are not as long term as her husband's and after 65 her condition begins to worsen. This decline in the economic situation of elderly women stands out prominently because the number of widows far outnumbers widowers, one of the main causes being the age difference between husband and wife. Other causes are that widowers tend to remarry, while social indoctrination often prevents widows (especially those over 50) from remarrying. Thus, with limited inheritance rights and consequently little or no access to resources widows are at best dependents of their sons[3] and at worst fend for themselves fulfilling the categories of the 'poorest of the poor' as de jure female headed households.

A women, however, will find herself as head of household not only when she is a widow but also when pressure on land and lack of alternative employment opportunities force the male household head to migrate in search of jobs. In most cases her household will be only about 8 years old with less than an acre of land and every earning member will be supporting about 2 non-earning members. In some cases, however, her household may be older (about 12 years old) and owning more land (3 acres) but economic dependency is very high, every earning member supporting 5 non-earning members.

Besides migration, other ways that men cope with a worsening economic condition is by remarrying for dowries although the custom of dowry has been declared illegal in Bangladesh. This leads to divorce and abandonment of young girls, 56 per cent of the divorced women in the BIDS survey being between the ages 15–24. She is, thus, forced into a labour market unable to absorb her, the unemployment rates of women 10–29 years being very high compared to those of 30 years and above.[4] On an average she will have about four children and by her 30th year she will be participating in the labour force at a rate higher than any other age group (BIDS estimated the LFPR of 30–34 year old rural females at 22 per cent). As seen earlier this is the economically depressed period of her life and she copes with the situation by going out to work. She will, however, enter and withdraw from the labour force depending on the mix of time and income she needs to commit to her young children (Lloyd, 1990).

By the time she reaches her fiftieth year she stands a good possibility of becoming and remaining widowed. If she survives upto the age of 60, she stands a better chance of living upto the age of 70 than a man[5], but whereas most of her male counterparts are withdrawing from the labour market, a woman over 65 years old in the rural areas shows a higher participation rate than a woman immediately younger than her. This trend is a reflection of the de jure widow-headed households as seen earlier.

Throughout her life-cycle and at all age groups a Bangladeshi woman will endure a health status that is inferior to her male counterpart especially in the rural areas. The main cause of her inferior health status is social discrimination leading to lower nutritional status even before she reaches the age of 4. The survey shows that in her younger years, she will suffer from cold related illnesses such as influenza and bronchitis, as well as diarrhoea and skin diseases. Later gynaecological illnesses will be added to her problems and in old age chronic diseases like rheumatism will be among her chief adversaries. The amount of money spent on her treatment will not generally exceed Tk 25 annually. Her literacy situation, however, records an improvement: where in 1981 only 16 out of every 100 females aged 5 years and above were literate, in 1989, 29 out of every 100 women were so. Compared to male rates, however, female literacy still remains low and there is no narrowing of the grip in evidence.

It is very likely that a woman participating in the labour market will come from a household owning less than 0.50 acres of land and facing food shortages at least part of the time. The household's main source of income will be agricultural or non-agricultural wage labour. Her own occupation will most likely be home-based self-employment, such as poultry and livestock raising, kitchen gardening, paddy husking and making handicrafts. Her choice of employment will remain the same even if credit were made available to her for investment[6], although the rate of return on capital investment of her choice is very low[7]. To compensate she will continue to engage in multiple income-earning activities. She will choose these occupations mainly because they will enable her to remain near the homestead to cook, clean and take care of the children, the elderly and the sick. On an average she will also be spending 9 to 11 hours daily on expenditure-saving activities, such as collecting leaves and twigs for fuel and fodder, collecting and making dung cakes, collecting edibles along the banks of ponds and rivers, fishing in flooded paddy fields, growing vegetables in the kitchen garden for consumption and gleaning paddy from harvested fields (Hamid, 1989). These expenditure-saving activities will augment the household income by as much as 15 per cent (see chapter 13). These diverse responsibilities will force her to frequently move in and out of the labour market and will be one of the major causes for her low wage rate and lack of bargaining power and choice in fixing the terms of labour arrangements. But although she will be participating in the labour force and adding to the household income she will be more deprived that the male member in the intra-household distribution of resources.

The social marginalisation of women extends to their standing in government priorities. Interest in WID (Women in Development) issues has been generated almost entirely by donors whose influence in this sector has perhaps increased proportionately to the aid dependency of WID programmes—a dependency that has tripled since 1980. According to one estimate, between 1980 and 1986 about 19 per cent of project allocations by donors have gone to projects where women are targeted as beneficiaries. Of those, 55 per cent went to population and family planning projects, 2 per cent to health, 8 per cent to education and 25 per cent to self-help projects. Thus, resource allocation pattern by donors highlight women's reproductive roles and that too in the context of controlling women's fertility and not reproductive health or reproductive rights (Jahan, 1989).

The Government of Bangladesh has been more receptive to women's concerns in social sectors than in economic ones. For example the Ministries of Agriculture and Forestry have been more resistant to gender issues than those of health and education. Amongst the NGOs, Grameen Bank, BRAC and Proshika have gained international reputation for involving large numbers of women. However, none have achieved significant breakthrough in helping women to move to higher productivity or to activities with higher economic returns. Again, small NGOs which have successfully provided safe, accessible and effective reproductive health services to women have failed to achieve significant scale or coverage (Chen, 1990). Also, since the dimensions of poverty that women experience are not necessarily only material but also social, cultural and knowledge-based, little of significance has been achieved on these front either by small NGOs like Soptogram, Nari Swanirbhar Parishad or government sponsored programmes like the Socioeconomic Development Programme for Women (Asad & Akhter, 1990).

Many of the factors which constrain a greater participation of women in social and economic life are rooted in attitude biases. Change in attitudes can be brought about through positive projection of women aimed at both men and women so as to break down age old conceptions of their roles and status in and outside the household. One of the ways could be the public media of radio which was found to be accessible to 60 per cent of the men and 40 per cent of the women in the rural areas. These projections must also be accompanied by concrete actions, such as providing women with equal inheritance rights, encouraging and training women to actively participate in politics and making a genuine effort to raise the image and the status of women to the young generation through text books and school syllabi.

To encourage women to graduate into activities with higher returns, small and appropriate technology must be developed to provide the necessary opportunities. Examples of these would include the production and dissemination of driers using solar energy (made from indigenous raw materials) to use for drying fish, fruit, vegetables, spices and coconut to sell in the market (Waring, et al., 1989). Such driers have proved very successful in Nepal. Again ovens made from metal drums for baking bread for selling in the market has proved very successful in some parts of Africa.

In the social sectors, programmes, like free secondary school education for girls, will have little impact if the life style of rural women are not taken into consideration. Because girls become mother surrogates to younger siblings in the absence of the working mother, drop-out rates for girls are very high. Any female literacy programmes have to take these constraints into account and devise appropriate formats which help to deliver education to the doorsteps of those who are culturally or economically forced to drop out of schools.

The multi-dimensional aspects of women's poverty in Bangladesh have developed over generations through social, cultural and economic deprivation. The layers are deep, resistant to change and difficult to permeate. Poverty-alleviation for women must, therefore, be aimed at the individual rather than the household since men and women are distinctive in their economic access and similarly have distinct self interest within the family. Male and female goals within nuclear and inter-generational households are typically pursued not through playing out cooperative plans but rather through institutionalised inequalities. In the interest of equality and economic progress policymakers must take these facts into cognisance (Bruce and Dwyer, 1988). Otherwise Virginia Woolf's plaintative cry made more than half a century ago about why one sex (male) was so safe and prosperous and the other (female) so poor and insecure will continue to echo through the generations without any major change in one of the core issues of human existence (Woolf, 1929).

Notes

1. The survey shows that 72 per cent of the households are either nuclear or joint households.
2. The probability of dying for a male child 1–4 years old is 0.047 compared to 0.059 for a female child of the same age (BBS Statistical Year Book 1990). Whereas that at birth for females is 0.105 compared to 0.120 for males. See also Chen et al., 1981, for a discussion on sex biases.
3. For a discussion on this see Cain, 1986.
4. LFS 85–86, BBS 1990 puts these values at:
   10–19 year old rural females—7.7
   20–29 year old rural females—8.0
   30 + year old rural females—0.9
5. BBS Statistical Yearbook 1990 p.67-68
6. 84 per cent of all loans disbursed to women by the Grameen Bank in 1986 were utilised for livestock, poultry raising and fisheries and processing and manufacturing (Hossain, 1988).
7. 'The rates of return on capital invested in individual activities range from 10 to 40 per cent, the rates being higher for trading and modern industrial activities and lower for traditional processing and artisanal activities. (Ghai, 1984).

References

Asaduzzaman, M. and **Akhtar F.**, 1990, *Womens' Programmes for Alleviation of Poverty* BIDS.
Bangladesh Bureau of Statistics (BBS), *Statistical Pocket Book 1989*.
BBS, *Statistical Yearbook 1990*.
Cain, M. 1986, 'The Consequences of Reproductive Failure: Dependence Mobility and Mortality among the Elderly of Rural South Asia', *Population Studies*, 40 (3).
Chen, M. 1990, *Review of the Ford Foundations' Programming for Women in Bangladesh*, Ford Foundation.
Chen, Huq and **D'Souza,** 1981, 'Sex bias in the family allocations of food and health care in rural Bangladesh', in *Population and Development Review*, Vol. 7, Number 1, March 1981.
Dwyer D. and **J. Bruce** (ed.), 1988, *A Home Divided*, Stanford University Press, California.

Ghai, D. 1988. *An evaluation of the Impact of the Grameen Bank Project*, Grameen Bank 29.

Hamid, S. 1989. *Women's Non-Market Work and GDP Accounting: The Case of Bangladesh*, BIDS Research Report, No.116.

Hossain, M. 1988. *Credit for Alleviation of Rural Poverty*, IFPRI/BIDS, Research Report No.65.

Jahan, R., 1989. *Women and Development in Bangladesh Challenges and Opportunities*, Ford Foundation, Dhaka.

Jain, D. (ed.), 1985, *The Tyranny of the Household*, New Delhi.

Lloyd, C.B. 1990, *Understanding the Relationship between Women's Work and Fertility*, Working Papers No.9, The Population Council.

Report on Labour Force Survey 1985-86, Bangladesh Bureau of Statistics.

Sen, A. 1987, *Gender and Cooperative Conflicts*, WIDER Working Papers WP18.

UNDP. 1990, *Human Development Report*, New York, Oxford University Press.

Waring, M., C. Joshi and S. Hamid, 1989, 'Strategies to Incorporate Women in the Attainment of the Goals of the Fourth Five Year Plan', UNDP/The Planning Commission, Government of Bangladesh, Dhaka.

Woolf, V. 1929, *A Room of One's Own*, Hogarth Press Ltd., Great Britain.

III

The Social Composition of Poverty

9

Socioeconomic Characteristics of the Poor

MAHABUB HOSSAIN

Introduction

Who constitute the rural poor? What are their characteristics? We have inadequate knowledge about these issues because of lack of information at the national level. The target group for anti-poverty programmes is usually defined on the basis of ownership of land. But land is not the only determinant of the level of living of the people. Since this study generated information at the household level, it is possible to identify the poor with respect to various socioeconomic characteristics. The main variables that we have used for classification of the households are: land ownership, land tenure, principal source of income and the level of education of the head of the household. This section presents the findings from the survey on these aspects.

Profile of the Poor

The bulk of the poor households belong to the land-poor category. The incidence of poverty is about 78 per cent for households having no cultivated land and 71 per cent for the marginal landowners compared to 31 per cent for medium farm households and only 9 per cent for households owning more than 5 acres (Table 9.1). The functionally landless households contain nearly 60 per cent of the poor, the marginal landowners another 21 per cent.

TABLE 9.1
Incidence of Poverty: By Size of Land Ownership, 1989–90

Land ownership group (acres)	Extreme poverty		Extreme and moderate poverty	
	Incidence of poverty (per cent)	Share of the poor (per cent)	Incidence of poverty (per cent)	Share of the poor (per cent)
No cultivated land	47.0	53.0	78.3	43.9
Up to 0.49	42.3	19.1	71.4	16.0
0.5–1.49	24.8	17.4	60.9	21.2
1.5–2.49	11.8	4.5	44.5	9.1
2.5–4.99	8.4	4.1	31.2	7.7
5.0 and more	3.4	1.5	9.1	2.1
Total	27.5	100.0	55.4	100.0

Source: Analysis of Poverty Trends Project, BIDS: 62 Village Survey.

Nearly 53 per cent of the 'hard core' poor are concentrated in households having no cultivated land and 90 per cent in households owning less than 1.5 acres. This suggests that poverty inflicts mostly landless and marginal land owning households. This is not surprising since land remains the most important income earning asset within the rural economy. The anti-poverty programmes in rural Bangladesh mostly target households owning upto 0.5 acres. This group contains nearly 72 per cent of the extreme poor and 60 per cent of the extreme and moderate poor. Another 21 per cent of the poor belong to households with 0.5 to 1.5 acres of land. There is a need to bring these households under poverty alleviation programmes.

Access of land through the tenancy market does not improve the poverty situation of the landless households (Table 9.2). The incidence of extreme poverty is almost the same for the landless non-cultivator households as for the pure tenant farmers (44 per

TABLE 9.2
Incidence of Poverty: By Land Tenure, 1989-90

Land tenure group	Extreme poverty		Extreme and moderate poverty	
	Incidence of poverty (per cent)	Share of the poor (per cent)	Incidence of poverty (per cent)	Share of the poor (per cent)
Landless Non-cultivator	46.7	47.9	78.8	39.2
Pure-tenant	44.0	13.1	78.7	11.7
Tenant-owner	24.7	9.7	60.8	11.9
Owner-tenant	16.5	6.6	38.4	7.6
Owner cultivator	14.9	22.6	39.3	29.6
Total	27.5	100.0	55.4	100.0

Source: Analysis of Poverty Trends Project, BIDS: 62 Village Survey.

cent) who rent their entire holding. This is also the case with extreme poverty. The mixed tenants however improve their economic position by renting in land. The tenant cultivators who own the major portion of their holding are as well off as the owner cultivators. Only 15 to 17 per cent of the population belonging to these households are 'hard core' poor. The landless non-cultivator households and pure tenants constitute about 41 per cent of rural households but contain 60 per cent of the 'hard core' poor.

The level of education of the head of the household is also found to be an important factor influencing poverty (Table 9.3). The incidence of poverty is about 69 per cent for households whose head had no formal schooling, compared to only 27 per cent for household heads who passed secondary schools. Households whose heads had no formal schooling contain 60 per cent of the 'hard core' poor while those with above secondary level education, only 5 per cent. Nearly 88 per cent of the 'hard core' poor remain in households whose heads are either illiterate or have attended only primary schools. The importance of education in alleviation of poverty is amply demonstrated by this findings.

Among various occupational groups the cultivator households have the lowest incidence of poverty (Table 9.4). Only 16 per cent of the population in the cultivator household were 'hard core' poor

TABLE 9.3
Incidence of Poverty: By Education Status, 1989–90

Education level of the head	Extreme poverty		Extreme and moderate poverty	
	Incidence of poverty (per cent)	Share of the poor (per cent)	Incidence of poverty (per cent)	Share of the poor (per cent)
No formal schooling	37.5	60.1	68.5	54.5
Primary	22.2	28.2	56.0	32.3
Secondary	16.9	7.9	35.9	7.6
Above secondary	10.4	4.5	26.7	5.6
Total	27.5	100.0	55.4	100.0

Source: Analysis of Poverty Trends Project, BIDS: 62 Village Survey.

TABLE 9.4
Incidence of Poverty: By Occupation, 1989–90

Principal occupation	Extreme poverty		Extreme and moderate poverty	
	Incidence of poverty (per cent)	Share of the poor (per cent)	Incidence of poverty (per cent)	Share of the poor (per cent)
Agricultural wage labour	54.5	30.6	84.5	23.6
Non-agricultural wage labour	42.8	16.6	85.6	15.4
Cultivator	16.1	28.1	40.9	35.4
Trader	19.9	6.9	53.2	9.2
Services	27.8	10.9	47.1	9.2
Others	38.5	6.9	61.5	7.2
Total	27.5	100.0	55.4	100.0

Source: Analysis of Poverty Trends Project, BIDS: 62 Village Survey.

and another 25 per cent moderately poor. At the other end, households who depend entirely on manual labour, such as agricultural and non-agricultural wage workers, and transport and construction workers, have the highest incidence of poverty. About 85 per cent of the population in wage-labour households are poor.

With respect to 'hard core' poverty, however, non-agricultural labour households are better off (43 per cent) compared to agricultural labour households. Non-farm households with capital (trader) and better quality human resources (service holder) are substantially better off than the wage labourers. The incidence of 'hard core' poverty is 20 per cent among traders and 27 per cent among service holders. An overwhelming proportion of the 'hard core' poor (75 per cent) are located in marginal cultivator and wage labour households.

Since ownership of land, education and non-agricultural employment opportunities are all important correlates of poverty, it is necessary to dissociate the effect on one from the other in order to assess their independent effects. This has been attempted by estimating the incidence of poverty in various education and occupational categories controlling the size of landholding. The findings are presented in Tables 9.5 to 9.8. It is found that education contributes to a substantial reduction in poverty only when the households own some land. For functionally landless households education has only a marginal effect in reducing poverty. The incidence of poverty in these households is about 82 per cent when the head had no formal schooling, 76 per cent with primary and secondary level education and as much as 71 per cent with higher education.

For cultivator households the incidence of poverty is obviously highly correlated with the size of landholding, varying from 83 per cent for those owning less than 0.5 acres to only 9 per cent for large

TABLE 9.5
Incidence of Extreme Poverty by Educational Level, Controlling Landholding Size, 1989–90

(Per cent of population)

Educational status	Landholding size (acres)			
	Less than 0.50	0.5–2.49	2.5–4.99	5.00 and above
No Formal Schooling	53.1	24.7	20.2	3.5
Primary	39.7	15.1	0.0	0.0
Secondary	47.6	22.8	3.9	5.4
Above Secondary	38.5	14.4	3.0	3.2

Source: Analysis of Poverty Trends Project, BIDS: 62 Village Survey.

TABLE 9.6
Incidence of Extreme and Moderate Poverty by Educational Level, Controlling Landholding Size, 1989–90

(Per cent of population)

Educational status	Landholding Size (acres)			
	Less than 0.50	0.5–2.49	2.5–4.99	5.00 and above
No Formal Schooling	82.5	63.5	42.0	19.9
Primary	75.7	53.5	47.8	0.0
Secondary	75.9	61.2	36.6	11.7
Above Secondary	70.7	39.9	11.0	7.7

Source: Analysis of Poverty Trends Project, BIDS: 62 Village Survey.

TABLE 9.7
Incidence of Extreme and Moderate Poverty by Occupation Controlling Landholding Size, 1989–90

(Per cent of population)

Occupation	Landholding size (acres)			
	Less than 0.50	0.5–2.49	2.5–4.99	5.00 and above
Cultivator	83.4	55.6	31.2	8.8
Wage Labour	85.9	80.5	*	*
Traders	60.0	58.4	12.2	14.6
Service	76.8	51.4	17.1	16.4
Others	76.5	42.1	47.3	4.3

Source: Analysis of Poverty Trends Project, BIDS: 62 Village Survey.

landowners (over 5.0 acres). For the functionally landless there is little difference in the incidence of 'hard core' or moderate poverty between cultivator and wage labour households, but those engaged in trade and services are substantially better off. Thus, the disadvantage of being land-poor is substantially redressed if the household is engaged in trading. The finding suggests that poverty could be substantially reduced if the land-poor are given access to capital and provided education and training for human resource development.

TABLE 9.8
Incidence of Extreme Poverty by Occupation Controlling Landholding Size, 1989–90

(Per cent of population)

Occupation	Landholding size (acres)			
	Less than 0.50	0.5–2.49	2.5–4.99	5.00 and above
Cultivator	54.1	18.9	7.5	3.0
Wage Labour	57.9	39.9	*	*
Traders	25.6	13.6	12.2	14.6
Service	35.8	20.5	17.1	16.4
Others	49.5	25.5	21.8	4.3

Source: Analysis of Poverty Trends Project, BIDS: 62 Village Survey.

Socioeconomic Characteristics

The socioeconomic characteristics of the 'poor' and the 'non-poor' households and their access to various resources may be reviewed from Table 9.9. It will be noted that the poor not only have limited access to land, they are also disadvantaged with regard to the access to new agricultural technology. The proportion of area irrigated and the land allocated to modern varieties of rice was found to be about one-third lower for the extremely poor households compared to the non-poor. With regard to the access to land from the tenancy market, there is no significant difference between poor and non-poor households.

The poor and non-poor households are also found to differ in respect of some demographic characteristics. The extreme and moderately poor households have larger number of children below age 10, fewer members in the income-earning age group, and higher child–women ratio which is an indicator of higher current fertility, compared to the non-poor. Thus, the poor not only have lower income-earning capacities, they have to bear a proportionately heavier burden of investment on human resource development, i.e., on nutrition, health and education of children. In practice, however, the poor cannot afford to invest much on human resource

TABLE 9.9
Characteristics of the Poor and Non-Poor Households, 1987–88

Variables	Extremely poor	Moderately poor	Non-poor
1. Land and New Technology			
(a) Land Owned (ac.)	1.02	1.14	2.15
(b) Land Cultivated (ac.)	1.59	1.85	2.72
(c) Per cent Area under Tenancy	23.1	25.00	21.5
(d) Per cent Area under Modern Variety Rice	30.9	37.10	45.1
(e) Per cent Area Irrigated	24.2	26.10	35.1
2. Demographic Characteristics:			
(a) Family Size	6.53	5.96	5.85
(b) Age of the Household	42	41	43
(c) Proportion of Children below Age 10	34.6	31.6	24.2
(d) Proportion of Males above Age 10	33.3	35.0	42.7
(e) Per cent of Adult Males (16 years +)	24.1	26.8	33.4
(f) Child-Woman Ratio	78.7	69.2	56.9
3. Education:			
(a) Per cent of Students in age group 6–15			
Male	52.8	63.0	70.0
Female	43.0	56.5	61.8
(b) Per cent of Illiterate Adult Members	85.5	63.6	47.0
(c) Per cent of Literate Adult Members with High Education	9.7	14.4	24.7

Source: Primary data provided by Dr. Mahabub Hossain from Differential Impact Study, BIDS (This Study had the same sample coverage and was carried out in 1987–88).

development, which is suggested by the differentiation of the households with regard to education. Nearly 86 per cent of adult members in the extremely poor households were illiterate, compared to 47 per cent in the non-poor households. The proportion of students in the school-going age of 6 to 15 was about 53 per cent for male and 43 per cent for female for the extremely poor, compared to 70 per cent and 62 per cent in the non-poor households. The average age of the household head is almost similar across the poverty scale. This may suggest that with respect to health and longeivity, the poor and the non-poor are not highly differentiated.

Sources of Income

The structure of household income for the 'poor' and 'non-poor' groups may be reviewed from Table 9.10 (Figure 9.1). The sectoral composition of income are almost similar. The extremely poor derive two-thirds of their incomes from agricultural sources and one-third from non-agriculture; for the non-poor the dependence on non-agriculture is marginally higher (38 per cent). But there are significant differences within these groups with respect to dependence on activities within the broad sectors. First, as expected the

TABLE 9.10
Composition of Rural Household Incomes: For Poor and Non-Poor Households

Source of Income	Extremely poor		Moderately poor		Non-poor	
	Tk per annum	Per cent	Tk per annum	Per cent	Tk per annum	Per cent
Agriculture:	7,553	66.6	14,990	63.5	38,253	61.8
Crop cultivation	2,516	22.2	7,515	31.9	27,053	43.7
Kitchen garden	1,039	9.2	1,904	8.1	3,611	5.8
Non-Crop Agriculture	841	7.4	2,650	11.2	6,122	9.9
Agricultural wage	3,157	27.8	2,921	12.4	1,467	2.4
Non-agriculture:	3,789	33.5	8,616	36.5	23,681	38.2
Industry	562	5.0	1,153	4.9	2,997	4.8
Trade	770	6.8	2,465	10.4	9,906	16.0
Service	837	7.4	1,883	8.0	4,244	6.9
Transport and construction	276	2.4	550	2.3	1,574	2.5
Non-agriculture wage	777	6.9	1,568	6.6	977	1.6
Remittances	567	5.0	997	4.2	3,983	6.4
Total	11,342	100.0	23,606	100.0	61,934	100.0

Source: Analysis of Poverty Trends Project, BIDS: 62 Village Survey.

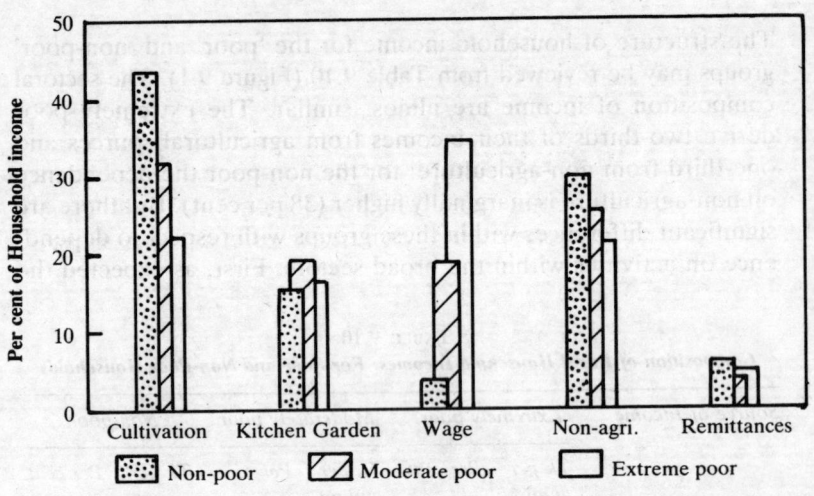

FIGURE 9.1
Composition of Rural Household Income by Poverty Status

poor depend substantially more on the labour market for their livelihood than the non-poor. Nearly 35 per cent of the income of the extremely poor is on account of wages, 28 per cent from agricultural labour market and 7 per cent from the non-agricultural labour market. The corresponding share is 19 per cent for the moderate poor and only 4 per cent for the non-poor households. Second, while the poor get a smaller proportion of their incomes from crop cultivation because of unfavourable endowment of land, their dependence on the kitchen garden is higher than that of the non-poor. Third, like the ownership of land, involvement in trading activities seems to have a poverty-alleviating effect. The non-poor households get nearly 16 per cent of their income from trading compared to 10.4 per cent for the moderate poor, and only 6.8 per cent for the 'hard core' poor. The relative share of industry, services, transport and construction in total household income is almost similar for the poor and the non-poor groups.

Wage Earnings

Since the poor depend to a large extent on the labour market for their earnings, an important determinant of the poverty situation would be the wage rate prevailing in the market and to change over time. The survey collected information on money wages and prices of rice from the 62 survey villages at different points of time. The estimates from this information of real wages and its change during the 1988–1991 period are shown in Table 9.11. This table also reports the differences in wages for different groups of villages classified by land and labour endowment and infrastructural facilities.

The daily wage for agricultural labourers is estimated at Tk 36.05 for a day's work in 1990. The average price of coarse rice during that time was found to be Tk 10.97 per kg. Thus, an agricultural wage labourer got 3.29 kg equivalent of rice for the day's work. The estimate for 1987 was 3.49 kg. It would then appear that the real wage rate declined by about 5.7 per cent over this period. This appears consistent with the deterioration in extreme poverty reported earlier. The money wage rate increased at 3.9 per cent but prices of rice increased 7.1 per cent per year during 1987–90 period, which reduced the purchasing capacity of the poor.

The variation of the real wage rate across villages was not related with the land endowment of the village. In fact, the real wage rate was found to be somewhat lower in villages with higher land endowments which is contrary to a priori expectation. Presumably apart from the endowment of land the use of modern technology and the availability of non-agricultural jobs determine wages. The wage rate is found higher in villages where the labour market is tight. The real wage rate in villages reporting labour shortage was about 19 per cent higher in 1987 and 11 per cent in 1990 compared to villages with labour surplus.

Development of infrastructure facilities and the diffusion of new agricultural technology exert a positive influence on the wage rate. The real wage rate was about 18 per cent higher in villages with developed transport facilities compared to less developed villages for both year of survey. Villages with more than 50 per cent of the area under modern rice varieties had about 23 per cent higher wages in 1987 and 12 per cent higher in 1990, compared to villages with lower proportion of area covered by the new technology.

TABLE 9.11
Level and Changes in Agricultural Wages in Villages Classified by Land and Labour Endowment and Development of Infrastructure

Village groups	Nominal wages (Tk/day)		Price of rice (Tk/Kg.)		Real wage rate (Kg. of rice/day)	
	1987	1990	1987	1990	1987	1990
Villages with Land per household:						
Up to 1.0 acre	33.86	36.43	8.82	11.24	3.84	3.24
1.0 to 2.0 acres	33.80	37.20	8.65	10.83	3.91	3.44
2.0 acres & above	28.17	34.33	9.35	10.82	3.01	3.17
Villages Reporting Labour Shortage:						
Yes	34.27	37.61	8.86	10.92	3.87	3.44
No	29.35	34.08	9.01	11.03	3.26	3.09
Village Reporting Access to Immigration						
Yes	32.80	36.55	8.86	10.76	3.70	3.40
No	31.74	35.79	9.03	11.08	3.51	2.23
Transport Infrastructure:						
Developed	34.27	41.50	8.84	11.25	3.88	3.69
Less Developed	29.35	34.02	8.96	10.87	3.28	3.13
New Agricultural Technology						
Developed	34.62	38.92	8.54	11.02	4.05	3.53
Less Developed	30.36	34.20	9.19	10.94	3.30	3.13
Total	32.10	36.05	8.92	10.97	3.60	3.29

Source: Differential Impact Study and Analysis of Poverty Trends Project, BIDS: 62 Village Survey.
* With more than 50 per cent of the cultivated area under modern rice varieties.

Wage Rate as a Poverty Monitor

Since estimation of poverty involves a process of data collection which is tedius, time-consuming and subject to errors, it is often suggested that the level and trend in real wages may be used as a proxy for monitoring poverty. In order to test this proposition we have related the village level estimates of poverty with the estimates of real wages. The association between the two variables is found statistically significant, but the coefficient of determination is found to be very low (see Table 9.12). The weak statistical relationship may be due to the fact that only a small proportion of the income of the poor originates from their participation in the agricultural and non-agricultural labour market. In rural Bangladesh self-employment in farm and non-farm activities is the predominant source of income, which is not affected by wages. Thus, while estimation of real wages may be one of the suggested indicators for monitoring poverty, it is not a perfect substitute for direct estimation of poverty.

TABLE 9.12
Relationship between the Incidence of Poverty and the Real Wage Rate, Regression Estimates, 1989–90

Explanatory Variables	Extreme Poverty	Extreme and Moderate Poverty
Constant	13.49	76.08
Average size of landholding	3.03	−8.75**
	(0.92)	(−2.28)
Proportion of area under modern varieties	3.16	2.64
	(0.64)	(0.46)
Proportion of landless households	22.84*	−4.22
	(1.68)	(−0.26)
Development of infrastructure facilities	−7.99*	−6.48
	(1.82)	(1.27)
Real wage rate	−4.96**	−5.29*
	(−2.09)	(−1.92)
R^2	0.20	0.18

Note: Figures within parentheses are estimated 't' values.
  * Denotes statistical significance of regression coefficients at 10 per cent probability and
 ** At 5 per cent level.

10

The Poor and the Poorest

BINAYAK SEN

Differentiation within the Poor

Using a number of criteria (i.e., income/calorie measure, self-categorisation of households according to surplus/deficit status, living standard indicators, etc.), one can examine whether a sharp differentiation exists within the poor community. Income measures of poverty previously revealed that 55 per cent of the rural population in 1989–90 lived in absolute poverty (chapter 4). This poor population is almost evenly divided into two distinct groups—moderately poor (27.9 per cent) and 'hard core' poor (27.5 per cent).[1] In other words, in 1989–90 about half of the poor population fell into the category of 'hard core' poor. An immediate question which arises is the nature of the trend in 'hard core' poverty over time.

Two types of evidence may be considered: one based on the BBS data and the other based on the BIDS survey data. Since the data on 'hard core' poverty from these two sources are not strictly comparable, we shall consider the findings of these two sources separately in order to capture the underlying trend in this regard. Analysing BBS data, Osmani (1990) has shown that during these period between 1973–74 and 1983–84, the proportion of 'hard core' poor has increased from 25–29 per cent to 38 per cent, even though one witnesses a reduction in moderate poverty.[2] The recent report on the 1988–89 HES carried out by the BBS also indicates that the proportion of 'hard core' poor has been on increase during the period between the 1985–86 HES and 1988–89 HES (from 22 per cent to 29.5 per cent).[3] It is argued that increase in 'hard core' poverty levels during the 1986–89 period may have been due to the adverse impact of the 1988 flood. The latter has had a more adverse impacts on the 'hard core' poor than on the moderately poor. However, from this otherwise valid observation, it does not necessarily follow that as one moves from a 'flood-affected' year to a 'flood-free' year, the proportion of 'hard core' poor would show a decline. There may be considerable rigidity in the 'trickle-down' mechanism which works against a rapid recovery in the situation of the 'hard core' poor.[4] Indeed, the BIDS survey findings which are based on household level panel data stand as a pointer to this. As is known, the year 1987–88 when the BIDS survey of 62 villages was initially carried out was a severely flood-affected year. The re-survey has taken place in 1989–90 which was by all measures a 'normal' (even 'good') agricultural year. Assuming that the 'trickle-down' mechanism based on overall economic recovery works smoothly, one would expect the level of 'hard core' poverty to come down. Contrary to this expectation, one finds that the share of 'hard core' poor population has not been reduced over the 1987–90 period, but has registered a slight increase from 25.8 to 27.5 per cent.

As per consumption (calorie) measure, one may identify several layers amongst the poor. Such an identification procedure is sensitive to the assumption to be made regarding 'per cent deviations' from the normative calorie line. BBS, for instance, considers two extreme poverty lines: one corresponds to 1805 K. cal. per day per person (i.e., about 85 per cent of the absolute poverty line of 2122 K. cal. per day per person); the other line corresponds to 1600 K. cal. per day per person (i.e., about 75 per cent of the absolute poverty line). Despite the arbitrariness involved in ascertaining the second extreme poverty line, it relays an alarming message. Even if one takes 1600 K. cal. per day per person as a cut-off mark for severest poverty[5], the proportion of rural population living below that line would be 19 per cent in 1988–89. As a proportion of the rural poor in 1988–89, this translates into an alarming figure of 40 per cent.[6]

The above picture of sharp differentiation amongst the poor is also confirmed by the perception survey. According to the self-categorisation of the respondents of the BIDS survey, in 1989-90 the number of rural households who lived in chronic deficit throughout the year was about 24 per cent, while households facing occasional deficit stood at 50 per cent.[7] The bulk of the chronic deficit households (about 84 per cent) belong to the lowest end of the land-poor categories, i.e., landless and functionally landless. This should not necessarily lead to the conclusion that most of the landless and functionally landless households are also chronic deficit households. BIDS findings suggest that land-poor households are not uniformly disadvantaged. There is in particular an important differentiation within the land-poor groups into those who are in chronic and those in occasional deficit. Thus, landless households divide into 44 per cent who are in chronic deficit, 44 per cent who are in occasional deficit and 12 per cent who are not in deficit. Similarly, functionally landless households divide into 39 per cent (chronic deficit), 49 per cent (occasional deficit) and 12 per cent (no deficit). Even upto small land-owner category the share of households above poverty, i.e., not in deficit is restricted to 25 to 36 per cent.[8]

Two implications of these findings may be considered. First, such differentiation within the land-poor groups suggests a limited scope for mobility within the ranks of the land-poor, the mobility scopes being limited to a movement from chronic deficit to occasional deficit status and not primarily from a deficit to surplus status. Second, while applying the principles of targeting, say, in case of NGO-led programmes, access to land ownership as a yardstick for demarcating the 'hard core' poor from the moderately poor and the non-poor is far from satisfactory. While targeted wage-employment programmes would more readily address the need of 'chronic deficit' households in the landless and functionally landless categories, the same does not apply to 'occasional deficit' households belonging to the same land ownership category. As for the latter, various targeted self-employment programmes need to be undertaken.

The housing indicator is more directly expressive of the poverty scale compared to the income or self-evaluation indicators. It is also useful in identifying the poorest from the average poor. From Table 10.1, one can see that the housing indicator identifies an

TABLE 10.1
Distribution of Rural Households by Housing Status and by Income Measures of Poverty, 1989–90

(Figures represent percentages of total households)

Housing status	Income measures of poverty*			Total
	Hard-core poor	Moderately poor	Non-poor	
Jhupri	3.4	2.7	3.1	9.2
Single structure	9.6	6.6	7.0	23.3
Thatch and 1 + structure	9.0	7.5	9.1	25.7
Others	6.1	10.4	25.2	41.8
Total	28.1	27.3	44.6	100.0

* Per capita annual hard-core poverty line is taken as Tk 2810 while the matched figures for moderate poverty line is Tk 4790.

even more extreme level of distress. The 'single structure' category represents 23 per cent and the 'jhupri' category represents 9 per cent of rural households. If one focuses on 'hard core' poor households in these two categories at the bottom end of the housing scale, one may capture the most vulnerable segment (the poorest of the poor) within the rural poor community. This segment represents about 13 per cent of rural households and constitutes 23 per cent of the rural poor community.

Chronic and Transient Poverty

Household level panel data generated by the BIDS provides a unique opportunity to capture the movement of the households across various poverty groups over time. As may be seen from Table 10.2, there appears to be considerable fluctuations (both of upward and downward mobility) in the poverty status of rural households over time, fluctuations that are not captured by the trends in head count ratio. A number of aspects cannot escape our attention on this score.

First, about 42 per cent of the households classified as 'hard core' poor in 1987–88 persisted in 'hard core' poverty during

TABLE 10.2
Movement In and Out of the Poverty, 1987–90

Poverty level (Col %) 1987–88	Poverty level 1989–90			Total
	Hard-core poor	Moderately poor	Non-poor	
'Hard core' poor	124	84	88	296
	(41.9)	(28.4)	(29.7)	(24.3)
Moderately poor	140	130	157	427
	(32.8)	(30.4)	(36.8)	(35.0)
Non-poor	79	119	299	497
	(15.9)	(23.9)	(60.2)	(40.7)
Total	343	333	544	1220
	(28.1)	(27.3)	(44.6)	(100.0)

Source: Analysis of Poverty Trends Project, BIDS: 62 Village Survey.
Note: 1. Income measures of poverty have been used for capturing movement in and out of poverty since expenditure module was not executed during the 1987–88 survey.
2. Figures in parentheses indicate row percentages except for the last column where they show column percentages.

1989–90. They constitute about 10 per cent of rural households and represent the chronically 'hard core' poor with little chance to escape from even the net of 'hard core' poverty. Second, only 37 per cent of the households who were termed as 'moderately poor' in 1987–88 could cross the poverty line. 33 per cent of them registered further deterioration, being classified under the re-survey as the 'hard core' poor households. The remaining 30 per cent continued to persist in moderate poverty. Third, the proportion of rural households who lived in chronic poverty (taking into account both 'hard core' and moderate poverty) during the 1987–90 period would be about 39 per cent.[9] These chronically poor households represent about 71 per cent of households classified as poor during the re-survey.[10] Fourth, out of 497 households who were classified as 'non-poor' during the 1987–88 survey, about 40 per cent of them went below the poverty line. (They constitute about 29 per cent of the poor households identified in course of the re-survey in 1989–90). On the other hand, about 34 per cent of households classified as 'poor' in 1987–88 had moved out of the poverty trap by 1989–90.[11] These households provide an example of transient poverty (see Figure 10.1).

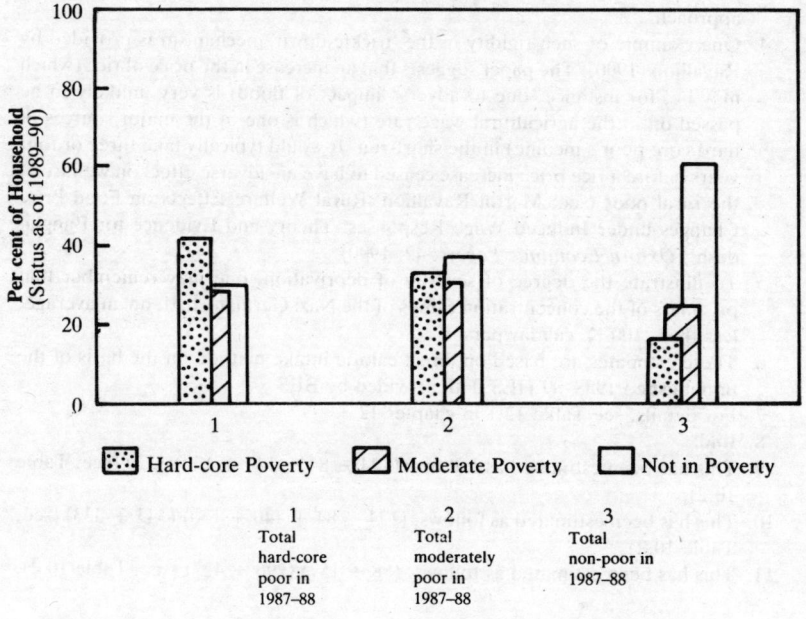

FIGURE 10.1
Chronic and Transient Poverty: Inter-Class Mobility 1987–88 to 1989–90

Notes

1. 'Moderately poor' households have access to a daily calorie intake of 2112 K. cal. (plus 30 per cent allowance for meeting non-food basic needs). As distinct from this group, 'hard core' poor (alternatively called extreme poor) households have access to daily calorie intake of 1740 K. cal. only (plus 30 per cent allowance for meeting non-food basic needs). It may be mentioned that the BBS estimates of 'hard core' poverty are based on the norm of daily calorie intake of 1805 K. cal.

2. See, S.R. Osmani, 'Structural Change and Poverty in Bangladesh: The Case of a False Turning Point,' *The Bangladesh Development Studies*, Vol. 18, No. 3, September 1990.
3. Osmani (1990) and the report on the 1988–89 HES have used the graph-fitting method (using calorie–expenditure graph) to derive the estimates on hard-core poverty, while the approach adopted in the current study is one of fixed-bundle approach.
4. One example of such rigidity in the 'trickle-down' mechanism is provided by Ravallion (1990). The paper suggests that an increase in the price of rice (which may be, for instance, due to adverse impact of flood) is very unlikely to be passed on in the agricultural wage rate (which is one of the major sources of hard-core poor's income) in the short-run. It would typically take three or four years before a rice price increase ceased to have an adverse effect on welfare of the rural poor (see, Martin Ravallion 'Rural Welfare Effects on Food Price Changes under Induced Wage Responses: Theory and Evidence for Bangladesh', *Oxford Economic Papers*, 42, 1990).
5. To illustrate the degree of severity of deprivation, one may remember that prisoners of the concentration camps of the Nazi Germany had, on an average, less than '100 K. cal/day/person'.
6. These estimates are based on direct calorie intake method on the basis of the unpublished 1988–89 HES data provided by BBS.
7. For details, see Table 12.1 in chapter 12.
8. Ibid.
9. This has been estimated as follows: $(124 + 84 + 140 + 130)/1220$ (see, Table 10.2).
10. This has been estimated as follows: $(124 + 84 + 140 + 130)/(343 + 333)$ (see, Table 10.2).
11. This has been estimated as follows: $(88 + 157)/(296 + 427)$ (see, Table 10.2).

11

Female Headed Households

SHAMIM HAMID

Introduction

Female headed households are formed through a historical, social and economic process. Pressure on land, lack of employment opportunities and increasing population, force the normal male household head to migrate leaving behind the wife/mother to manage the farm household to the best of her ability. Again, because of the big age difference between husband and wife[1], the proportion of widows is much higher (8 per cent) than the proportion of widowers (0.8 per cent). Together with divorced and abandoned women, these widows without any extended family system or any adult male members to support them also add to the female headed households. It is these latter households which are more prominent and commonly recognised as female headed households in the rural areas. This chapter first offers a definition of female headed households and then examines their socioeconomic profile to highlight the disparities between male headed households and those headed or managed by women.

Defining a Female Headed Household (FHH)

Although female headed households have always been known to exist and have also been known to be economically and socially disadvantaged, little attention has been focussed on them in Bangladesh. Some studies have mentioned them in passing (Agriculture Sector Review 1988, Rahman 1980) while others which have looked at them in more detail draw upon a limited data base (Islam 1990, Saldert 1984, Alam 1985, Arif 1988).

Estimates of the proportion of female headed households in Bangladesh include that made by a micro study in the village of Madhupur which found that 'only 21 female heads of households are reported and even these cases are by default, i.e., death of husbands, absence of grownup sons, etc.' (Rahman, 1980). Under this definition 5.7 per cent of the households were found to be female headed. The Bangladesh Population Census Sample Survey 1982 estimated this figure to be 15 per cent, while the Bangladesh Labour Force Survey 1984–85 put the percentage at 7.2 per cent without precisely defining the concept. In 1988 the Agriculture Sector Review also came up with the same figure as the Population Census Sample Survey 1982 (15 per cent) using participation in agricultural decisionmaking as a basis for identifying de facto female headed households.

A later study (Islam, 1991) identified 5 categories of female headed households incorporating those with no adult male members, invalid normal male household heads, migrant male household heads and those with widows who are in charge inspite of the presence of an adult son. The study was based on three villages relatively close to the city of Dhaka and the proportion of female headed households was estimated to be 9 per cent. Because of the sociocultural milieu of Bangladesh, our definition, like that of other studies, was based on the absence of certain male members from the household. Female headed households were identified as being of two basic types—de jure and de facto:

1. De jure households were defined as those with no males over 18 years of age present in the household. These would include widowed, divorced and abandoned women who are solely responsible for their own and their children's survival.

2. De facto households were defined as those where the male head of household normally worked and lived outside the village and only occassionally visited the household and there were no close male relative (such as father, son or brother of the male migrant) between the ages of 18–70 years living as permanent members of the household. The oldest adult female member was then taken as the head of household and this was normally the wife/mother of the absent male head. The lower and upper age limits of male relatives living in the household were based on the observation that adult male relatives in this age group normally take over the management functions of the absent head.

Using the above definition the BIDS survey estimated that 9 per cent of rural households in Bangladesh were managed or headed by women.

Characteristics of Female Headed Households

Looking at the sex of household members (Table 11.1) we see that compared to the national figures female headed households (FHH) had a significantly higher proportion of women (54 per cent) and this was more evident in de jure FHH where the proportion of females was 62 per cent. The average household size in FHH was 5 which was smaller than the total population average of 6.3 as well as the national average of 5.7 (BBS 1990). De jure FHH on the other hand had the smallest households with an average of 3.6 members. Children 0–9 years old were marginally higher in FHH (31 per cent) than in the total population (29 per cent) but de facto FHH had a significantly higher proportion (34 per cent) of children than de jure FHH (20 per cent). The presence of elderly persons 65+ years was low (1.8 per cent) in FHH compared to the population (3.7 per cent) but the variation between de facto and de jure FHH was insignificant.

De jure FHH had a very high proportion of earning members (40 per cent) compared to both de facto FHH (25.6 per cent) and the population (28 per cent). Consequently economic dependency ratio (the number of non-earning members divided by the number

TABLE 11.1
Demographic and Economic Indicators

Variables	All hh	Female headed hh (%)		
		Total	De facto	De jure
1. Sex of hh members (%)				
Male	53	46.3	49.0	38.0
Female	47	53.7	51.0	62.0
2. Average hh size	6.2	5	5.8	3.6
3. Children 0–9 years (%)	29	30.5	34	20
4. Elderly 65 + (%)	3.7	1.8	1.9	1.5
5. Economic dependency ratio	2.54	2.42	2.90	1.49
6. Earning members (%)	28	35.3	25.6	40.0
7. Monthly income per hh (Tk)	3100	1700	1800	1300

Source: Analysis of Poverty Trends Project, BIDS: 62 Village Survey.

of earning members) was lowest (1.49) for de jure FHH compared to de facto FHH (2.9) and the population (2.54). It may be noted that de facto FHHs had an economic dependency ratio which was higher than not only the sample ratio but also the national ratio of 2.35 in rural Bangladesh (LFS 1984–85).

The monthly household income showed that FHH in general had an income which was 55 per cent of that earned by the average household with the de jure FHH being the poorest of the poor with an income which was 42 per cent of the average household income.

The poverty level of the households showed that the overwhelming majority (96 per cent) of the FHH were poor (Table 11.2) and none of the female headed households were among the 3 per cent of the non-poor households. Further probing however showed that while de jure FHH were relatively stable in their poverty de facto FHH faced a deteriorating situation with 21 per cent of the households having less land now than at the inception of the household, compared to 11 per cent of de jure FHH facing the same situation (Table 11.3).

While most rural households have multiple occupations, there is normally one that provides the major source of income. For 43 per cent of the total population, farming was the principal source of income (Table 11.4) and for another 32 per cent wage labour, both agricultural and non-agricultural, provided the main source. For

TABLE 11.2
Poverty Level

Types of households	All hh (%)	Female headed hh (%)		
		Total	De facto	De jure
Poor	82	96	95.8	94.8
Moderately Poor	15	4	4.2	5.2
Non-poor	3	0	0	0

Source: Analysis of Poverty Trends Project, BIDS: 62 Village Survey.

TABLE 11.3
Dynamics of Land Ownership

Status of land ownership since inception of hh	All hh (%)	Female headed hh (%)		
		Total	De facto	De jure
Worsened	27	17.3	20.8	10.5
Unchanged	52	71.8	65.3	84.2
Improved	21	10.9	13.9	5.3

Source: Analysis of Poverty Trends Project, BIDS: 62 Village Survey.

TABLE 11.4
Principal Source of Income

Principal source of income	All hh (%)	Female headed hh (%)		
		Total	De facto	De jure
1. Farm	43	19	19.4	21.1
2. Agricultural labour	19	15	15.3	18.4
3. Non-agricultural labour	13	21	15.3	28.9
4. Homebased self-employment	2	4	1.4	7.9
5. Outside home self-employment	13	16	20.8	7.9
6. Service	10	21	26.4	7.9
7. Financially Assisted	0.5	4	1.4	7.9
	100	100	100	100

Source: Analysis of Poverty Trends Project, BIDS: 62 Village Survey.

female headed households, a comparatively higher proportion (36 per cent) depended on wage labour and twice as many female headed households (21 per cent) were dependent on services as a principal source of income as the total population (10 per cent). De facto FHH were highly dependent on services and outside the home self-employment (47 per cent) while for de jure FHH the single major source of income was wage labour (47 per cent).

A look at asset ownership of households shows (Tables 11.5 to 11.7) that female headed households in general owned less livestock, as well as fewer personal, household and vocational assets than the

TABLE 11.5
Livestock Ownership

Types of livestock owned	All hh (%)	Female headed hh (%)		
		Total	De facto	De jure
1. Cow	35	20.9	25	13.2
2. Calf	32	20.9	26.4	10.5
3. Bull	27	10.9	12.5	7.9
4. Buffalo	2	0.9	1.7	0.0
5. Goat/Sheep	29	19.1	16.7	23.7

Source: Analysis of Poverty Trends Project, BIDS: 62 Village Survey.

TABLE 11.6
Ownership of Other Assets

Types of asset owned	All hh (%)	Female headed hh (%)		
		Total	De facto	De jure
1. Modern irrigation equipment	4	1.8	1.4	2.6
2. Boat	5	2.7	2.8	2.6
3. Cart	5	1.8	2.8	0
4. Bicycle	17	6.4	8.3	2.6
5. Artisanal equipment	8	5.5	8.3	0

Source: Analysis of Poverty Trends Project, BIDS: 62 Village Survey.

population. Within the female headed households, the de jure households were clearly the worst off. It was only in the ownership of goats and sheep that the de jure FHH held advantage over the de facto households with 24 per cent owning goats and sheep

TABLE 11.7
Ownership of Consumer Durables

Types of asset owned	All hh (%)	Female headed hh (%)		
		Total	De facto	De jure
1. Cot/almirah	53	45.5	55.6	26.3
2. Ratio/cassette player	22	15.5	19.4	7.9
3. Television	3	1.8	1.4	2.6*
4. Watch	31	19.1	26.4	5.3
5. Ornaments	27	25.5	34.7	7.9

Source: Analysis of Poverty Trends Project, BIDS: 62 Village Survey.
* The seeming contradiction is because only one household in each type of FHH owned a television, thereby giving these percentages.

compared to 17 per cent of de facto FHH. However, the ownership of small animals was itself an indication of the higher poverty level of de jure households. Table 11.8 shows that even in the ownership of basic clothing female headed households were worse off, with de jure FHH being significantly worse off compared to de facto FHH.

TABLE 11.8
Ownership of Basic Clothing

Types of clothing owned	All hh (%)	Female headed hh (%)		
		Total	De facto	De jure
1. A minimum pair of clothes	83	77.9	84.3	58.4
2. Winter clothes	78	68.1	73.7	51.1
3. Footwear	76	60.0	66.2	41.6

Source: Analysis of Poverty Trends Project, BIDS: 62 Village Survey.

A self-evaluation by households on their deficit status showed that 24 per cent of the population was chronically short of food and another 50 per cent was occasionally deficit. The corresponding figures for female headed households was much higher with 33 per cent of FHH having chronic food shortage (Table 11.9). But whereas about 27 per cent of the de facto FHH were always short of food as much 45 per cent of the de jure FHH had to face a

TABLE 11.9
Deficit Status

Food availability	All hh (%)	Female headed hh (%)		
		Total	De facto	De jure
Deficit	24	33.0	26.8	44.7
Occasionally Deficit	50	40.4	45.1	31.6
Stable	18	19.3	22.5	13.2
Surplus	8	7.3	5.6	10.5

Source: Analysis of Poverty Trends Project, BIDS: 62 Village Survey.

similar situation. Defining the households that are chronically short of food as the 'hard core' poor and the occasionally deficit moderate as poor, Figure 11.1 shows the distribution of such households among the female headed as compared to other households.

The living standards of the households (Table 11.10) showed that although more than 85 per cent of all types of households used water from tubewells for drinking, only 58 per cent of the de jure FHH had access to such drinking water. Again where 44 per cent of all households had no latrines and used the open fields, the corresponding figure for de jure FHH was 76 per cent. Here the de facto FHH were relatively better off with only 32 per cent using open fields. The structure of housing showed (Table 11.11) that 58 per cent of female headed households lived in single roomed structures with thatched roofs or in jhupris made of leaves and twigs compared to 33 per cent of the total population living in such structures. This figure was highest (69 per cent) for de jure FHH.

Stratification of Female Headed Households

Female headed households have so far been defined entirely on the basis of the absence from the household of specific males of certain age groups. From the preceding section it is also clear that female headed households were generally at a greater economic disadvantage than male headed ones, the disadvantage being more

FIGURE 11.1
Poverty Distribution in Different Types

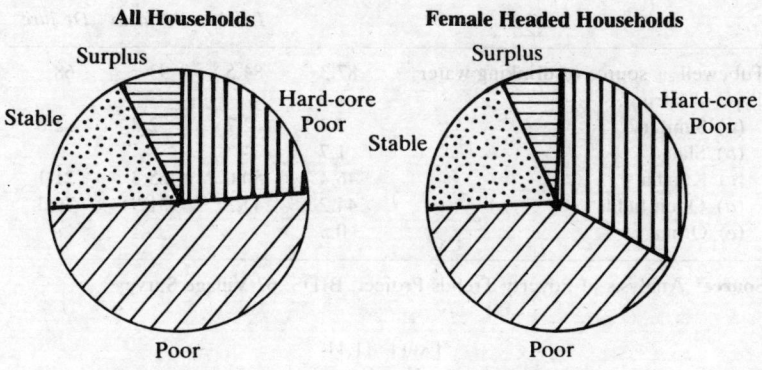

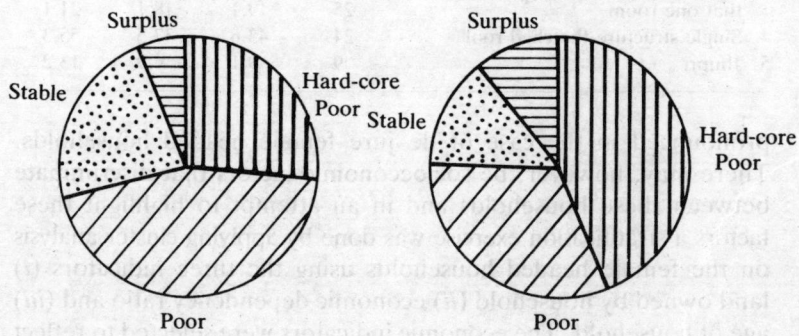

TABLE 11.10
Standard of Living Indicators

Indicator	All hh (%)	Female headed hh (%)		
		Total	De facto	De jure
Tubewell as source of drinking water	87.3	84.5	93	68
Type of latrine				
(a) Sanitary	7.2	2.7	2.8	2.6
(b) Slab	1.7	–	–	–
(c) Kutcha	46.4	50.0	65.3	21.1
(d) Open fields	44.2	47.3	31.9	76.3
(e) Other	0.5	–	–	–

Source: Analysis of Poverty Trends Project, BIDS: 62 Village Survey.

TABLE 11.11
Housing

Types of Households	All hh (%)	Female headed hh (%)		
		Total	De facto	De jure
1. Durable	15	11.8	13.9	7.9
2. Semi-durable	27	16.4	23.6	2.6
3. Thatched roof with more that one room	25	19.1	18.1	21.1
4. Single structure thatched roof	24	43.6	37.5	55.3
5. Jhupri	9	9.1	6.9	13.2

pronounced in the case of de jure female headed households. There may, however, be socioeconomic factors that discriminate between these households and in an attempt to highlight these factors a stratification exercise was done by applying cluster analysis on the female headed households using the three indicators (*i*) land owned by household (*ii*) economic dependency ratio and (*iii*) age of household. The economic indicators were selected to reflect the income-earning capacity of the household and the age of the household was chosen to cover the demographic aspect.

The result of the exercise (Tables 11.12a and 11.12b) shows that female headed households may be classified into three distinct groups. The age of the household was the factor that best explained the variance between the groups while economic dependency ratio

TABLE 11.12a
Classification of Female Headed Households Through Clustering Exercise

Group	No. of households*	Mean age of household (years)	Average land owned (acres)	Economic dependency ratio
1.	9 (8)	30.33	1.59	1.83
2.	23 (22)	11.52	3.05	5.17
3.	74 (70)	8.41	0.93	2.23
Total	106 (100)	10.94	1.44	2.83

Source: Analysis of Poverty Trends Project, BIDS: 62 Village Survey.
* Total number of households was reduced from 111 to 106 because 5 households which survived on financial assistance reported zero earning members so that the dependency ratio could not be calculated and the cases were hence dropped from the clustering exercise.

TABLE 11.12b
Analysis of Variance

Variables	Between group variation	DF	Within group variation	DF	F	Prob.
1. Age of household	22.93	2	0.4986	103	45.99	0.0
2. Land owned	21.84	2	0.6017	103	36.29	0.0
3. Dependency ratio	19.64	2	0.6382	103	30.77	0.0

was the best explanatory factor for within group variation. The three groups are described below.

1. Most (70 per cent) of the female headed households were relatively newly formed with an average age of 8 years; these owned less than one acre of land and economic dependency ratio was 2.23, i.e., every earning member supported more than two non-earning members. These could include both de jure and de facto types of female headed households.
2. A significant proportion (22 per cent) of the female headed households were large households, 11–12 years old and owning on an average around 3 acres of land. They had a very high economic dependency ratio of 5.17, i.e., every earning

member supported more than 5 non-earning members. These would be de facto FHH where the pressure on land forced the male to seek alternate sources of income through migration.
3. A relatively small percentage (8 per cent) of female headed households were mature households of about 30 years and had been formed through death of husband and moving out of adult sons if any. Economic dependency ratio was low at 1.83 and land owned was about 1.50 acres on an average. These would be de jure FHH largely headed by widows.

Conclusions

From the preceding sections we see that while female headed households were worse off than other households in almost all aspects, it was the de jure female headed households, i.e., those headed by widows and divorced/abandoned women that are in the worst possible economic situation. Again, while female headed households had a high proportion of females in general, the de jure households had an exceptionally high proportion (62 per cent) of female members, although the average household size was roughly half that of the average Bangladeshi household. However, the proportion of earning members in de jure households was very high (40 per cent) and the economic dependency ratio was consequently very low (1.49). While this indicated high employment rate amongst the de jure households, it also implied that a larger portion of the income-earning burden was being borne by children and the elderly in such households compared to de facto and other households.

De facto female headed households on the other hand had larger households, more children but a very high dependency ratio of 2.90. This implied that while children and the elderly were spared income-earning responsibilities in de facto households, the total burden of the household subsistance fell on a few male members. It also implied that even when the women managed the household she was not recognised as an income earner in the normal sense. A further implication was that although de facto FHH are deteriorating in their economic stability, social customs prevent women and other members of the household to freely participate in the labour market, thus, continuing the vicious cycle of a worsening poverty situation.

Although there were more earning members in de jure households, the earners were all women and children whose income-earning capacity was lower than the de facto households. De jure FHH not only had less access to land but also their major source of income was from wage labour, where the female wage ratio was 40 to 44 per cent of male wage rates and children's rates were even lower. De facto households, on the other hand, received income from services and from self-employment which was not home based, both activities involving adult male members and both having relatively higher returns than female wage labour. Thus, average income per month for de jure female headed households was Tk 1300, that for de facto households was Tk 1800 while the average income of all households was Tk 3100.

It may be mentioned here that the proportion of elderly persons in both de facto and de jure households was significantly lower than in the population. This could have two implications: one, that elderly people cannot survive the hardship of such households and two that the household is too young to have old, inter-generational members. The first may be true in the case of de jure households which face the highest economic deprivation but more research would be needed to verify this. The second would appear to hold true for de facto households since the average age of these households was about 11 years. It may be pointed out that although de jure households were relatively poorer than de facto households, the trend in land ownership indicated that de jure households remained stable in their poverty situation, while de facto households (starting off from a better off position vis-à-vis the de jure households) faced a situation that was worsening over the years.

In the final analysis we see that to cope with the deteriorating economic situation in rural areas relatively new households were adopting the strategy of male out-migration leaving the households to be managed by women in the absence of a surrogate male head. For households with little or no assets, the strategy adopted by the male was in the form of divorce or abandonment of wife and children. Added to these were the households headed by widows who were either unable to realise even their limited inheritance rights or had nothing to inherit either from husband or parents.

Female headed households in rural Bangladesh are being formed not through women's emancipation or through any desire or economic capability on their part. They are being forced to manage the households through a combination of economic, demographic and social factors which hold no advantage for them in any form. They are the end product of a pauperisation process and represent the poverty situation in its most acute form. While programme aimed at such households can provide temporary aid for these households, an arrest in the growth of such households can be affected only through poverty-alleviation programme for the whole country. In the mean time the existence of the different types of female headed households must be taken into cognisance and programmes aimed at such households must take their diverse socioeconomic situation into consideration to ensure any degree of success.

Note

1. The average age difference between married couples in the survey was 10 years.

References

Agriculture Sector Review, 1988, *Women's Roles in Agriculture, Present Trends and Potential for Growth*, Rothschild and Mahmud, UNDP/UNIFEM.

Alam, S. 1985, *Women and Poverty in Bangladesh*, Women Studies International Forum 8.4.

Arif, F. 1988, 'Self-employment for Rural Distressed Female Headed Households—A Case Study of a Pilot Project in Bangladesh', paper prepared for the National Workshop on *Female headed households and Development*, ILO, New Delhi, April 1988.

Bangladesh Bureau of Statistics, *Statistical Yearbook 1990*.

Bangladesh Population Census Sample Survey 1982-cited in BBS Statistical Yearbook 1990.

Islam, M. 1991, *Women Heads of Household in Rural Bangladesh: Strategies for Survival*, Narigrantha Probartana, Bangladesh.

Rahman, H.Z., 1980, *Report from Raipur*, BIDS, Mimeo.

Saldert, C. 1984, *Female Headed Households in Rural Bangladesh*, Working Paper, Development Study Unit, Department of Anthropology, University of Stockholm, Sweden.

IV

Aspects of Poverty Process

12

Income-Earning Environment of the Poor: Aspects of Dislocation, Adjustment and Mobility

BINAYAK SEN

Aspects of Dislocation

Dislocation of the rural poor focuses on those aspects of deprivation which are primarily related to command over resources. Accessibility of the poor in terms of land and non-land income-earning assets, institutional support mechanism, such as credit and extension services, etc., are some of the variables which measure the extent of their dislocation within the overall income-earning environment prevailing in the rural areas.

Access to Land Assets

Consider first the land ownership criterion as one particular aspect of dislocation.[1] The findings presented in Table 12.1 indicate the presence of significant inequality in the distribution of land ownership. Nearly 16 per cent own practically negligible land (less than 0.5 acre) and another 33 per cent own upto 0.5 acres, and can be considered near landless. These two groups together constitute the

TABLE 12.1
Land Ownership Location of Deficit Households, 1989–90

Land ownership category (in acres)	% of households	% distribution of deficit households		Intra-group percentage distribution			Total
		Chronic or occasional deficit	Chronic deficit only	Chronic deficit	Occasional deficit	No deficit	
Landless (less than 0.05)	16	19	29	44	44	12	100
Functionally Landless (0.05–0.49)	33	40	55	39	49	12	100
Marginal Owner (0.50–1.49)	21	21	11	12	63	25	100
Small Owner (1.50–2.49)	11	10	4	8	56	36	100
Medium Owner (2.50–4.99)	12	8	1	2	46	52	100
Large Owner (5.00+)	7	2	–	5	20	75	100
All Households	100	100	100	24	50	26	100

Source: Analysis of Poverty Trends Project, BIDS: 62 Village Survey.

bottom 50 per cent as per the land ownership scale and control only 4 per cent of the total land. At the other end of the spectrum, households owning more than 5.0 acres represent the top 7 per cent of rural households, but they own nearly 50 per cent of the total land. The concentration ratio of land ownership distribution is estimated at about 0.63. Table 12.1 further shows that most of the chronic deficit households (about 84 per cent) belong to the lowest end of the land-poor categories, i.e., landless and functionally landless. Similarly, the bulk of the deficit category (including both chronic and occasional deficit types) are made up of land-poor households: landless and functionally landless households constitute 59 per cent of the deficit category while marginal and small land-owners account for an additional 31 per cent. Thus, lack of land emerges as a major initial disadvantage for the rural poor.

Access to Non-Land Assets

Data on non-land income-earning assets are available from two sources: (*a*) the 1983–84 agricultural census carried out by BBS, and (*b*) the 1989–90 BIDS survey. Evidence from both these sources shows that the disadvantage of being land-poor is not significantly compensated by the ownership of non-land assets. There is in fact a strong correlation between the ownership of land and non-land assets which makes the position of 'hard core' poor all the more vulnerable.

According to the census data, households belonging to the land-poor category accounted for 70 per cent of the farms, but they owned only 44 per cent of cattle, 54 per cent of goats and 56 per cent of poultry birds (Table 12.2). Differentiation in respect of

TABLE 12.2
Control Over Resources by Size of Landholding, 1983–84

Size of operational holdings (in acres)	Per cent of farms	Share of land operated (per cent)	Share of homestead water bodies and orchard (per cent of cultivated land)	Per cent share of		
				Cattle	Goats	Poultry birds
Less than 0.5	23.9	2.6	35.2	6.3	13.8	14.6
0.5–2.49	46.1	26.1	13.3	37.4	39.7	41.6
2.5–4.99	18.2	27.6	9.1	27.3	23.6	22.6
5.0–7.49	6.7	17.5	9.0	13.7	11.2	10.3
7.5 & more	5.1	26.2	9.5	15.3	11.7	10.9
Total	100.0	100.0	11.0	100.0	100.0	100.0

Source: Bangladesh Bureau of Statistics: *Bangladesh Census of Agriculture and Livestock: 1983–84*, Vol. III (Sample Enumeration of Agricultural Characteristics), Dhaka, 1988.

non-land income-earning assets becomes even more transparent when these indicators are measured along the land ownership scale. Thus, Table 12.3 records only 8 per cent to 20 per cent of landless and functionally landless households as owning cows/bulls compared to 62 per cent to 75 per cent for medium and large land owning groups. Similar trends may be observed with regards to the ownership of artisanal equipments, irrigation equipments and transport equipments (see Table 12.4) indicating limited option of

Table 12.3
Percentage Distribution of Livestock Ownership among Land Ownership Categories, 1989–90

Land ownership category (in acres)	% of households in each land category owning		
	Cow	Bulls	Goat/Sheep
Landless (less than 0.05)	20	8	19
Functionally Landless (0.05–0.49)	18	9	22
Marginal Owner (0.50–1.49)	40	29	31
Small Owner (1.50–2.49)	47	48	39
Medium Owner (2.50–4.99)	62	56	44
Large Owner (5.00+)	72	75	48

Source: Analysis of Poverty Trends Project, BIDS: 62 Village Survey.

Table 12.4
Percentage Distribution of Non-Land Asset Ownership by Land Ownership Categories, 1989–90

Land Ownership Category (in acres)	% of households in each land category owning				
	Artisanal equipment	Irrigation equipment	Boat	Cart	Rickshaw
Landless (less than 0.05)	6	2	2	1	2
Functionally landless (0.05–0.49)	8	–	4	1	3
Marginal owner (0.50–1.49)	6	3	5	1	1
Small owner (1.50–2.49)	16	6	4	7	1
Medium owner (2.50–4.99)	9	9	10	12	–
Large owner (5.00+)	10	24	17	30	–

Source: Analysis of Poverty Trends Project, BIDS: 62 Village Survey.

the 'hard core' poor for non-crop self-employment. This makes them critically vulnerable to the availability of wage-employment opportunities during the agriculturally slack seasons.

Since asset-accessibility is one of the major determinants of income, the pattern of assets owned will significantly influence the flow as well as the structure of future income streams. Extreme land-poor households are likely to be more dependent on non-farm income sources than larger land owning households. As seen from Table 12.5, 53 to 58 per cent of landless and functionally landless households have reported wage income as their principal

TABLE 12.5
Principal Income Sources of Households by Land Ownership Status, 1989–90
(Figures represent percentages of row total)

Land Ownership Category (acres)	Principal source of Income						Total
	Farm	Agri. labour	Non-agri. labour	Cottage industry	Business	Services	
Landless (less than 0.05)	12	38	20	2	21	7	100
Functionally landless (0.05–0.49)	17	31	22	4	14	12	100
Marginal owner (0.50–1.49)	56	10	8	2	14	10	100
Small owner (1.50–2.49)	77	3	3	–	6	11	100
Medium owner (2.50–4.99)	80	–	–	2	8	10	100
Large owner (5.00+)	86	–	–	–	90	5	100
All households	43	19	13	2	13	10	100

Source: Analysis of Poverty Trends Project, BIDS: 62 Village Survey.

income source, while the figure sharply declines to 18 per cent in case of marginal landowners and drops further to 6 per cent in case of small land owners. Households with farming as principal source of income rises sharply from 12 to 17 per cent in case of landless and functionally landless households to 56 to 77 per cent recorded for marginal and small land owning groups. On the other hand, the proportion of households with 'trading and commercial ventures' as a principal source of income is higher for the landless and functionally landless categories than in case of small land owning group (14 to 21 per cent vis-à-vis 6 per cent). The table, thus, brings out sharp contrast between the extreme land-poor and the moderate land-poor categories in respect of household income structure.

Some immediate policy implications of these findings can not escape our attention here. Given significant variation which already exists within the rural poor community in terms of their differential access to land as well as non-land assets, poverty-alleviation policies should be suitably attuned to the differential need of particular poverty groups. Expansion of wage employment opportunities and non-farm (specially non-agricultural) sector-oriented programmes should figure prominently in poverty-alleviation packages targeted at the landless and the functionally landless poor. Small land owning group will benefit significantly from the targeted farm programmes which promote adoption of new agriculture (improved seed–chemical fertiliser–controlled water) technology with strong poverty-alleviation effects. As for the marginal land owning group, the emphasis should be on a mix of both farm and non-farm self-employment programmes.

Access to Capital

As mentioned earlier, dislocational characteristics of a rural poor household focus on various aspects of its command over resources, of which asset-accessibility is only one item. Lack of capital which acts as the major constraint to enhancement of non-land assets can largely be addressed by increasing access of the poor to institutional credit sources. The latter includes sources as diverse as government owned scheduled banks, private commercial banks, cooperatives, such as those under the Bangladesh Rural Development Board (BRDB), NGOs. As may be seen from Table 12.6, as of June 1989, only 23 per cent of rural households have reported access to institutional credit. Even this otherwise very low figure conceals considerable variation between land-poor and land-rich households. For instance, the proportion of landless and functionally landless

TABLE 12.6
Access to Institutional Credit Sources, 1989–90

Land ownership group (acres)	% of house-holds	Institutional credit sources			
		% of loanee households in each landowing group	% of total volume of institutional credit	Average loan per loanee household (TK)	Average loan per household in the group (Tk)
Landless and functionally landless (upto 0.49)	48.8	15.3	17.3	3524	541
Marginal owner (0.50–1.49)	21.4	27.0	22.8	6037	1630
Small owner (1.50–2.49)	11.1	29.4	11.0	5156	1516
Medium owner (2.50–4.99)	11.9	34.9	22.2	8195	2863
Large owner (5.00+)	6.8	36.6	26.7	16711	6114
All Groups	100.0	23.2	100.0	6614	1532

Source: Analysis of Poverty Trends Project, BIDS: 62 Village Survey.

households constitute bottom 50 per cent of rural households, but their share in total institutional credit flow is only 17 per cent. By contrast, large and medium land owning groups accounting for only a fifth of all rural households, have accumulated almost 50 per cent of the total volume of institutional credit. The average loan amount per household estimated for each land owning group also varies significantly, the corresponding figure for landless and functionally landless groups being only one-tenth of the loan amount received by the large land owning group.

Aspects of Adjustment

While dislocation in terms of limited command over resources constitutes a major initial disadvantage for the rural poor, this disadvantage is not necessarily an absolute one. The working of various markets (such as tenancy, creditor labour) may unleash a process by way of which benefits would trickle down to the poor. Existence of such a mechanism may be seen as essentially an adjustment process which partly compensates for the adverse effects of the initial dislocation experienced by rural poor households in terms of their limited command over resources. Indeed the participation rate as well as terms and conditions of participation in these markets may vary considerably not only between two different land owning groups, but also within the same landholding category. This may largely explain why some households are better off in terms of aggregate income and welfare even within the ranks of same land owning status. Data presented in Table 12.1 are revealing in this regard. The table shows 44 per cent of landless households as 'chronic deficit', 44 per cent as 'occasional deficit' and 12 per cent as 'no deficit'. Significant intra-group differentiation has been observed for other land-poor categories as well.

Adjustment through Tenancy Market

Some of the salient features of the working of various markets which are related to the adjustment process, are mentioned below. Consider first the adjustment process through the tenancy market.[2] The tenancy market appears to have some moderating effect on the inequalitarian consequences of concentration of land ownership, specially in areas of expansion of new technology. Two major issues are considered here. The first relates to the directionality issue of land transfer in the tenancy market (i.e., 'who rents in' vis-à-vis 'who rents out'). The second issue focuses on the nature of participation in the tenancy market (i.e., terms and conditions of tenancy).

As seen from Table 12.7, about 88 per cent of total rented-in land (measured as a proportion of total cropped area) are cultivated by the land-poor group with cultivated owned land upto 2.49 acres. A substantial proportion of land under tenancy (i.e., 46 per cent) is rented-in by the extreme land-poor tenants (such as the landless and the functionally landless). By contrast, about 87 per cent of total rented-out are supplied by medium and large land owning groups (data not shown in Table). This shows that the land-poor

Table 12.7
Dependence of the Land-Poor on Tenancy Market, 1989–90

Tenant category (owned cultivated land status)	% of total tenant households	% of HH renting-in land in each group	Rented in land as proportion of gross cropped area %	% of HH renting-out land in each group
Landless (0)	30.6	23.2	27.2	0.0
Functionally landless (0.01–0.49)	21.2	41.8	18.8	10.0
Marginal owner (0.50–1.49)	26.9	35.9	30.8	19.4
Small owner (1.50–2.49)	12.6	37.6	11.3	29.6
Medium owner (2.50–4.99)	6.7	20.0	9.1	32.0
Large owner (5.00+)	2.0	10.9	2.8	54.7
All	100.0	29.4	100.0	14.6

Source: Analysis of Povety Trends Project, BIDS: 62 Village Survey.

groups are 'net-takers' in contrast to medium and large land owner groups who are 'net-givers' in the tenancy market.

Table 12.7 also provides some insights on the status of pure tenant category in the tenancy market. Pure tenants are defined here as those having no cultivated land of their own, as opposed to the BBS agricultural census definition of having no land at all. Using this definition, the 1989–90 survey found pure tenants as 31 per cent of all tenant households. The proportion of landless households who participate in the tenancy market as 'pure tenants' has also increased over time (from 17 per cent in 1987–88 to 23 per cent in 1989–90).[3] Since landless tenants are generally better off than landless agricultural labourers, participation of a certain section of landless (and functional landless) households in the tenancy market will lead to some differentiation within the extreme land-poor group with some prospects for upward mobility on the part of pure tenants.

Additional data further reveal considerable presence of kinship network in the tenancy market (about 37 per cent of total rented-in land falls under this arrangement). This average figure, however, conceals significant variation amongst the various land-poor groups (see Table 12.8). The incidence of kinship network is prominently visible with respect to marginal and small tenants vis-à-vis landless and functionally landless tenants. Thus, in case of marginal and small tenant groups, 42 to 62 per cent of their total rented-in land are taken from the category of 'relatives' as opposed to only 17 to 36 per cent for functionally landless and landless tenants.

TABLE 12.8
Adjustment through Tenancy Market: Relevance of Kinship Network
(*Figures represent percentage of area rented-in measured as a proportion of total cropped area*)

Tenant (owned cultivated land status)	Relationship with landlord					All
	Close relative	Distant relative	Non-relative in same village	Non-relative in other village	Non-relative in urban area	
Landless (0)	26.5	9.8	28.3	35.1	0.2	100
Functionally landless (0.01–0.49)	11.6	5.3	64.4	11.7	7.0	100
Marginal owner (0.50–1.49)	33.5	8.6	36.3	21.3	0.3	100
small owner (1.50–2.49)	44.9	17.0	17.1	19.1	1.9	100
Medium owner (2.50–4.99)	31,4	6.8	52.1	8.7	0.9	100
Large owner (5.00+)	29.3	–	10.2	53.3	7.2	100
All tenant households	28.5	8.8	38.0	22.7	2.0	100

Source: Analysis of Poverty Trends Project, BIDS: 62 village Survey

The spread of new technology in agriculture appears to have a positive adjustment impact on the income and welfare status of the tenant farmers. The dominance of small farms and the widespread practice of tenancy have not emerged as 'structural constraints' to technological progress in agriculture. Indeed, with respect to the use of modern inputs, the smaller farmers are found to be better adopters than the larger farms while owner-cum-tenants are better adopters compared to owner farmers (Hossain and Sen, 1992). If diffusion of technology can be encouraged through increased supply of credit and modern inputs to the small and marginal farmers, then potential benefits that can be reaped by land-poor groups even from the prevailing tenurial arrangement would be much higher than are currently derived under conditions of traditional technology.[4] Spread of new technology in agriculture also appears to be associated with an increasing incidence of cost-sharing of inputs under share tenancy and a relatively high practice of fixed-rent tenancies in 'high-adopter' villages compared to 'low-adopter' villages. These changes associated with the expansion of new technology in agriculture are likely to have a strong positive impact on tenant farmers' income.

Adjustment through Informal Credit Market

Limited access to government-owned institutional credit sources make the land-poor groups particularly dependent on alternative sources of credit. Credit programmes of NGOs offer such an alternative but only in a limited sense. Even though NGOs currently cover more than 10 per cent of landless and functionally landless households of the country, only a few of them promote targeted credit programmes; the rest being involved in functional education, training and other support services. But the main reason why the access of a vast majority of land-poor would be limited under NGO arrangement lies in the very nature of the targeted credit programmes. Experiences of the Grameen Bank suggest that the expansion potential of these programmes (specially if they are to be made cost-effective) critically depends on the capacities of the prospective loanees to select clearly viable projects. This obviously requires some entrepreneurial talent which will then become a limiting factor for the otherwise extremely vulnerable poor in getting access to such programmes. Apart from such a self-selection principle on the basis of which these programmes should normally operate, there is also uncertainty regarding the number of viable projects that can be financed under conditions of local economy.

The number of such projects will largely depend on how the local economy develops and how the potential borrowers perceive the evolving market conditions.[5] It means, therefore, that the rural poor cannot readily count on NGOs as one routine source of credit support. And this also explains why the rural poor turn to informal credit sources for support in times of risks.

At this juncture, it is important to note that informal credit market (ICM) is a highly generalised category with significant intra-sectoral differentiations in respect of terms and conditions of credit classified by borrower and lender types, size, duration and end-use nature of loans. Table 12.9 shows that the land-poor

TABLE 12.9
Access to Non-Institutional Credit Sources

Land Ownership group (acres)	Non-institutional credit			Av. loan (institutional and) non-institutional per household in the group
	% of loanee households*	Av. credit per loanee household	Av. loan per household (Tk) in the group	
Landless and functionally landless (upto 0.49)	15.9 (8.5)	4806	762 (329)	1303
Marginal (0.50–1.49)	22.4 (13.3)	5308	1191 (690)	2821
Small (1.50–2.49)	17.6 (13.2)	9206	1624 (1328)	3140
Medium (2.50–4.99)	13.0 (6.2)	9537	1241 (860)	4104
Large (5.00+)	9.7 (3.6)	18,175	1773 (695)	7887
All groups	16.7 (9.5)	6426	1074 (606)	2606

Source: Analysis of Poverty Trends Project, BIDS: 62 Village Survey; Table 12.6.
* Figures in parantheses measure the degree of accessibility to non-institutional credit sources *excluding* loan cases relating to 'friends and relatives' category.

groups are in general characterised by higher dependence on ICM vis-à-vis the more land-endowed groups, but the accessibility of the poor decreases substantially if one excludes the 'friends and relatives' category from the lender sample. This is quite expected in view of the scarcity of collateralisable assets in the land-poor groups for 'large' borrowings. A further breakdown of informal credit flow in Table 12.10 reveals significant vulnerability of the extreme land-poor groups vis-à-vis more well off borrowers. Extreme land-poor groups (upto 0.49 acres) account for about 40 per cent of total credit advanced by professional/semi-professional lenders who charge high interests on credit compared to other lender categories.[6]

Most of the poor borrowers, however, have little collateralisable assets with little prospects for risk-coping through routine access to informal lenders, specially those who charge collaterals and/or high interests on loans. Borrowers of this kind are faced with two options. The first option relates to the likelihood of personal attachment to the lenders. One type of 'asset' that a poor household may build up is to attach itself to a lender who has full information on its capacity to repay and who control its members' lives sufficiently in order to minimise the risk of default. Such a personalised relationship with lenders is indeed an asset for a poor household, particularly in times of risks.[7] Purchases of commodities on credit from shopkeepers-cum-lenders in times of acute shortage, *dadan* trade advances (i.e., loans against sales of output in advance), landlords credit to tenants, employers credit to wage labourers are some of the examples of this type of loan transactions. For such transactions to be effective, they must take place in the context of a long-term relationship between the two parties. The threat of credit cessation acts in these cases as an effective enforcement mechanism since poor borrowers expect repeated transactions in future in times of unanticipated crisis and risks.

The second option to which the collateral-poor households may take recourse is to borrow from 'friends and relatives'. Here again 'relationship with lender' emerges as an important asset for the borrower, but this time the transaction operates within a kinship network. Because of the collaterals and interest-free nature of these loans, they are regarded by the poor as the most favoured form of risks insurance. This also explains why the category of 'friends and relatives' account for a substantial proportion (44 per cent) of informal loanable funds (see Table 12.11). However, for a large section of extremely poor households, the prospect for such soft loan does not exist in reality, as likely to be the case with respect to destitute female headed households who usually lack such kinship network.

TABLE 12.10

Pattern of Distribution of Credit Advances amongst Different Land Owning Groups, by Lender Types*
(figures represent percentage distribution of amount of loans)

Land ownership group (acres)	% of house-holds	Distribution of institutional credit	Non-institutional credit sources				Total non-inst. credit sources	Total non-inst. sources (excluding 'friends & relatives')	All sources (inst. + non-inst.)
			Prof./semi-Prof. money lenders	Rich pea-sant/ landlords	Traders/ shop-keepers	Friends and rela-tives			
Landless and functionally landless (upto 0.49)	48.8	17.3	39.2	19.2	49.9	45.2	34.9	26.5	24.4
Marginal (0.50–1.49)	21.4	22.8	19.6	29.5	25.3	22.6	23.7	24.6	23.3
Small (1.50–2.49)	11.1	11.0	17.5	41.8	1.5	7.0	16.7	24.3	13.4
Medium (2.50–4.99)	11.9	22.2	21.1	6.6	23.3	9.7	13.7	16.9	18.6
Large (5.00+)	6.8	26.7	2.6	2.9	–	15.5	11.0	7.7	20.3
All Groups	100.0	100.0	100.0	100.0	100.0	100.0	100.0	100.0	100.0

Source: Analysis of Poverty Trends Project, BIDS: 62 Village Survey

TABLE 12.11
Breakdown of Informal Credit Flow by Lender Types
(Figures represent percentages of loan amount)

Prof./ semi-prof. money-lenders	Rich peasants/ landlords	Traders shop-keepers	Friends and relatives	Other lenders*	Total
11.5	18.3	6.5	43.5	20.2	100.0

Source: Analysis of Poverty Trends Project, BIDS: 62 Village Survey.
* 'Other' lenders include miscellaneous types such as service-holders, etc., who would not otherwise fall under conventional categories.

TABLE 12.12
Risk-Insurance through Access to Emergency Loans
(figures represent row percentages for each landowning group)

Land ownership groups (acres)	% of households having access to			
	First lender	Second lender	Third lender	Fourth lender
Landless (less than 0.05)	50.2	22.3	5.6	0.5
Functionally landless (0.05–0.49)	52.3	24.4	7.8	2.4
Marginal (0.50–1.49)	53.9	28.6	9.6	1.5
Small (1.50–2.49)	59.5	36.8	14.1	0.7
Medium (2.50–4.49)	58.3	28.1	12.0	2.6
Large (5.00+)	56.0	40.2	14.6	6.1
All	54.1	27.8	9.5	3.1

Source: Analysis of Poverty Trends Project, BIDS: 62 Village Survey.

This analysis is empirically validated by data presented in Table 12.12 through 12.14. Three broad tendencies emerge from these tables. First, the degree of accessibility to emergency loan funds declines sharply as one moves from 'first lender' to 'fourth lender'

TABLE 12.13
Dependency of Lenders Supplying Emergency Loans
(figures represent row percentages for each landowning group)

Land ownership group*	% of borrower households dependent on first lender	% of borrower households dependent on second lender	% of borrower households dependent on third lender	% of borrower households dependent on fourth lender
Landless	52.9	33.3	30.8	–
Functionally landless	51.8	42.2	33.3	30.8
Marginal	47.0	43.7	20.5	25.0
Small	47.2	38.5	24.0	50.0
Medium	41.1	39.7	24.0	–
Large	26.2	32.5	23.5	16.7
All	47.0	39.7	25.9	22.5

Source: Analysis of Poverty Trends Project, BIDS: 62 Village Survey.
* Land Ownership classification is same as in Table 12.12.

TABLE 12.14
Kinship Lineages with Lenders Supplying Emergency Loans
(Figures represent row percentages for each landowning group)

Land ownership group*	% of borrower households having kinship lineages with first lender	% of borrower households having kinship lineages with second lender	% of borrower households having kinship lineages with third lender	% of borrower households having kinship lineages with fourth lender
Landless	52.1	50.0	46.2	–
Functionally landless	51.8	50.4	36.2	30.8
Marginal	61.6	49.5	52.5	62.5
Small	65.1	50.7	40.0	33.3
Medium	57.0	60.4	56.0	57.1
Large	54.9	62.5	64.7	50.0
All	56.5	52.5	50.3	43.6

Source: Analysis of Poverty Trends Project, BIDS: 62 Village Survey.
* Land Ownership classification is same as in Table 12.12.

(from 50 to 52 per cent to less than 2 per cent in case extremely land-poor categories). While this tendency is uniformly observed for all borrower types, it has particularly adverse implications for the poor borrowers with limited options for alternative sources of borrowings in times of risks. Second, the borrowers are found to be highly dependent on lenders who supply emergency loans and the extent of this dependency is in general higher for land-poor categories compared to larger land owning groups (52 per cent as against 26 to 41 per cent). Third, while the dependency on emergency-lenders declines as one moves from 'first lender' to 'fourth lender', the degree of accessibility to emergency loans also declines at the same time. This implies strong correlation between dependency on lenders and the likelihood of risks insurance. Fourth, the declining trend in the ratio of dependent borrowers observed in case of borrowings from 'third' and 'fourth' lenders does not necessarily imply that emergency loans in these cases are obtained through routine credit market operations. As Table 12.14 reveals, kinship lineages emerge as a prominent relationship even in case of the 'fourth lender' where apparently incidence of 'no dependency' is also reported to be very high.

Thus, for a large rural poor with little collateralisable assets, dependency on non-relative lenders and kinship networking with the 'friends and relatives' category emerge as two major avenues for ensuring emergency credit. Evidently, those vulnerable poor households who are able to borrow at all (even at high interest rates) would be a very selective few. Many poor households are likely to be rationed out of the credit market altogether, because their income prospects are so poor that their capacity to repay is in doubt or they lack effective kinship network. If they can not thus borrow in times of risks, they will have to fall back upon their own meagre resources to survive with strong adverse consequences on nutrition; health and welfare.

Adjustment through Labour Market

The adjustment process takes place in case of labour market as well. For instance, an important feature of the survival pressure on the rural poor is the necessity to combine a variety of income sources such as wage labour, trading, kitchen gardening, livestock rearing etc. to make up a subsistence income. Table 12.15 shows that multiple occupation pattern cuts across all land ownership categories. The dominant tendency is for dual income sources. For the lower land ownership categories, a significant number varying from 31 per cent for the landless to 42 per cent for the marginal owner take recourse or have access to more than 2 occupations. Some implications of this increased dependence on multiple sources on the part of rural households may be considered.

TABLE 12.15
Incidence of Multiple Occupation by Land Ownership Categories

Land ownership group (in acres)	% distribution of households by no. of income sources				
	1	2	3	4	5
Landless (less than 0.05)	27	42	26	4	1
Functionally landless (0.5–.49)	26	36	28	9	1
Marginal owner (0.50–1.49)	13	45	28	11	3
Small owner (1.50–2.49)	22	46	25	6	1
Medium owner (2.50–4.99)	21	55	18	6	–
Large owner (5.00+)	23	56	19	2	–

Source: Analysis of Poverty Trends Project, BIDS: 62 Village Survey.

The land-poor households take recourse to multiple occupations in order to compensate for low wages and under-employment in the crop sector. The growing importance of low-productivity non-crop and non-farm employment in the lower echelons of rural households as reflected in their dependence on multiple income sources is mainly due to 'push' rather than the 'pull' effects of the crop sector development. It is equally important to note that 87 per cent of marginal owners and 78 per cent of small owners have multiple occupations. Growing importance of non-farm activities in the occupational profile of marginal and small owners contributes to the persistence of small landholdings. By contrast, dependence of large land owning groups on multiple income sources implies integration of different businesses which further stimulates the concentration of economic power in the higher echelon of the rural society.

Additional data presented in Tables 12.16 through 12.18 reveal several important aspects of the rural labour market.[x] First, the participation rate is found to be inversely related to the size of the landholding. Nearly 30 per cent of the population in the landless

TABLE 12.16
Participation in Income-Earning Activities by Land Ownership and Surplus Deficit Status

	Workers as a per cent of family Members	Female workers as a per cent of Total workers
A. Land Ownership (acres)		
Landless (less than 0.05)	29.4	3.5
Functionally landless (0.05–0.49)	27.4	6.8
Marginal (0.50–1.49)	28.0	1.5
Small (1.50–2.49)	24.4	4.3
Medium (2.49–4.49)	18.0	1.7
Large (5.00+)	20.6	–
B. Surplus/Deficit Status (as per self-categorisation)		
Chronic deficit	33.1	7.6
Occasional deficit	24.3	2.5
Break-even	25.9	2.4
Surplus	20.4	2.1
All	26.1	3.6

Source: Analysis of Poverty Trends Project, BIDS: 62 Village Survey.

households participated in the labour force, compared with 21 per cent in the large land owning group (Table 12.16). Since income is highly and positively associated with the size of land owned, this suggests that the higher income households supply fewer workers, an indication of a greater preference for leisure over work. Second, the proportion of female workers declines sharply as the size of land owned increases, participation being negligible in the highest land owning group (see Table 12.16). In Bangladesh there is a social stigma against women working in the field or performing

TABLE 12.17
Days of Labour in 1990, by Land Ownership Group

Land ownership group (ac.)	Annual days of employment/ household	Annual days of employment/ worker
Landless (less than 0.05)	417	342
Functionally landless (0.05–0.49)	430	302
Marginal (0.50–1.49)	370	287
Small (1.50–2.49)	399	267
Medium (2.50–4.49)	540	335
Large (5.00+)	510	285
All Households	426	304

Source: Analysis of Poverty Trends Project, BIDS: 62 Village Survey.

TABLE 12.18
Composition of Annual Employment per Household by Surplus Deficit Status

Surplus/ Deficit group	Days of employment per household			
	Self	Casual wage (including formal sector services)	Contract	Total
Chronic Deficit	169	179	82	430
Occasional Deficit	227	100	60	387
Break-even	343	20	128	491
Surplus	339	15	119	473

Source: Analysis of Poverty Trends Project, BIDS: 62 Village Survey.

manual labour on another account. Hence, the higher presence of female workers in case of the landless and the functionally landless occurs mainly under the pressure of poverty. This trend is clearly revealed when deficit/surplus status of the household is taken into consideration. 'Chronic deficit' households are characterised by the highest presence of female workers compared to 'surplus' households (7.6 per cent vis-à-vis 2.1 per cent). Indeed, women workers from the land-poor group are increasingly being involved in recent years in market-oriented income-earning activities, including petty trading, construction, agricultural labour over and above their traditional spheres of involvement in livestock rearing, homestead gardening, and cottage industry activities. Third, days of labour are found to be inversely related to the size of land owned, again suggesting that at higher levels of income, people substitute labour for leisure. In 1990, a worker in the large land ownership group, for example, put in 285 days of labour, compared with 342 days for a worker in the landless group, i.e., about 20 per cent fewer days (Table 12.17).

Important differences appear to persist in the composition of employment observed for the two respective categories of the poor, i.e., chronic deficit and occasional deficit groups. As may be calculated from Table 12.18, the share of self-employment in total employment is much higher for the occasional deficit group vis-à-vis the chronic deficit group (59 per cent vis-à-vis 40 per cent). Additional data (not shown in the table) show that the crop sector accounts for the largest share (43 per cent) in self-employment of the occasional deficit group, while the matched figure is only 23 per cent in case of the chronic deficit group. By contrast, chronic deficit households spend more time within self-employment on miscellaneous homestead and expenditure-saving activities compared to the occasional deficit group (28 per cent as against 15 per cent). Trading is another sector which figures prominently in self-employment of the poor accounting for a quarter of total days of self-employment across the two deficit groups.

As expected, break even and surplus households are only marginally dependent on casual wage-labour which represents only 3 to 4 per cent by their total employment. This may be contrasted to 42 per cent recorded for the chronic deficit households, indicating the extent of vulnerability of this group in the labour market. Occasional deficit households are less vulnerable in this regard, the share of casual wage-labour in total employment of this group being 26 per cent. It is widely believed that contract labour has emerged as an important form of wage-employment in recent years. This change in the rural labour market may have important implications for the two groups of the poor. Although longitudinal data on the share of contract labour in total wage-labour supply is not available, data presented in Table 12.18 provides some important insights on this score.

Contract labour (i.e., *chukti*) constitutes a significant proportion (about 31 to 37 per cent) of total wage-employment recorded for the deficit groups. The term 'contract labour', however, includes different types of activities ranging from formal service sector employment to piece-rate arrangements in agricultural wage labour and hence, it has differing implications for various groups of rural households. For the chronic deficit group, contract labour would be mainly related to activities carried out by them as labourers attached to well off farms for a certain period (varying from 3 to 9 months) in a year. These are mostly low-productivity activities in informal services, construction or agricultural sectors. It appears that involvement of chronic deficit households in contract labour is driven mainly by pressure of underemployment and poverty. In going for a shift from casual to contract labour, the principal consideration of chronic deficit households has been more to secure wage-employment of longer duration as attached labourers, rather than to switch over from low-paid to high-paid labour activities. Occasional deficit households are somewhat better placed in this regard; part of their contract labour activities (about 17 per cent of total days of contract labour) are related to piece-rate jobs in agriculture and informal services with potentials for higher return to labour vis-à-vis casual (time-rate) labour. Thus, it was estimated from the 1990 survey that average return per hour of contract labour in agricultural sector is Tk 7.4 compared to Tk 3.5 recorded for casual agricultural wage labour. A shift from casual (time-rate) to contract (piece-rate) arrangements may have important poverty-alleviating effects in another important way. Such a shift allows that labourer to save time by intensifying work-input on the contract and use the time thus saved for additional earning or expenditure-saving activities. However, this trend to shift from casual (time-rate) to contract (piece-rate) is yet to become strongly pronounced. For instance, within agricultural wage-employment the share of contract labour is assessed at an average figure of only 11 per cent for the sample. Besides, as pointed out above, only the occasionally deficit households could reap the advantage of this change in the rural labour market, the chronic deficit households being restricted to only the lower end of the contract labour activities.

In contrast to the deficit group, the term contract labour as applied to the break-even and the surplus categories mainly points to formal service sector jobs falling under contract employment category. Thus, the formal service sector's share in contract labour is over 80 per cent for the break-even and the surplus categories as against only 38 per cent registered for the chronic deficit group. It appears that lack of education and networking capacity acts as barriers to entry to formal services sector for the extreme poor households.

So far we have briefly touched upon some selected features of adjustment process. The immediate issue that springs up is: what would be the net outcome of initial dislocational features the negative effects of which are only partly 'compensated' by the working of various markets? Will the instability of poor households' existence improve over time? Will there be any viable prospect of upward mobility for a vast majority of the rural poor? It is difficult to construct a single indicator which would adequately capture the dynamics of household existence in the land-poor group. Keeping this limitation in mind and given the dearth of reliable longitudinal data, one can consider land-stability and upward mobility along the land ownership scale as two important indicators of change, which would capture the aggregate impact of the adjustment process on the rural poor. To this issue, we now turn.

Aspects of Mobility

Going through Table 12.19 to 12.22, several aspects can be noted. In the first place, the land stability index (LSI) (which is defined as the ratio of 'total land currently owned by the household' to total land owned by the household at inheritance') shows that differential access to various markets has led to considerable intra-group as well as inter-group variations. For instance, deficit households divide into 32 per cent with declining LSI, 59 per cent with 'stable' LSI and only 9 per cent with 'improved' LSI. On the other hand, 55 per cent of the surplus households are characterised by 'improved' LSI while the corresponding figure for occasional deficit households is only 19 per cent (Table 12.19). Similar trend may be observed for other land owning categories as well (see Table 12.20). Secondly, only a fraction of households with 'improved' LSI in a particular land ownership category have the potentials for upward (inter-class) mobility, (i.e., the capacity to move up into

TABLE 12.19
Land Stability of Deficit/Surplus Status, 1989–90
(figures represent percentages of row total, while figures in parentheses show column percentages)

Land Stability Index (LSI)*	Deficit/Surplus category				Total
	Deficit	Occasional deficit	Stable	Surplus	
Worse (LSI < 0.9)	29	55	12	4	100
	(32)	(29)	(18)	(12)	(27)
Stable (0.9 < LSI < 1.1)	27	49	18	5	100
	(59)	(52)	(54)	(33)	(52)
Improve (LSI > 1.1)	10	45	23	22	100
	(9)	(19)	(28)	(55)	(21)
Total	24	50	18	8	100
	(100)	(100)	(100)	(100)	(100)

Source: Analysis of Poverty Trends Project, BIDS: 62 Village Survey.

* Land stability index is calculated as follows:

$$\text{Land stability index (LSI)} = \frac{\text{Total land at present}}{\text{Total land at inheritance}}$$

TABLE 12.20
Land Stability by Land Ownership Status, 1989–90
(Figures represent percentages of row total, while figures in parentheses show column percentages)

Land ownership group (acres)	Land Stability Index*		
	Worse (LSI < 0.9)	Stable (0.9 < LSI < 1.1)	Improve (LSI > 1.1)
Landless (less than 0.05)	33 (19)	67 (20)	–
Functionally landless (0.05–0.49)	27 (34)	60 (38)	13 (20)
Marginal owner (0.50–1.49)	32 (26)	43 (18)	25 (25)
Small owner (1.50–2.49)	28 (12)	44 (9)	28 (15)
Medium owner (2.50–4.49)	17 (7)	40 (9)	44 (24)
Large owner (5.00+)	8 (2)	43 (6)	49 (16)

Table 12.20 (Continued)

Land ownership group (acres)	Land Stability Index*		
	Worse (LSI < 0.9)	Stable (0.9 < LSI < 1.1)	Improve (LSI > 1.1)
All	27 (100)	52 (100)	21 (100)

Source: Analysis of Poverty Trends Project, BIDS: 62 Village Survey.

* Land stability index is calculated as follows:

$$\text{Land stability index (LSI)} = \frac{\text{Total land at present}}{\text{Total land at inheritance}}$$

TABLE 12.21
Incidence of Land Stability by Age of Household and by Non-Land Income status
(figures represent intra-group weight of households with LSI greater than 0.9, i.e., 'land-stable' households)

% of non-land income in total income				Age of household* (Yrs.)				All house-holds
0	0.1–<40	40–<80	80+	1–5	6–10	11–15	16+	
58.1	80.5	78.8	68.3	61.8	65.8	68.1	60.3	62.9

Source: Analysis of Poverty Trends Project, BIDS: 62 Village Survey.

* 'Household age' refers to the period when the current household head assumed the role of household head.

the next category along land ownership scale. Table 12.22 compares the proportion of households reporting 'improved' LSI in each land owning group with the incidence of upward (inter-class) mobility recorded for each group. It appears that, for a sheer majority of cases, households with 'improved' LSI have mobility only in a limited sense, their mobility being restricted to a narrow band with little prospects for escaping from the land-poverty trap.

To illustrate the point just made, one may record 64 to 81 per cent of extreme land-poor households as having 'improved' or 'stable' LSI as against only 12 to 28 per cent who could 'cross over' to the next land owning group. The former tendency, thus, points to the overwhelming presence of 'banded mobility' whereby land-poor households may move slightly up or slide downward along the land ownership scale with fluctuating LSIs over time, but on

TABLE 12.22
Incidence of Inter-Class Mobility* vis-à-vis Land Stability by Land Inheritance Group

Land inheritance group (acres)	% of 'land-stable' households within each group, i.e., with LSI > 0.9	% of households in each land owning group having			% of 'surplus' households within each group as per self-categorisation	Mean household age** (yrs)
		Downward inter-class mobility	No inter-class mobility	Upward inter-class mobility		
Landless (less than 0.05)	64	–	72	28	1	11
Functionally landless (0.05–0.49)	81	11	77	12	1	17
Marginal (0.50–1.49)	65	23	63	14	5	18
Small (1.50–2.49)	61	31	50	19	14	20
Medium (2.50–4.49)	58	35	54	11	21	20
Large (5.00+)	60	34	66	–	40	24
All Households	63	19	66	15	9	18

Source: Analysis of Poverty Trends Project, BIDS: 62 Village Survey.

Note: * 'Inter-class mobility' in this case essentially measures the likelihood of a household to corss over to the immediate next land owning group. For example, the LSI index of a household may fluctuate over time within a certain band without actually elevating the household into the next land ownership category.

** 'Household age' refers to the period when the current household head assumed the role of household head.

the whole they are compelled to remain restricted well within the band. In contrast to this, inter-class mobility would have increased the likelihood of substantial improvement for the rural poor in terms of systemic dislocational characteristics discussed earlier. However, and this needs to be underlined, even an upward mobility of the second kind is also possibly limited to a movement from chronic deficit to occasional deficit status and not primarily from a deficit to surplus status. Thus, while productivity increases and non-land opportunities appear to permit some mobility to the land-poor, the lack of land remains as yet a limiting disadvantage not allowing a comprehensive escape from the poverty trap. Thus, we can see that even up to small land-owner category the percentage of households above poverty, i.e., not in deficit, remain significantly below 50 per cent.

Notes

1. Direct evidence on changes in the distribution of land ownership is not available because previous agricultural censuses reported findings on the distribution of landholdings rather than on land ownership. But there is some indirect evidence which indicates that the concentration of land ownership may have increased over time. Hossain (1986) further shows that the number of landless households also must have increased at faster rate than population (2.5 vis-à-vis 2.2 per cent per annum during the period between 1960 and 1983–84).
2. There is controversy over the extent of land cultivated under tenancy arrangements—23 per cent according to the land occupancy survey of 1978, 18.5 per cent according to the 1983–84 agricultural census, 22.7 per cent according to the 1987 BIDS survey. The latest 1989–90 survey puts the figure at 26.7 per cent.
3. However, the overall weight of the pure tenant category in total rural households is quite low (9 per cent only).
4. Given the short duration of tenancy and prevailing discriminatory practice of output sharing on a 50:50 basis implementation of tenurial reforms is considered by many as an avenue for increasing small farmers tenurial security. However, such reform measures are extremely difficult to implement and likely to be declarative as was the case with the 1984 tenancy reforms.
5. Constraints to the rapid expansion of NGO-sponsored programmes as an instrument for poverty-alleviation have been spelt out in the recent literature. For details, see Osmani (1989).
6. A survey carried out in ecologically vulnerable *haor* areas indicates that average implicit interest rate charged by professional moneylenders can be as high as 200 per cent compared to 80–125 per cent for other categories of lenders. For details see, Sen (1989).

7. For details on these issues, see Siamwalla (1990).
8. The employment data were generated through one-week survey during June 1990 which may be roughly considered as a 'normal' agricultural period. The survey, although executed in the 16-village cluster sample on account of the greater time and resources needed in the collection of the data, relates to a representative sub-set of the 62-villages originally selected for the study.

References

Hossain, M., 1986, 'A Note on the Trend of Landlessness in Bangladesh, *The Bangladesh Development Studies*, Vol. 15, No. 2.
Hossain, M. and B. Sen, 1992, 'Rural Poverty in Bangladesh: Trends and Determinants', *Asian Development Review*, Vol. 10, No. 1.
Osmani, S.R., 1989, 'Limits to the Alleviation of Poverty through Non-farm Credit', *The Bangladesh Development Studies*, Vol. 17, No. 4.
Sen, B., 1989, *Moneylenders and Informal Financial Markets: Insights from Haor Areas of Rural Bangladesh* Research Report No. 100, BIDS.
Siamwalla, A., 1990, 'Rural Credit and Rural Poverty,' Thailand Development Research Institute, (mimeo.).

13

Ecological Reserves and Expenditure-Saving Scope for the Poor

Hossain Zillur Rahman

Introduction: Income-Earning and Expenditure-Saving

Productive activities of rural households in Bangladesh as in many other countries fall into two major categories: income-earning and expenditure-saving. Working for a wage in agriculture is an income-earning activity while collecting firewood to meet the fuel needs of the household is an expenditure-saving activity. Overall household welfare is an outcome of both types of activities. For poor households with low levels of income in particular, the expenditure-saving scope may be an important determinant of their well-being and survival capacity.

Analysis of household welfare based on income estimation frequently overlook this additional dimension of household sustenance. From a measurement point of view, adequate cognisance of the expenditure-saving scope helps to correct for any underestimation of household welfare arising from traditional income calculations. Equally importantly, from a dynamic point of view, the nature and durability of the scope of expenditure-saving can shed important light on routine survival and crisis-coping capacities of rural households. In the latter aspect, the expenditure-saving scope may also be seen as a safety net in the survival process of the rural poor.

The scope for expenditure-saving for rural households lie in three major sources. The first such source is the fuller use of the household's own homestead resources as, for example, in the consumption of supplementary food items, such as fruits and vegetables. Secondly, the access poor households may enjoy to the unutilised and residual products on the property of more affluent neighbours as, for example, in crop-gleaning on neighbours' fields provides another source. Third and not the least source in this regard is the contribution of common property resources, such as village woodlots and free-access water bodies. Poor households in particular derive a variety of benefits from such resources in the form of fuel items, supplementary foods including protein sources, such as fish and house-building materials. The use of such common property resources for expenditure-saving purposes have long antecedents in the community culture of rural Bangladesh and such practices are quite in harmony with sustaining the environment as for example in the widespread community practice of slack-season fishing in the autumn.

Common Types of Expenditure-Saving Scopes

The most frequent areas of expenditure-saving for rural households were found to be the following:

1. Fuel use
2. House-building materials
3. Supplementary foods, i.e., fruits and vegetables
4. Fishing
5. Livestock grazing
6. Crop-gleaning

Among fuel items which can be collected without cost, the most important are cow-dung, firewood and miscellaneous leaves and sticks. Of the house-building materials the most significant are *chon* (thatch), bamboo, jute-sticks, cane, straw, *hogla, gol* and other leaves. Supplementary food items collected without cost are various types of fruits, *shak* or leafy green vegetables, *kochu* or arum, sweet potato, and various types of pot-herbs. Fishing opportunities cover a variety of fish-grounds ranging from small water-holes in *bil* and *khal*. These sweet water fish grounds yield a wide variety of protein-rich indigenous fishes.

The range of expenditure-saving scopes listed above does not of course imply that they are either uniformly and/or abundantly available for all areas of the country and for all categories of the village population. The overall intensity of vegetation and tree cover, actual size of common and *khas* property resources both land and water bodies, and last but not the least, whether or not poorer households enjoy effective access to such resources or whether such access is monopolised by the village influentials, all these factors determine the actual scope for expenditure-saving for any one particular area. Of particularly negative impact in this regard is the indiscriminate turn over to commercial leasing of erstwhile common property resources.

Taken all together, the opportunities for expenditure-saving constitute an ecological reserve which play an important role in the sustenance of rural household besides contributing to the environmental health of the country. Such opportunities should not all be seen automatically as distress activities but should instead be seen as a routine component of rural household economy. However, a few of these activities, i.e., collecting leaves for fuel and house-building and crop-gleaning do fall within the distress category in that better-off households are unlikely to participate in them.

Survey Findings on the Importance of Expenditure-Saving

Extent of Household Participation in Expenditure-Saving

Five major areas of expenditure-saving activities were enquired into: fuel, house-building materials, supplementary foods, slack-season fishing and crop-gleaning. Tables 13.1 and 13.2 describe

TABLE 13.1
Extent of Household Participation in Expenditure-Saving

Expenditure-saving items	Percentage of household involved in expenditure-saving				
	Landless/ Functionally Landless	Small Land Owners	Middle Land Owners	Large Land Owners	All Bangladesh
Cow-dung	66	68	69	59	67
Firewood	69	70	72	70	70
Other Fuel	49	41	34	25	44
Fuel: Total	**76**	**76**	**73**	**59**	**75**
Straw	16	23	31	32	21
Jute-stick	15	34	42	50	27
Bamboo	25	43	51	59	36
Other materials	12	13	11	18	13
All House-building Materials	**100**	**100**	**100**	**100**	**100**
Fruit	24	39	51	59	34
Leafy Vegetable	48	59	63	73	55
Arum/kochu	29	35	33	41	32
Pot-herb	35	51	58	68	45
Other fruit/vegetable	2	1	1	–	1
Supplementary Foods: Total	**54**	**53**	**50**	**39**	**53**
Crop-gleaning	17	8	4	2	11
Slack-season Fishing	56	58	59	48	57

Source: Analysis of Poverty Trends Project, BIDS: 62 Village Survey.

the extent of household participation in such activities by region and land owning groups. The most frequent areas of expenditure-saving for the country as a whole are seen to be in firewood and cow-dung collection for fuel (70 per cent and 67 per cent of households respectively), collection of leafy green vegetables or *shak* (55 per cent of households) and slack-season fishing (57 per cent of households). Consolidating the percentages for the individual items under their broad headings, however, we see that nearly all households save on expenditure on house-building materials of one kind or another while 75 per cent of households

TABLE 13.2
Division-Wise Household Participation Rate in Expenditure-Saving

Expenditure-saving items	Percentage of household involved in expenditure-saving				
	Chitta-gong Division	Khulna Division	Dhaka Division	Rajshahi Division	All Bangla-desh
Cow-dung	53	79	63	70	67
Firewood	72	80	64	65	70
Other Fuels	37	36	66	35	44
Fuel: All Categories	**69**	**60**	**89**	**80**	**75**
Straw-collection	19	24	17	25	21
Jute-stick	6	28	41	29	27
Bamboo	27	42	41	33	36
Other materials	8	14	22	6	13
House-building Materials	**100**	**100**	**100**	**100**	**100**
Fruit	32	41	40	24	34
Leafy vegetable	51	62	58	49	55
Arum (*kochu*)	28	48	24	29	32
Pot-herb	45	53	49	34	45
Other furits/vegetables	2	2	1	–	1
Supplementary Foods: All Categories	**58**	**28**	**83**	**41**	**53**
Crop-gleaning	4	10	7	23	11
Slack-season Fishing	56	47	65	60	57

Source: Analysis of Poverty Trends Project, BIDS: 62 Village Survey.

partially or wholly save on fuel expenditure. Furthermore, 53 per cent and 57 per cent partially or wholly save on fruit/vegetable and fish consumption expenditures respectively.

Table 13.1 also underscores the fact that expenditure-saving as an activity is not confined to the poor alone but cuts across all classes. Indeed, while the need for such activities is the greatest for the poor, it is the better-off households, i.e., the middle and large land owning groups, who appear to enjoy better access to such opportunities. Such differential access is most clearly demonstrated in the area of 'house-building materials' and 'fruits'. The higher percentages for the land-poor households in 'crop-gleaning' and 'other-fuel' (i.e., fallen leaves, etc.) only emphasise the same point since both these activities are essentially of a distress nature and better-off households are in any case likely to shun them.

Coming to the regional pattern, the percentages for the major categories of 'firewood', leafy vegetable and 'slack-season fishing' are uniformly high for all areas ranging from 64 per cent in Dhaka division to 80 per cent in Khulna division in the case of 'firewood', 49 per cent in Rajshahi division to 62 per cent in Khulna division in the case of 'leafy vegetable' and 47 per cent in Khulna division to 65 per cent in Dhaka division in the case of 'slack-season fishing'. Taking the consolidated percentages for the broad item heads, the most intensive recourse to expenditure-saving appears to be in the Dhaka division with above 80 per cent of households saving on expenditure on fuel, house-building materials and supplementary foods while it also records the highest participation in slack-season fishing (65 per cent). Dhaka is closely followed by Chittagong division in this regard. Rajshahi division has the highest percentage (23 per cent) for the distress activity of crop-gleaning followed by Khulna division (10 per cent). As a whole, Khulna division appears to have the least scope for expenditure-saving activities. Such regional differences do not of course have any single explanation but may reflect both lower need on the part of households due to higher average incomes and/or better availability of ecological reserves. To determine which of these explanations apply, it will be necessary to juxtapose the regional pattern with information on income levels, the size of common property resources and the power balance between the rich and the poor in terms of their access to such activities.

Estimating the Contribution of Expenditure-Saving to Household Welfare

Depending on availability and access, not all households in all areas were able to save on expenditure in particular on the major items listed earlier. Information was also collected on whether actual expenditure if any had been incurred on each of the items by any of the households in each of the areas surveyed. Actual expenditure figures provided a basis for imputing the savings on expenditure by households who had obtained such items free of cost. This procedure was, of course, difficult to apply in the case of very marginal items like fallen leaves for fuel and house-building and stray fruits and vegetables. However, for most of the items it was possible to obtain a reasonably realistic estimate of what the items would cost if they had to be purchased. We were unable, however, to impute a value to the 'crop-gleaning' and 'slack-season fishing' activities. Following the procedure indicated above, we estimated annual savings on expenditure on three major heads: fuel, house-building materials and fruits/vegetables.

Table 13.3 presents estimates of average annual household savings on expenditure on fuel, house-building materials and fruit/vegetables. The major omission here is the saving on slack-season fishing. The savings presented in the Table arise, as we have noted earlier, from three sources: household's own homestead and orchards, access to homestead and orchards of more affluent neighbours and various open-access land and waterbodies falling under the rubric of common property resources. The exact proportion in which savings arise from each of these three sources could not be disaggregated but richer households are more likely to draw upon their own homestead and orchard properties while for poorer households, ecological reserves are likely to play the more significant role.

Average annual household expenditure saved on fuel, house-building materials and fruit/vegetables stand at Taka 6767. Of this, 40 per cent come from savings on fuel, 6 per cent from savings on house-building materials and 54 per cent from savings on fruit/vegetables. This proportional breakdown when disaggregated by land owning status shows broadly the same pattern across groups.

Table 13.3 also juxtaposes the expenditure-saving figures with average annual household income figures. It should, of course, be pointed out that current procedures for calculating household income do not incorporate savings on expenditure. Nor do income calculations based on expenditure data fully take account of such savings in particular the savings arising from access to residual and unutilised products of affluent neighbours and common property resources. From this standpoint, total household welfare is the sum of household income and household savings on expenditure. Following from this, expenditure-saving scopes arising from homestead and community forestry contribute on average 15.4 per cent to annual household welfare (Figure 13.1). For the land-poor

TABLE 13.3
Annual Savings on Expenditure and Annual Household Income

Land-owning category	Average annual household savings				Average annual household income	Expenditure-savings as % of the sum of income and savings
	Fuel	H-B materials	Fruits/vegetable	Total		
	(in Takas)					
Landless	2240	665	1810	4715	19,193	20
Functionally Landless	2391	657	2750	5798	25,971	18
Marginal Landowner	2106	663	6070	8839	31,693	22
Small Landowner	4133	655	5077	9865	39,080	20
Middle Landowner	3775	608	3469	7852	56,649	12
Large Landowner	1548	976	1952	4476	117,410	4
All Groups	2683	429	3655	6767	37,246	15.4

Source: Analysis of Poverty Trends Project, BIDS: 62 Village Survey.

FIGURE 13.1
The Importance of Ecological Reserves for Rural Households

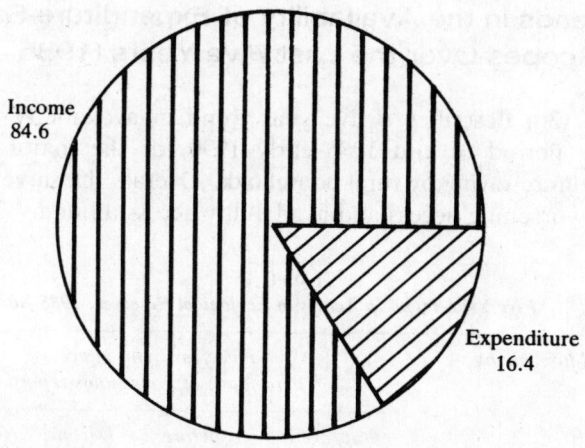

Note: Income and expenditure–savings from ecological reserves together describe the magnitude of household welfare in rural Bangladesh. The expenditure–savings considered here are in fuel (6%), fruits/vegetables (8%) and house-building materials (1%). An important category of savings which could not be calculated was consumption of fish.

households ranging from the landless to marginal landowners, this percentage averages to 20 per cent and it declines to 4 per cent in the case of large land owners.

Even though of an indicative nature, the above estimates bring to light a significant though largely obscured source of household sustenance in rural Bangladesh. Ecological reserves whether in homestead forestry, product residuals or common property resources have a significance in particular for resource-poor households which appear to escape the attention of policymakers and the informed public. Contributing as it does nearly a fifth to annual household welfare of the poor, ecological reserves combine both a poverty-alleviating function with an environment sustaining function which may all too easily be put at risk by ill-considered commercial and other encroachments. In the next section, we review how the access of rural households to such reserves have been evolving over the recent past.

Trends in the Availability of Expenditure-Saving Scopes Over the Last Five Years (1985–90)

Table 13.4 describes a five year trend in availability from the survey period of end 1985–early 1990 for the major areas of expenditure-saving by rural households. Overall, the survey findings show worsening access and availability across all items. The most

TABLE 13.4
Five Year Trend in Access to Ecological Reserves, 1985–90

Expenditure-saving items	Five year trend in access (Percentage of households reporting)			
	Improved	*As before*	*Decline*	*Non-response*
Cow-dung	7	14	46	33
Firewood	7	15	48	30
Other fuel	12	12	27	49
Jute-stick	3	7	16	74
Straw	3	6	12	79
Bamboo	5	11	20	64
Other materials	1	4	7	88
Fruit	3	8	22	67
Leafy vegetables	7	16	33	44
Arum/kochu	3	10	18	69
Pot-herb	6	14	25	55
Other fruit/vegetables	–	–	1	99
Crop-gleaning	1	1	9	89
Slack-season fishing	1	3	68	29

Source: Analysis of Poverty Trends Project, BIDS: 62 Village Survey.

dramatic decline is in the area of slack-season fishing (68 per cent of all households reporting worsening access). Such a large decline not only underscores the negative impact of indiscriminate turn over of state and common property resources to commercial encroachment, it also highlights the tragic neglect by the nation of the waterways and waterbodies of this deltaic land.

This decline is less grim in the case of supplementary foods and house-building materials with the percentages of households reporting a decline only slightly higher than the percentages reporting constant or improved availability. The situation is clearly worse in the case of fuel items in particular in the two substantive items of cow-dung and firewood. This may reflect both greater intensity of demand arising from population pressure and also ill-considered depletion of ecological reserves.

The regional picture as shown in Table 13.5 brings out certain interesting features. The decline in fishing opportunities is most pronounced in Rajshahi and Dhaka divisions. Both these divisions also report significant decline in fuel item access. Despite such declining trends, households in Dhaka division as yet continue to enjoy the best access to ecological reserves though the coming future may well be very different (Table 13.2). The modest decline figures for Khulna division must of course be read with the knowledge that access to ecological reserves is already the lowest in this region (Table 11.2). In terms of both current access and past trends, it is the Chittagong division which probably shows the most positive picture. Strikingly enough, not a single major item shows an overall improvement in access and availability except for the single item of 'fruit' in the case of Rajshahi division.

Conclusions

An important proportion of the productive time of rural households in Bangladesh is devoted to activities which are expenditure-saving. Previous attention to such activities, if any, have focused only on those which are of a distress nature. Our survey findings clearly show, however, that the significance of such activities extend much beyond their distress nature. Indeed, such activities are very much integrated in the routine functioning of the rural household economy. Their significance is underlined by the fact that they contribute as much as a fifth to the annual household welfare of the rural poor.

The scope for expenditure-saving activities is dependent on the size and availability of ecological reserves in an area. In this context, the appropriate use of such activities potentially carries a

TABLE 13.5
Division-Wise Five Year Trend in Access to Ecological Reserves, 1985–90

Expenditure-Saving	Chittagong			Khulna			Dhaka			Rajshahi		
	Increased	As before	Decreased	Increased	As before	Decreased	Increased	As before	Decreased	Increased	As before	Decreased
Cow-dung	9	9	34	8	21	50	4	18	41	9	9	52
Firewood	10	13	48	6	24	51	2	15	46	9	9	48
Other fuel	3	14	20	3	10	23	8	18	39	4	6	25
Jute-stick	–	1	5	4	8	14	5	10	27	5	6	16
Straw	4	7	7	3	7	15	1	5	11	6	4	15
Bamboo	3	8	15	8	17	19	3	11	27	5	10	18
Other materials	1	4	5	1	5	8	3	7	10	–	1	5
Fruit	1	7	24	4	11	25	3	10	26	3	16	5
Leafy vegetables	8	11	31	5	21	39	6	19	31	7	13	30
Arum/kochu	1	7	17	3	17	26	4	8	11	5	7	19
Pot-herb	7	11	27	4	21	28	6	14	26	5	10	20
Other fruit/vegetables	1	–	1	–	–	2	–	–	–	–	–	–
Crop-gleaning	2	–	2	–	2	8	1	1	5	3	2	18
Slack-season fishing	1	3	56	–	7	58	2	3	74	–	1	80

Source: Analysis of Poverty Trends Project, BIDS: 62 Village Survey.

double significance combining a poverty-alleviation dimension with an environment sustaining dimension. Survey findings show the highest savings to occur in the areas of fuel items and supplementary foods. Collection of house-building materials in which nearly all households participate yield comparatively a much smaller amount of savings. One area on which information could not be gathered is the savings arising in open-access fishing opportunities. Figures on participation rates clearly underline the overall importance of this activity for the rural households. What is noteworthy is that such expenditure-saving activities have long antecedents in the community culture of rural Bangladesh and as such they require no cultural mediation to be encouraged. The lack of understanding and attention to their significance, if any, has rather been on the part of policymakers and the public.

Expenditure-saving activities are not a substitute for income-earning activities but they are rather their complement. For the rural poor, life becomes paradoxical when increase in income is counter balanced by reduction in expenditure-savings. For development to be meaningful, such paradoxes need to be avoided and this means giving appropriate and adequate attention to strengthening ecological reserves and the access of the poor to them. A particular pitfall to be avoided is the indiscriminate turning over of ecological reserves for commercial exploitation. In terms of the major policy measures which merit attention here are homestead and community forestry, free stocking of fish in open-access waterbodies and the removal of such waterbodies from the ambit of commercial considerations and ensure free access of the rural public. From a long term point of view, however, the most important step in this regard is likely to be the reversal of the nation's neglect of its silted-up waterways and waterbodies.

14

Mora Kartik: Seasonal Deficits and the Vulnerability of the Rural Poor

HOSSAIN ZILLUR RAHMAN

Introduction

An unusually intense political debate in the autumn of 1991 helped to throw the spotlight on a major dimension of the vulnerability of the rural poor in Bangladesh, namely, the perennial nature of seasonal deficits which grip the countryside, some parts more severely than others, at certain times of the year. *Kartik* (in the title) is the Bengali month coinciding with October. *Mora* refers to hunger and deprivation. *Mora Kartik* is the bane of the rural poor, the season of half-meals and debt bondage. Elsewhere in this book, the importance of seasonality for any discussion of rural poverty has already been underscored (chapters 3 and 7). In this chapter, we shall look at the dynamics at work from the vantage-point of the heightened political attention which briefly invested the routine suffering on the poor with a measure of 'national' importance. The analysis is supplemented by a rapid survey which was carried out during October, 1991. The arguments advanced are of an indicative nature.

Lean Seasons in Bangladesh

Rural life in Bangladesh still revolves around the agricultural cycle. Traditionally, there has been two major periods of seasonal deficits, one starting in late September and extending upto early November and the other starting in late March and extending upto early May (Figure 14.1). With the widespread expansion of winter planting of rice, the incidence of the early summer lean season has significantly declined. However, the autumn lean season coming after the planting of the *aman* crop and with harvest time still a month or more away remains very much the routine order of the day affecting nearly all parts of the country. Indeed, the success of the green revolution in terms of winter planting has accentuated the autumn deficit because the winter rice, *boro* crop has largely displaced the secondary early summer, *aus* crop which was harvested in the autumn.

The nature of this routine seasonal crisis is brought out in Tables 14.1 and 14.2 which report the average drop in income flows during October for the two major categories of the rural poor—those mainly dependent on wage labour and; those mainly dependent on petty trade.

TABLE 14.1
Percentage of Labour Households Going Without any Work for 4–7 Days a Week

Division	10–20 October, 1991	Normal time
Chittagong	50	4
Khulna	67	–
Dhaka	69	2
Rajshahi	65	2
Bangladesh	62	2

Source: Analysis of Poverty Trends Project, BIDS: Rapid Survey, 1991.

The Tables compare work availability and average daily earning during the (October) lean month and normal times when various agricultural activities are in full swing. For Bangladesh as a whole, while only 2 per cent of labourer households reported going without any work for 4–7 days a week during normal time, this figure

TABLE 14.2
Average Daily Earning of Petty Trader Households During 10–20 October, 1991 vis-à-vis Average Daily Earning in Normal Time

Division	% of Households reporting			
	No Change	Increase	Moderate decline	Severe decline
Chittagong	23	2	37	38
Khulna	3	2	48	47
Dhaka	13	1	35	51
Rajshahi	8	–	59	33
Bangladesh	11	2	46	41

Source: Analysis of Poverty Trends Project, BIDS: Rapid Survey, 1991.

jumps to 62 per cent during the crisis month of October. Such a pattern broadly holds true for all parts of the country though Chittagong division appears to be somewhat better placed in terms of access to compensatory non-farm and non-crop opportunities.

The petty trader households fare slightly better than wage labour households but at 41 per cent of such households reporting a severe decline in daily earning during October, the seasonal deficit is very much of a crisis nature for this category of the rural poor too.

The same picture of a routine seasonal decline can also be seen in the variation in average daily wage rates provided in Table 14.3. For Bangladesh as a whole, there is an average drop of 30 per cent in the daily wage rate during October compared to the normal time. Such a drop is relatively the largest for the Rajshahi Division (37 per cent) and the smallest for Chittagong Division (20 per cent). At a more disaggregated level, the greater districts of Rangpur (50 per cent), Pabna (47 per cent), Tangail (40 per cent) and Jessore (40 per cent) experience the largest seasonal drop in wage rate.

Though the two Tables present information only on 1991, a seasonal crisis in October is hardly peculiar to that year. The routine nature of such crisis has already been brought out in chapters 3 and 7. However, even within the routine occurrence of seasonal crisis, there may be an escalation in vulnerability in any particular year due to a number of contingent factors. Two major

TABLE 14.3
Comparison of Daily Wage Rates during October 1991 and Normal Time

Greater district	Average wage rate during 10–20 October, 1991 (Tk.)	Average wage rate in normal period (Tk.)	Average drop in wage rate during October (%)
Comilla	29	39	25
Noakhali	29	38	23
Chittagong	49	60	18
Sylhet	35	40	12
Chittagong Division	**35**	**44**	**20**
Khulna	23	36	36
Jessore	22	37	40
Kushtia	29	31	6
barisal	25	38	34
Khulna Division	**25**	**36**	**30**
Faridpur	25	30	17
Dhaka	23	33	30
Tangail	21	35	40
Jamalpur	24	35	31
Mymensingh	23	35	34
Dhaka Division	**23**	**34**	**32**
Dinajpur	24	32	25
Rangpur	13	26	50
Bogra	22	36	39
Rajshahi	25	37	32
Pabna	19	36	47
Rajshahi Division	**21**	**33**	**37**
Bangladesh	**26**	**37**	**30**

Source: Analysis of Poverty Trends Project, BIDS: Rapid Survey, 1991.

considerations here are the possibility either of a production failure or of an entitlement failure in terms of a collapse of purchasing power and coping capacities.

Natural Calamities in 1991 and their Impact on Agricultural Production

Bangladesh witnessed more than its routine share of natural calamities during 1991. The April cyclone devastated much of the coastal belt. At the same time flash floods in northern pockets, such as Netrokona damaged the boro crop, thus, creating a stock shortage for poorer households to last them through the aman season. Over the summer, several parts particularly in greater Rangpur, Pabna, Rajshahi, Kushtia, Jamalpur, Tangail and Sylhet experienced two rounds of floods. Most other parts of the country experienced continuous heavy rain through much of the late summer. By contrast, greater Dinajpur and Kushtia suffered the opposite problem of a drought for part of the summer.

Table 14.4 provides local estimates of the aman cropped area affected by these natural calamities and to what extent replanting was subsequently possible. It can be seen for the country as a whole, a quarter of the aman cropped area was estimated to have been affected. However, the greater districts of Sylhet, Jamalpur, Rangpur, Kushtia and Pabna were seen to have been the most affected.

The sequence of natural calamities is not, however, likely to have any uniformly adverse impact across the country. Indeed, some areas stood to derive an above average harvest as others stood to lose. Table 14.5 summarises local estimates of production forecasts on the coming aman harvest. Such a countrywide perspective at once puts the prospects of scarcity within clear focus. For the country as a whole, 57 per cent of thanas expect normal production, 16 per cent expect a definite shortfall and 27 per cent expect an above average production according to local estimates. This would put the aggregate production estimates at very much around the normal level.

While the overall estimates indicate near-normal production, there are several regional pockets where significant production shortfalls are likely to occur. These pockets are concentrated in the north, specifically in the areas of greater Rangpur, Dinajpur and Pabna and smaller pockets in Kushtia and Tangail. All these pockets are in the low-lying belts along the Padma, Jamuna and Teesta rivers. 43 per cent of thanas in greater Rangpur, 36 per cent in greater Dinajpur and 33 per cent in greater Pabna reported an expected shortfall in production. For the northern division of Rajshahi as a whole, 28 per cent of thanas expect a shortfall. As against this, 15 per cent expect an above average production while 57 per cent expect normal levels of production.

TABLE 14.4
Impact of Flood/Excess Rain on Aman/Aus Crop: Local Estimate of Loss and Recovery

Name of greater district	No. of thanas surveyed	Local estimate of average % area affected	Local estimate of average % of area replanted	Estimated net cropped % of area affected
Comilla	12	7.00	4.20	6.70
Noakhali	9	10.60	–	10.60
Chittagong	7	4.20	–	4.20
Sylhet	20	46.90	20.50	37.28
Chittagong Division	**48**	**17.10**	**5.20**	**16.22**
Khulna	15	2.60	4.00	2.50
Jessore	13	–	–	–
Kushtia	7	41.70	4.30	39.90
Barisal	20	43.70	59.00	25.78
Khulna Division	**55**	**22.00**	**16.80**	**18.30**
Faridpur	22	12.60	–	12.60
Dhaka	18	29.10	34.70	19.00
Tangail	5	47.00	45.00	25.85
Jamalpur	20	57.50	44.20	32.09
Mymensingh	11	40.90	30.40	12.43
Dhaka Division	**77**	**37.40**	**30.90**	**25.84**
Dinajpur	14	12.10	–	12.10
Rangpur	21	35.90	2.70	34.93
Bogra	11	16.80	–	16.80
Rajshahi	17	45.60	27.80	32.92
Pabna	9	86.60	48.80	44.33
Rajshahi Division	**72**	**39.40**	**15.90**	**25.23**
Bangladesh	**251**	**30.00**	**18.00**	**24.6**

Source: Analysis of Poverty Trends Project, BIDS: Rapid Survey, 1991.

Purchasing Power and Coping Capacities in Autumn, 1991

Even if there was no overall scarcity in foodgrains, the vulnerability of poorer households could still increase if opportunities for work and income collapse and the established coping capacities of the poor become threatened. Any rise in such vulnerability would

TABLE 14.5
Expectation of 1991 Aman Production vis-à-vis Normal Year

Name of greater district	No. of thanas surveyed	Percentage of thanas reporting		
		No shortfall	Shortfall	Excess
Comilla	12	33	–	67
Noakhali	9	25	–	75
Chittagong	7	29	–	71
Sylhet	20	15	20	65
Chittagong Division	**48**	**25**	**8**	**67**
Khulna	15	86	7	7
Jessore	13	100	–	–
Kushtia	7	43	43	14
Barisal	20	85	5	10
Khulna Division	**55**	**84**	**9**	**7**
Faridpur	32	45	–	55
Dhaka	18	88	6	6
Tangail	5	80	20	–
Jamalpur	20	60	10	30
Mymensingh	11	66	5	27
Dhaka Division	**76**	**65**	**6**	**29**
Dinajpur	14	57	36	7
Rangpur	21	57	43	–
Bogra	11	9	–	90
Rajshahi	17	88	12	–
Pabna	9	67	33	–
Rajshahi Division	**72**	**57**	**28**	**15**
Bangladesh	**251**	**57**	**16**	**27**

Source: Analysis of Poverty Trends Project, BIDS: Rapid Survey, 1991.

immediately be reflected in the intensity of shortage in food intake at the household level. Table 14.6 reports the level of household distress in terms of food intake shortage during 10–20 October, 1991 and contrasts this with the level of distress during the same period in 1990. Of the households surveyed, 18 per cent reported to being in distress (on 1 meal a day for 1–3 days in the week) and 9 per cent reported to be in extreme distress (on 1 meal a day for 4–7 days in the week) during October, 1991. This contrasts with the percentages for the previous year when 8 per cent reported to be in distress and 4 per cent in extreme distress. It would, thus, appear

Seasonal Deficits and the Vulnerability • 241

TABLE 14.6
Intensity of Food Intake Shortage, 10–20 October, 1991

Name of greater district	No. of sample households	Distress households % of households on 1 meal a day for 1–3 days in the week		Extreme distress households % of households on 1 meal a day for 4–7 days in the week	
		This year	This time last year	This year	This time last year
Comilla	53	23	19	X	X
Noakhali	48	39	8	2	X
Chittagong	37	X	X	X	X
Sylhet	80	1	X	X	X
Chittagong Division	**218**	**15**	**6**	**X**	**X**
Khulna	54	13	X	X	X
Jessore	46	4	X	X	X
Kushtia	15	20	14	X	X
Barisal	79	6	1	X	X
Khulna Division	**194**	**9**	**1**	**X**	**X**
Faridpur	60	X	X	X	X
Dhaka	65	31	X	X	X
Tangail	19	39	X	X	X
Jamalpur	60	35	12	2	X
Mymensingh	37	32	3	X	X
Dhaka Division	**241**	**25**	**3**	**X**	**X**
Dinajpur	44	11	11	20	X
Rangpur	94	23	25	59	26
Bogra	46	33	28	2	X
Rajshahi	92	24	12	16	2
Pabna	36	17	X	27	X
Rajshahi Division	**213**	**22**	**18**	**29**	**13**
Bangladesh	**965**	**18**	**8**	**9**	**4**

Source: Analysis of Poverty Trends Project, BIDS: Rapid Survey, 1991.

that for the country as a whole there was some intensification in the degree of seasonal deficit during autumn, 1991.

The regional breakdown shows that the phenomenon of extreme distress was almost wholly confined to the areas of Rajshahi

Division specifically to the greater districts of Rangpur, Dinajpur and Pabna and to a lesser extent Rajshahi. In greater Rangpur, 26 per cent of households were in extreme distress in the previous year which by production and other standards was a normal year. In comparison, the proportion of extreme distress households this October jumped to 59 per cent clearly marking the gravity of the situation there. For the Rajshahi Division as a whole, the severity of the deficit in 1991 was of the order of an increase from 13 per cent extreme distress households in 1990 to 29 per cent last October.

Insofar as 1990 was a largely disaster-free, normal year (by Bangladesh standards), the comparison in Table 14.6 provides a basis for assessing to what extent the economic health of the countryside is worse off relative to normal standards. From the district-wise breakdown, it would appear that two separate discussions may be warranted. The first is about the intensity of the seasonal deficit in the northern districts as is indicated by the sharp rise in the proportion of 'severe distress' households. The second is about a possible economic recession as may be suggested by the across the board rise in the proportion of 'moderate distress' households in Khulna, Chittagong and Dhaka Divisions. We shall postpone the discussion on economic recession to a later section and concentrate here on the issue of an intensified seasonal deficit.

The thanas in the grip of an intensified seasonal deficit were in the greater districts of Rangpur, Dinajpur, Pabna and Jamalpur. A variety of factors contributed to the severity of this year's lean season. Nilphamari, Dinajpur and Thakurgaon witnessed both drought and flooding which disrupted the normal flow of agricultural activities. In addition, there was a widespread incidence of cattle disease; many cattle died and many farmers were forced to incur higher production costs on account of having to hire tractor services. One of the mitigating factors during the deficit month is the planting of various minor rabi crops and also potatoes. The supplementary income and employment opportunities arising out of these activities were seriously hampered on account of a major shortage of working capital. To tide over the deficit period, many labourer households were forced to contract forward sale of their labour at less than half the rate they could have earned normally.

Lalmonirhat witnessed two rounds of flooding and the flood waters took a long time to recede. The cultivation of rabi crops, vegetables and potatoes have been seriously hampered as a consequence. Recourse to various wild foods brought on an outbreak of diarrhoea. Another misfortune to befall this area was the widespread damage to housing. By contrast, there was no significant housing damage in the Rangpur, Gaibanda and Kurigram areas. However, these areas sustained major damage to standing crop on account of flooding with little opportunities for replanting and recovery, thus, intensifying the margin of deficit in these perennially vulnerable districts. The crisis of entitlement was compounded by the relatively slow response of relief efforts from government and non-government sectors at the outset. One serious lacuna here is the very limited range of activities in which slack-season relief effort is conducted. With excessive rain hampering the normal avenues of construction work, the administration of relief grinds to a standstill for lack of alternative avenues. From a longer-term perspective, this is clearly one priority area for the attention of crisis managers both within and outside the government.

There was some degree of distress sale of household assets, cattle and mortgaging of land, to tide over the deficit period. The vulnerability in this regard is highlighted in Table 14.7 which reports prevailing wage rates and market prices during the period 10–20 October, 1991 throughout the country. Eggs, chicken and cattle whose sale constitute the first line of defence for rural households in coping with crisis all show levels significantly below the national and even the division average in the case of greater Rangpur belt indicating a glut in supply on account of distress sale. Land prices too show a lower average for Rangpur but not sufficiently low to warrant any firm conclusions in terms of the incidence of distress sale. The more serious consideration here is the possibility that the deficit period may extend to the months of November and December requiring a sustained relief attention to the affected thanas in this area all through to the winter months.

An important factor in the severity of the deficit in Rangpur is that there are relatively few resource-rich rural households who could be a major source of crisis-period borrowing to tide over the deficit period. Any major shock to the slender balance of coping capacities, thus, escalates here into a generalised crisis.

Bogra as a whole was not significantly affected except for the pockets of Sariakandi and some areas in Joypurhat. There was

TABLE 14.7
Wage Rates and Market Prices, 10–20 October, 1991

Name of greater district	Average daily wage rate (Tk)	Average price of coarse rice (Tk per Kg.)	Average price of atta (Tk per Kg.)	Average price of milk (Tk per Kg.)	Average price of egg (Tk per 4 pcs.)	Average price of chicken (Tk per Kg.)	Price of average size cattle (Tk)	Average price of land (Tk per bigha)*
Comilla	29	11.80	10.00	13.00	11.00	51	4200	30,000
Noakhali	29	12.80	10.35	13.00	12.50	52	4200	27,000
Chittagong	49	12.85	10.00	12.00	12.75	60	5100	40,000
Sylhet	35	11.90	10.10	15.25	11.00	57	2890	20,000
Chittagong Division	**35**	**12.34**	**10.10**	**13.30**	**11.80**	**55**	**4116**	**29,000**
Khulna	23	11.40	9.30	11.85	10.00	57	2850	21,700
Jessore	22	12.50	9.25	12.50	9.80	58	2866	17,000
Kushtia	29	12.75	13.10	12.25	9.90	49	3825	27,125
Barisal	25	13.00	9.80	10.10	10.20	42	3255	8,600
Khulna Division	**25**	**12.42**	**10.40**	**11.70**	**9.95**	**52**	**3198**	**18,606**
Faridpur	25	13.35	9.80	12.35	9.65	50	4413	20,022
Dhaka	23	12.50	10.20	15.80	11.90	61	4082	52,916
Tangail	21	12.50	10.60	14.75	10.75	68	3375	32,375
Jamalpur	12	11.40	9.60	10.30	9.05	35	2666	22,250
Mymensingh	23	11.75	9.40	12.45	10.40	44	3100	27,125
Dhaka Division	**21**	**12.31**	**9.90**	**13.10**	**10.35**	**52**	**3527**	**30,937**
Dinajpur	24	11.20	9.57	9.00	18.20	28	2100	23,875
Rangpur	13	12.40	10.50	7.80	7.60	26	1724	19,912

Bogra	22	10.15	8.30	9.30	8.10	35	2520	25,950
Rajshahi	25	11.00	9.05	9.75	7.65	38	3400	28,058
Pabna	19	11.80	9.80	11.50	9.20	44	3055	24,222
Rajshahi Division	**21**	**11.30**	**9.45**	**9.50**	**10.15**	**34**	**2560**	**24,403**
Bangladesh	**25**	**12.10**	**9.97**	**11.90**	**10.60**	**48**	**3350**	**24,736**

Source: Analysis of Poverty Trends Project, BIDS: Rapid Survey, 1991.
* one bigha = 33 decimals.

significant housing damage in Sariakandi compounded by flood damage to the aman crop and the spread of sand on the land rendering the next planting uncertain. The deficit in Natore arose from the damage to the previous boro crop which has meant a lack of stocks to last poorer households through the deficit period.

The Pabna region also witnessed significant damage to its standing crop along the Jamuna belt. Rain also hampered planting of supplementary minor crops thus intensifying the crisis of employment and income. In addition, there was the massive disruption of communication which has hampered both relief efforts and movement of the affected population in search of work opportunities.

Like Rangpur, Jamalpur is also a perennially vulnerable area with a slender resource margin, in the aggregate. Though Jamalpur was also subjected to floods, it was unlikely to hamper aman production significantly as was borne out subsequently. However, the lack of employment opportunities was intensified because as in much of the whole country, excess rain has prevented the growing of supplementary minor crops and vegetables to mitigate the deficit season. With little non-farm opportunities, this meant a collapse in work opportunities. Floods also damaged many of the existing tubewells, thus, creating a sudden crisis of safe drinking water. Consequently, there was a major outbreak of diarrhoea.

In Netrokona, there was a major crisis of cattle fodder because the earlier damage to the boro crop meant a lack of straw and also because current grazing grounds went under water due to floods. Even many well-to-do households had to sell off cattle and enter into debt to repurchase cattle for the boro planting.

To summarise, a number of factors essentially arising from the sequence of natural calamities in 1991 greatly aggravated the seasonal deficit in a number of thanas in the northern districts. These factors may be listed as (*a*) damage to the aman crop, (*b*) damage to the prospects of supplementary minor crops, such as pulses, vegetables and potatoes on account of excess rain during October, (*c*) disruption in communication preventing the movement of people to search for work opportunities, (*d*) adverse impact on living standard via damage to housing and safe drinking water and (*e*) the limited response capabilities of relief efforts insofar as these rely almost exclusively on earth-work which can be easily hampered by rain as was the case last October.

Seasonal Deficit or Economic Recession?

Table 14.6 not only underscored the increased seasonal vulnerability of northern districts, it also pointed towards a much wider debate on a possible economic recession across the country. One indication of this could be the marked rise in the proportion of 'moderate distress' households across the entire country during October, 1991 compared to the same time the year before. Such a rise, it could be argued, was indicative of a general decline in purchasing power. Another angle from which to examine such a possibility is to compare the volume of sale on the most common range of sale items in rural shops/wholesalers during October 1991 vis-à-vis such sale in the same time the year before. Such a comparison is provided in Table 14.8.

In general, there has been a slight decline in the level of business activity across the country. However, the extent of this decline is not sufficiently pronounced to warrant any firm conclusions on any major economic recession. The reality appears to be closer to a situation of an intensified seasonal deficit against the backdrop of a generally stagnating economic situation. Interestingly, such a conclusion is supported from a different angle by what at first sight appears to be anomalous evidence, namely, the higher than average volume of sale of rice in the districts identified as those of greatest distress. Rangpur reports a 30 per cent rise in the volume of rice sale in retail and wholesale shops during this October vis-à-vis the same last year, while Jamalpur reports a 25 per cent corresponding rise. The most reasonable explanation for higher levels of food purchase in distress areas appears to be the following: flood damage to aman cultivation meant that normal levels of employment opportunities during August and September were disrupted. This forced wage-dependent households to consume any stocks they may have built up from the boro harvest before it could be put to use to mitigate the deficit period of October. In effect this meant that to stave off starvation, distress households had to engage in above-average participation in food purchase and the purchasing power for such participation had to be obtained through disadvantageous contracts, such as forward sale of labour at much cheaper rates, borrowing at very high levels of interest and distress sale of

TABLE 14.8
Trend in Business Activity

Name of greater district	No. of thanas surveyed	Shop/traders estimate of current level of business activity as a proportion of business activity same time last year								
		Rice	Attal Wheat	Sugar	Pulses	Saree	Crocke-ries	Tools and machine parts	Cosmetic	Medicine	Clothing
Comilla	12	87	89	83	99	114	NA	NA	67	NA	150
Noakhali	8	60	68	77	74	200	NA	NA	NA	NA	108
Chittagong	7	75	85	86	89	NA	NA	NA	NA	71	NA
Sylhet	20	102	97	122	91	96	NA	NA	NA	NA	115
Chittagong Division	**47**	**81**	**85**	**92**	**88**	**137**	**NA**	**NA**	**NA**	**NA**	**124**
Khulna	13	87	87	75	91	100	75	80	83	100	113
Jessore	12	80	90	82	100	77	78	67	83	88	82
Kushtia	10	93	96	90	94	80	NA	NA	NA	NA	70
Barisal	20	63	58	76	81	63	66	53	73	88	53
Khulna Division	**55**	**83**	**83**	**81**	**92**	**80**	**73**	**67**	**80**	**92**	**80**
Faridpur	40	96	95	107	104	103	NA	NA	91	90	105
Dhaka	17	70	97	78	72	50	83	100	57	84	38
Tangail	5	81	77	77	74	31	NA	NA	NA	61	71
Jamalpur	13	125	159	95	88	69	NA	133	82	NA	70
Mymensingh	18	86	107	88	82	77	92	116	116	109	76
Dhaka Division	**93**	**91**	**107**	**89**	**84**	**66**	**88**	**107**	**87**	**86**	**71**

Dinajpur	13	100	116	110	96	83	40	62	70	73	78
Rangpur	20	130	147	106	81	87	29	NA	17	47	76
Bogra	13	121	118	94	118	100	NA	NA	114	NA	100
Rajshahi	20	108	228	80	84	88	76	NA	81	70	84
Pabna	10	35	48	54	50	76	61	NA	74	80	94
Rajshahi Division	**76**	**99**	**131**	**88**	**86**	**87**	**51**	**NA**	**76**	**68**	**86**
Bangladesh	**271**	**84**	**103**	**88**	**87**	**88**	**67**	**83**	**81**	**80**	**87**

Source: Analysis of Poverty Trends Project, BIDS: Rapid Survey, 1991.

TABLE 14.9
Reasons for Lower Sale in Current Period as Provided by Traders

Name of greater district	Percentage of responses									
	Seasonal deficit	Cyclone rain flood drought	Price Hike	Decline in middle east remittance	Increase in no of traders	Disruption in communication	Low price of jute	Competition of Indian goods	Access to relief goods	Purchasing power exhausted on account of having to bribe survey and settlement personnel	Low expenditure by the wealthy for reasons of insecurity
Comilla	13	25	–	37	25	–	–	–	–	–	–
Noakhali	30	50	–	10	–	–	–	–	10	–	–
Chittagong	9	36	–	18	–	–	–	–	36	–	–
Sylhet	42	25	23	10	–	–	–	–	–	–	–
Chittagong Division	**30**	**26**	**14**	**12**	**2**	**–**	**–**	**–**	**5**	**–**	**–**
Khulna	42	16	26	–	3	–	3	–	–	10	–
Jessore	43	3	29	–	–	–	26	–	–	–	–
Kushtia	67	33	–	–	–	–	–	–	–	–	–
Barisal	45	31	15	–	–	8	–	–	–	–	–
Khulna Division	**43**	**20**	**20**	**–**	**1**	**3**	**8**	**–**	**1**	**2**	**1**
Faridpur	60	27	–	–	–	–	13	–	–	–	–
Dhaka	39	–	9	6	33	–	6	6	–	–	–
Tangail	55	9	9	–	18	–	–	9	–	–	–
Jamalpur	42	33	–	4	–	–	17	4	–	–	–
Mymensingh	45	18	–	9	9	–	9	9	–	–	–
Dhaka Division	**47**	**14**	**4**	**4**	**14**	**–**	**32**	**5**	**–**	**–**	**–**

Dinajpur	100	—	—	—	—	—
Rangpur	48	30	9	—	—	—
Bogra	59	12	29	—	—	—
Rajshahi	49	19	23	8	—	13
Pabna	26	47	27	—	—	—
Rajshahi Division	**47**	**26**	**19**	**4**	**1**	**4**
Bangladesh	**44**	**22**	**15**	**2**	**6**	**1**

Source: Analysis of Poverty Trends Project, BIDS: Rapid Survey, 1991.

household utensils and animal stocks. Field reports from these areas have indeed confirmed the greatly increased incidence of such injurious contracts. While the purchasing power generated through such distress means goes into food purchase, the participation in the purchase of not so immediately essential items of consumption fall sharply. Thus, we see that in Rangpur while rice purchase is 30 per cent above average for this period, purchase of crockeries is 70 per cent below average, purchase of cosmetics is 83 per cent below average and purchase of clothing is 24 per cent below average.

The generation of purchasing power through distress means to stave off current starvation brings out a less-discussed dimension of the dynamics of food shortage. For the situation under review, what it essentially implies is that while current starvation may be averted, distress conditions may extend into the periods of normal economic activities. Households who have contracted forward sale of their labour and sold households assets will continue to face various degrees of current income crisis well into December–January, when they will be working but not getting an income, this income having been consumed in October. In macro terms, this implies, not increased mortality in the distress areas, but increased vulnerability and must be addressed as such.

The generation of purchasing power through injurious contracts could not of course have mitigated on its own the intensity of this year's seasonal deficit. The importance of government and non-government relief efforts was no less important in this regard. Further elaboration on this, however, has not been possible due to the limitations of the survey.

Table 14.9 elaborates on the explanations offered by the traders themselves on the incidence of lower sale. Seasonal deficit, natural calamities, price hike, low price of jute, declining Middle East remittance income and proliferation of petty traders stand out as the major explanations offered for the reported decline in the volume of sale and the implied decline in purchasing power. Some of these factors are of a seasonal or temporary nature and others of a structural nature. On the aggregate, these factors are not specifically indicative of any major economic recession at work beyond the larger problem of a stagnating economy.

Conclusions

Mora Kartik has always been the bane of the rural poor, a season of half-meals and debt bondage to cope with the deficit. Even within this routine cycle, this year's litany of natural disasters have combined to produce significantly worse levels of vulnerability in certain parts of the northern districts. For the country as a whole, no major aggregate production shortfall is expected but a major coping mechanism in terms of supplementary minor crop production has been seriously hampered throughout the country. However, except in the northern pockets of severe distress, the economic revival coming with the harvest season is likely to pull the rest of the country out of the seasonal crisis. What will remain as a stark challenge for the nation and its leaders is not just to tide over a seasonal deficit but to pull the economy out of its stagnation and initiate a growth process which will render the bane of *Mora Kartik* a thing of the past.

V

Policy Environment and Poverty

V

Policy Environment and Poverty

15

Determinants of Poverty

MAHABUB HOSSAIN AND BINAYAK SEN

Introduction

The household level data collected in this study allow us to examine the relative significance of a number of factors having a bearing on rural poverty. Six major factors which have been considered are land ownership, new technology, education, occupation, physical infrastructure and family size. Admittedly, the factors considered may not exhaustively explain the determination of rural poverty in Bangladesh. Nevertheless, several useful insights emerge.

Determinants of Rural Income

A multivariable regression model has been estimated using household level data to analyse determinants of rural income. The income of a household would obviously depend on the amount of land owned (LND), the number of earning members in the household (LBR) and to some extent by the amount of capital employed in farm and non-farm activities. A household may also earn additional income by renting-in land from others (TNC). The higher the productivity of land, the higher would be the income of the household. The productivity of land would depend on the use of the new 'seed–fertiliser–water' technology, represented by the proportion of area allocated to the high yielding modern varieties (TCNLG). The income from labour may depend on the quality and composition of labour and the productivity of the activity in which labour is employed. Female workers (FLBR) may earn less than male workers, while the workers employed in non-agricultural activities (NAGL) may earn more than those employed in agriculture. The productivity of labour and the choice of economic activities would depend on the level of education of the worker. The state of development of infrastructure may also affect income by changing the input–output prices and providing scope for adoption of new agricultural technology and generating employment opportunities in rural non-farm activities. The most important infrastructural variables that have been considered here are the access to electricity (ELCT) and the state of development of transport facilities (TRN).

The regression equations are estimated in log linear forms. Natural logarithms are taken for the dependent variable income, and for land and workers. The tenancy and the technology variable is measured in ratio form i.e., by the proportion of cultivated area rented-in from others, and the proportion of area allocated to high-yielding varieties. The differential earnings of female workers and of the workers employed in non-farm activities is captured by measuring these variables in ratio forms, i.e., as a proportion of total workers. Since the level of education may not have a linear effect, dummy variables have been used to capture the effect of different levels of education of the household head, using 'no formal schooling' as control. The infrastructural variables have been measured in the form of village level dummy variables. For example, villages having access to electricity have been assigned value '1' and those without electricity, value '0'. The survey did not collect information on capital employed in production activities for the reference year of income, and hence, it could not be taken into account in this exercise[1].

The regressions have been estimated for the entire sample as well as for the farm and non-farm households (Table 15.1).

The amount of land owned by the household is found to be the most important determinant of rural income. But the elasticity of rural income with respect to land ownership is quite low. A doubling of the size of land ownership for an average rural household would increase income by only 26 per cent. The amount of land rented-in from the tenancy market also increases income but the return is about 60 per cent lower than that for owned land, a reflection of the exploitative terms and conditions in the tenancy market. The regression coefficient of the technology variable is found positive and statistically significant. This implies that the adoption of the new technology makes a significant positive contribution to rural incomes.

The contribution of labour to household incomes is found very high. The elasticity of income with respect to workers is estimated at 0.46, suggesting that a 100 per cent increase in the number of earners would increase incomes by 46 per cent. The contribution of a female worker is, on average, about 60 per cent lower than that of an average worker. This suggests that female workers are employed in low productive activities and/or they are paid lower wages than the male workers when they sell their services in the market. The low earnings of the female workers is particularly pronounced for non-farm households. For farm households the differential earning of the female worker is not statistically significant. The workers employed in non-farm activities contribute more to household income than an agricultural worker. The regression coefficient of the variable representing non-agricultural occupation is found positive and statistically highly significant in the income equations for both the farm and non-farm households.

The coefficient of the dummy variable representing primary and secondary education is found positive but *not* statistically significant. The households whose head had primary schooling had about 7 per cent higher income than those headed by persons having no formal schooling. The impact of primary education on income is found to be higher for non-farm households than for farm households. Those attending secondary schools had about 8 per cent higher income than the illiterates, but the effect is found more pronounced in case of farm households. Those who had secondary school certificate or higher degrees earned about 37 per cent higher incomes than the illiterates; the estimate is 34 per cent for farm households and 43 per cent for non-farm households. The positive coefficient for higher education is statistically highly significant. The findings suggest that with the present curriculum, the

TABLE 15.1
Determinants of Rural Household Income: Regression Estimates

Variables	Descriptions	All households		Farm households		Non-farm households	
		Regression coefficient	't' value	Regression coefficient	't' value	Regression coefficient	't' value
LND	Land owned (acres)	0.257	20.0**	0.274	14.03**	0.153	6.20**
TNC	Proportion of cultivated land under tenancy	0.159	2.7**	0.109	1.50	—	—
TCNLG	Proportion of cultivated land under modern variety	0.033	2.5**	0.023	1.80*	—	—
LBR	No. of earning members	0.460	11.15**	0.456	9.62**	0.342	4.14**
FLBR	Proportion of female earning members	−0.586	−5.43**	−0.178	−1.14	−0.667	−4.24**
NAGL	Proportion of non-agricultural earners	0.256	5.19**	0.265	4.28**	0.315	3.76**
PRY	Household head with primary education	0.073	1.28	0.052	0.78	0.098	0.92
SCND	Household heads attending secondary schools	0.080	1.47	0.082	1.35	0.034	0.32

HIGH	Household heads having higher certificate or higher degrees	0.365		6.74**	0.344		5.83**	0.434		3.69**
REM	Household receiving remittance	0.041		0.69	0.080		1.15	0.038		0.35
ELCT	Village with access to electricity	0.272		5.40**	0.227		3.81**	0.333		3.64**
TRN	Village with good transport facilities	0.110		2.48**	0.104		2.02**	0.138		1.70*
R^2		0.49			0.48			0.30	
No. of cases		1112			759			353	

Note: * Denotes significance at less than 10 per cent. The dependent variable is measured in logarithms of household income. The variables LND and LBR are also measured in logarithm forms.
** Denotes that the regression coefficient is significant at less than 5 per cent probability error.

drop outs from the secondary schools do not contribute much to increasing incomes particularly in non-farm households. This may be a reason for the low demand for secondary education in rural Bangladesh.

The regression coefficient of the dummy variables representing the state of development of infrastructure is positive and highly statistically significant. The average household income for a village having access to electricity is about 27 per cent higher than a village lacking such access. With access to electricity, the income of non-farm households increases at a higher rate (33 per cent) than that of a farm household (23 per cent). A village with good transport facilities has about 11 per cent higher income compared to a village with less developed transport network. The positive effect is higher for non-farm households (14 per cent) compared to farm households (10 per cent). The findings point to the beneficial effect of investment on rural infrastructures, particularly for generating employment opportunities in the non-farm sector.

Determinants of Income for Poor and Non-Poor Households

The multivariable regression model referred in the previous section has been used to analyse the determinants of income for the poor and non-poor households. The model helps us to identify the independent effect on income and poverty alleviation of various factors mentioned above. The results are presented in Table 15.2.

The ownership of land is found to be a statistically significant variable influencing income of both poor and non-poor households, but it is less important for the former than for the latter. The elasticity of income with respect to land ownership is 0.14 for poor household, compared to 0.20 for the non-poor. The poor depend more on the tenancy market for increasing their incomes. The tenancy variable is not found statistically significant for the non-poor households. The adoption of new agricultural technology increases income for both groups of households. The positive effect is, however, more pronounced for poor households than for the non-poor. This result is contrary to the prevailing notion that the new technology (so-called green revolution) has an anti-poor

TABLE 15.2
Determinants of Income of the Poor and Non-Poor Households

Variables	Description	Poor household		Non-poor household	
		Regression coefficient	't' value coefficient	Regression coefficient	't' value coefficient
LND	Land Owned (acre)	0.139	9.10**	0.203	11.52
TNC	Proportion cultivated land under tenancy	0.218	3.50**	0.043	0.52
TCNLG	Proportion of Cultivated land under modern variety	0.043	−1.84*	0.020	1.68*
LBR	No. of earning members	0.375	7.35**	0.489	10.44**
FLBR	Proportion of female earning members	−0.520	−4.38*	−0.437	−3.08*
NAGL	Proportion of non-agricultural earning members	0.131	2.28**	0.285	4.76**
PRY	Household heads attending only primary schools	0.121	1.87*	0.010	0.14
SCND	Household heads attending secondary schools	−0.004	−0.07	0.184	2.77**
HIGH	Household heads with high school certificates or higher degrees	0.150	2.03**	0.301	5.07**
REM	Households receiving remittances	0.029	0.38	0.112	1.70*
ELCT	Villages with access to electricity	0.140	2.18**	0.171	3.12**
TRN	Villages with good transport facilities	0.131	2.39**	0.060	1.18
R^2		0.29		0.49	
No. of cases		591		521	

Note: * At less than 10 per cent. The dependent variable is measured in natural logarithms of income. LBR and LND variables are also measured in logarithms.
** Denotes that the regression coefficient is statistically significant at less than 5 per cent probability error.

bias, that it makes rich richer and the poor poorer. Our findings suggest that in Bangladesh the diffusion of the new agricultural technology has poverty-alleviating effects.

The number of workers is found to be a significant determinant of income for both groups of households. The marginal return from workers is higher for the non-poor than for poor households. The elasticity of income with respect to labour is 0.38 for poor households compared to 0.49 for non-poor households. The income of the female workers is about 52 per cent lower than that for an average worker belonging to poor households. The corresponding figure is 44 per cent for the non-poor. Involvement in non-agricultural occupation increases household income through raising the productivity of labour. The returns from workers engaged in non-agricultural activities is about 13 per cent higher compared to an average worker for poor households. The corresponding figure is 29 per cent for the non-poor. The higher positive effect of occupational mobility from agriculture to non-agriculture on rural incomes for non-poor households may be because they are better endowed with capital and quality manpower than the poor. The findings suggest the significant role of the development of non-farm activities in the alleviation of poverty.

The impact of education on income varies with the level of education. The impact of primary education is found positive, but it is statistically significant at less than 10 per cent probability level only for poor households. By contrast, secondary education has a significant positive effect on income only for non-poor households. For poor households secondary education does not seem to have any effect on income at all. The coefficient of the dummy variable representing high school certificates or higher degrees is found statistically significant for both groups of households, but the positive effect is more pronounced for the non-poor households. Poor households whose head has passed secondary school earn 15 per cent more than the one whose head had no formal schooling. The differential income is 30 per cent for the non-poor households. The result suggests that education is more effective in raising income when it is combined with access to land and capital.

Access to electricity is found to have a positive effect on income even after disassociating the effect of other variables. Poor households in villages having access to electricity earn 14 per cent higher income than their counterparts in villages lacking this access. The differential income effect is 17 per cent for non-poor households.

Determinants of Poverty • 265

The state of development of transport facilities seems to have a positive effect on income only for the poor households. For non-poor household the income effect is positive but not statistically significant.

Infrastructure and Poverty

Irrigation

The impact of infrastructure on poverty is reviewed by considering the poverty impact of irrigation, electrification and transport facilities (Figures 15.1, 15.2 and 15.3). A major constraint in increasing

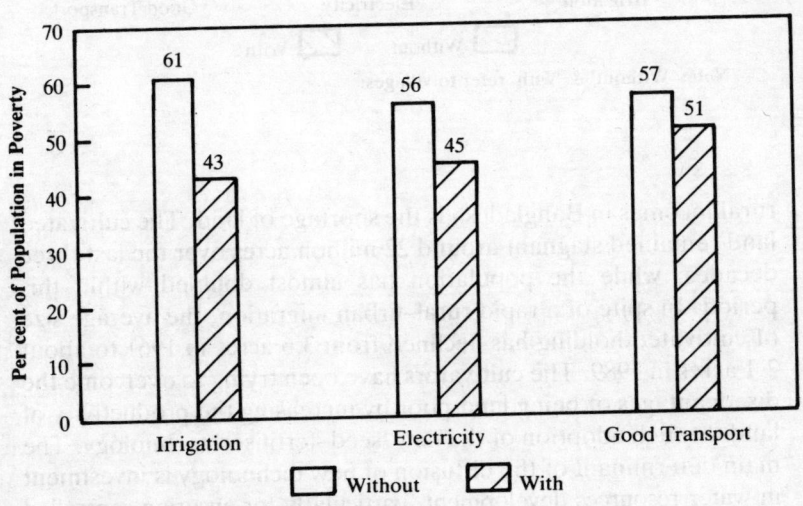

FIGURE 15.1
Impact of Infrastructure on Extreme and Moderate Poverty

Note: 'Without' & 'with' refer to villages.

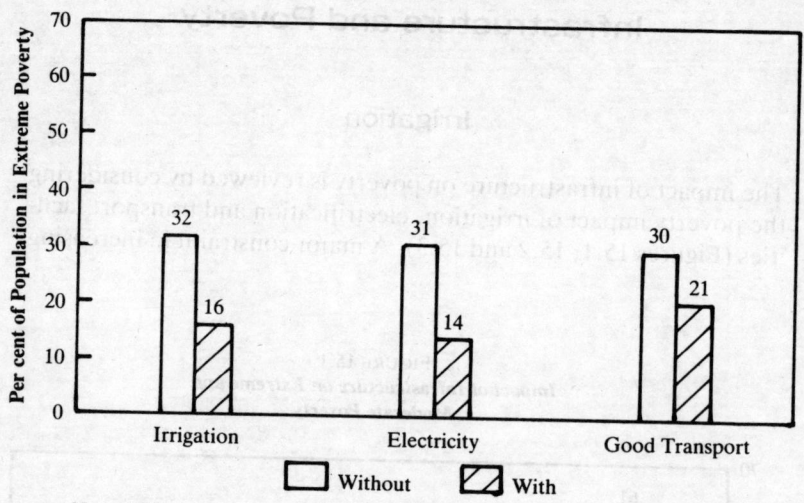

FIGURE 15.2
Impact of Infrastructure on Extreme Poverty

Note: 'Without' & 'with' refer to villages.

rural incomes in Bangladesh is the shortage of land. The cultivated land remained stagnant around 22 million acres over the last three decades, while the population has almost doubled within this period. In spite of a rapid rural–urban migration, the average size of cultivated holding has declined from 3.6 acres in 1961 to about 2.1 acres in 1989. The cultivators have been trying to overcome the disadvantages of being land-poor by increasing the productivity of land through adoption of the new 'seed–fertiliser' technology. The main determinant of the diffusion of new technology is investment in water resources development, particularly for ensuring controlled irrigation. The government has come forward to support farmers in this respect with assistance from donor agencies. Nearly 60 per cent of the public sector development resources allocated for agriculture over the last two decades was spent on water resource

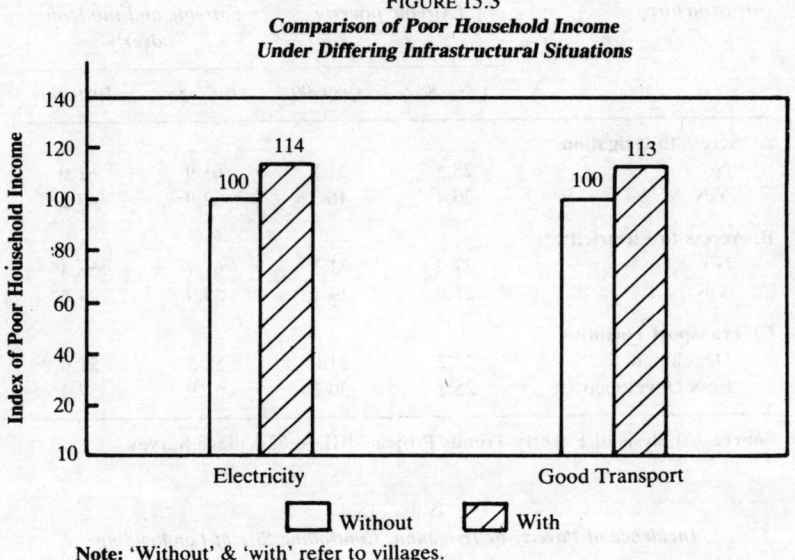

FIGURE 15.3
Comparison of Poor Household Income Under Differing Infrastructural Situations

Note: 'Without' & 'with' refer to villages.

development. It would be of interest to see the impact of the investment for development of irrigation infrastructure on alleviation of poverty.

We have estimated the incidence of poverty for households who have access to irrigation and compared it with that for households lacking this facility. The results are presented in Table 15.3 and Table 15.4. It is found that irrigation contributes substantially to reduction of poverty. In 1989–90, the 'hard core' poor were 16 per cent in households having access to irrigation compared to 32 per cent for households lacking this access. The estimates for moderate poverty are 27 per cent and 29 per cent respectively. Thus, the impact of irrigation is more pronounced for reduction of 'hard core' poverty than for moderate poverty.

A comparison with estimates for 1987–88 shows that the poverty

TABLE 15.3
The Incidence of Poverty by State of Development of Infrastructure
(Per cent of poor population)

Infrastructure	Extreme poverty		Extreme and moderate poverty	
	1987–88	1989–90	1987–88	1989–90
A: Access to Irrigation				
No	28.5	31.8	63.9	61.0
Yes	20.4	16.3	52.0	43.2
B: Access to Electricity				
No	27.3	31.3	61.7	58.4
Yes	21.0	14.1	55.0	44.6
C: Transport Facilities				
Developed	27.2	21.0	58.5	51.0
Less Developed	25.2	30.2	61.9	57.4

Source: Analysis of Poverty Trends Project, BIDS: 62 Village Survey.

TABLE 15.4
Incidence of Poverty by Irrigation, Controlling Size of Landholding

Size of landholding (acres)	Non-irrigated		Irrigated	
	Moderate Poverty	Moderate and extreme poverty	Moderate poverty	Moderate and extreme poverty
0.50	47.3	78.2	40.9	74.8
0.5–2.49	24.3	59.5	15.4	52.8
2.5–4.99	5.6	33.2	10.8	29.3
5.2 and more	1.9	7.3	Nil	6.8

Source: Analysis of Poverty Trends Project, BIDS: 62 Village Survey.

situation did not change for non-irrigated households; in fact 'hard core' poverty deteriorated. By contrast, the proportion of the poor was reduced substantially from 52 to 43 per cent for households with access to irrigation. The improvement is also noted for extreme poverty.

Electrification

Rural electrification reduces cost of irrigation, and facilitates the development of the rural non-farm sector. A number of donors, specifically the USAID, are supporting the government in spreading rural electrification in the country.

The incidence of poverty has been estimated for villages brought under the purview of rural electrification and compared with that for villages without access to electrification. The results show substantial effect of the spread of electrification on reduction of poverty. Only 14 per cent of the population in villages with electricity are 'hard core' poor compared to 31 per cent for villages lacking this access. The matched figures for moderate poverty is 27 per cent and 31 per cent respectively. It thus appears that the extreme poor benefit more from rural electrification than the moderate poor. The benefit may have originated more from generation of employment opportunities in the rural non-farm sector than from increasing the profitability per unit of land. It is found that the incidence of poverty is almost the same for households in the land-size category of 2.5–4.3 acres in the two groups of villages. But, for the functionally landless and the small farm households, poverty is substantially lower for villages with access to electricity (Table 15.5). 'Hard core' poverty improved substantially between 1987–88 and 1989–90 for villages with access to electricity. For villages lacking this infrastructure facility, the proportion of hard core poor increased from 27 per cent to 31 per cent (Table 15.3).

Transport Facilities

The development of transport facilities increases income of the farmers by lowering input prices, raising output prices, and enabling farmers to produce more profitable, perishable crops. It may also benefit the landless households by generating opportunities of employment in the rural non-farm sector and raising wage rates by making labour more mobile.

The incidence of poverty in two groups of villages differentiated by the state of development of transport facilities can be reviewed from Table 15.3. The proportion of poor population, both extreme and moderate, is found lower in developed villages than in less

TABLE 15.5
Incidence of Poverty by Access to Electricity: Controlling Landholding Size
(Figures in %)

Size of landholding (acres)	Villages without electricity		Villages with electricity	
	Extreme poverty	Moderate and extreme poverty	Extreme poverty	Moderate and extreme poverty
Less than 0.5	56.4	84.7	23.7	62.4
0.5–2.49	23.1	59.4	11.0	42.7
2.5–4.99	9.3	30.5	Nil	27.4
5.0 and more	4.4	10.3	Nil	6.3

Source: Analysis of Poverty Trends Project, BIDS: 62 Village Survey.

developed villages. It is also found that the poverty situation improved substantially between 1987–88 and 1989–90 in villages with developed transport facilities. For less developed villages, the proportion of the moderate poor improved marginally, but the proportion of 'hard core' poor increased from 25 per cent to 30 per cent.

Implications for Poverty-Alleviating Policies

Several conclusions emerge from the analysis in this chapter with strong implications for policy interventions. First, spread of new technology in agriculture has considerable effect on increasing rural income. An appropriate mix of pricing, subsidy, credit and extension policies should be undertaken to promote the expansion of new technology in agriculture. As argued earlier, the positive effect of the spread of new technology will be particularly strong for marginal and small farmers. The latter in general tend to be better adopters than the larger farmers. Moreover, land is usually transferred in the tenancy market from large to small and marginal owners. The moderating impact of the tenancy market on the marginal and small farmers is further increased by favourable changes in tenurial arrangement associated with the spread of new technology (such as cost-sharing between landlords and tenants with respect to inputs, higher incidence of fixed rent tenancy, etc.).

Second, conclusion to emerge is the critical importance of rural infrastructure. The poverty-alleviating effect of rural infrastructure is found to be even higher compared to the impact of the new agricultural technology. Within the rubric of infrastructure, rural electrification tends to have greater poverty-alleviating effect vis-à-vis the transport network. It may be noted that the positive effect of infrastructure is higher for non-farm households compared to farm households, because of strong linkage effects which infrastructure has on the expansion of the rural non-farm sectors, such as trade and services.

Third, promotion of non-farm activities will have strong poverty-alleviating effects. Indeed the most important factor behind the moderation of rural inequality is the income from non-agricultural sources. The concentration ratio of non-agricultural income across the land ownership scale is estimated at only 0.16 (see chapter 4). Thus, non-agricultural income is distributed fairly equally across land ownership groups. Land-poor households who manage to participate in non-agricultural activities move up in the per capita income ladder. This is the reason why non-agricultural income is found to be distributed highly unequally when measured in the per capita income scale. The concentration ratio is estimated at 0.47 (ibid.). Thus, access to non-agricultural employment provides scope for income mobility for the land-poor households. An implication of this finding is that anti-poverty strategy and policies should contain elements that empower landless and marginal farmers to participate in the non-agricultural sector. The importance of undertaking various targeted self- and wage-employment programmes under different institutional arrangements can hardly be over-emphasised in this regard.

Fourth, spread of education tends to have a significant impact on increasing rural incomes, and hence, on reducing poverty. The positive effect of education is higher for non-farm households vis-à-vis farm households. It seems that the kind of education provided in schools basically facilitates occupational mobility from relatively low-productive agriculture to relatively high productive non-agricultural activities. It does not pay enough dividends unless the student completes secondary schooling. In order to make schooling more attractive there is a need to change the curriculum and make it more work oriented so that it increases efficiency of labour at the work place and school drop outs can contribute more to household income than the illiterates. Knowledge about modern agricultural practices and their practical applications should be taught in schools so that parents find their children useful in raising farm incomes. The landless could be induced to send their children to schools if the educated landless were given access to credit so that they could use their skills for generating self-employment in non-agricultural activities.

Fifth, the above observations relating to education is equally applicable in the case of social sectors as a whole. For instance, as discussed in chapter 6, incidence of morbidity was found to be quite high across the land ownership groups (ranging from 46 per cent to 63 per cent). Little improvement has occurred in the primary health care sector outside the sphere of expansion of safe drinking facilities and immunisation programme for children upto 6 years. Direct provisioning of primary health care in the rural areas thus emerges as a priority area for state and NGO interventions.

Sixth, as mentioned earlier in chapter 10, about 13 per cent of rural households (which also constitutes about 23 per cent of the rural poor) represent the most vulnerable segment within the rural community. They live in most deplorable housing conditions (such as jhupri and single structure houses) and the aggregate income earned by them is quite inadequate, even to ensure as low as 75 per cent of normative calorie requirements. At most they can aspire to escape from the trap of 'hard core' poverty to moderate poverty, but even that scope is increasingly being whittled away by the caprice of nature or by the sudden and unanticipated fluctuations in the markets. In most cases, they are left out of the routinised market process, lacking land as well as non-land assets. The scope for their increased self-employment through GO and NGO programmes, thus, appears to be extremely limited. Their only factor endowment, the labour power, is gradually eroded over time as they become increasingly prone to sickness and diseases, thus, reducing their bargaining capacity even in the rural labour market. Without owning any collateralisable assets or having the capacity to develop personal attachment to prospective patrons, they are deprived of the benefits of both institutional and non-institutional credit markets. They often lack emergency lenders or any form of traditional social security which would have supported them in times of severe crisis. It is difficult to project any growth-induced trickle-down programme for this segment of population. They persist as a floating underclass beyond the pale of regular society. Social security programmes designed to eradicate their severe malnutrition and poverty seems to be in order in this case. Such income-transfer programmes for the lowest 10 per cent to 15 per cent of the rural population would require significant commitment of the government budget to poverty-alleviation programmes.

Note

1. Since presence of multi-collinearity may create problems for testing the hypothesis, the degree of correlation between the explanatory variables included in our specification of the income equation was cross-checked. None of the correlations was found to be significantly high. It may be further noted from the regression results presented in Tables 15.1 and 15.2 that all the explanatory variables display the intuitive signs and most of them are significant at standard levels of statistical significance.

16

The Political Economy of Poverty-Alleviation

HOSSAIN ZILLUR RAHMAN

The Poor in the Political Process

The political process in Bangladesh can be seen to cover two possible primary action arenas relevant to a discussion on poverty. Firstly, there is the arena of national and local government elections which could provide a scope for the political representation of the poor. Second, and no less significant, is the arena of local-level mobilisational politics aiming to act as pressure groups on the district and sub-district administration in their allocative and executive decisionmaking. The political representation of the poor through the electoral process suffers from a double handicap in the specific political environment of Bangladesh. Electoral politics as a whole in today's Bangladesh remains firmly set in a patron-client framework which militates against any independent political assertion by the poor. This is certainly true for the national level and also largely true for the local level. A dramatic illustration of the preponderance of this patron-client politics is the near total absence of any issue-based demands in the election manifestoes of candidates.

The patron-client orientation of the electoral process is additionally compounded by the frequent instances of electoral violence which tends to be an inhibiting factor on the poor's participation in the political process. A survey of local government elections over the 20 years since independence shows a secular increase in the use of violence by political entrepreneurs in their bid against rivals (Rahman, 1990). Such a culture of violence by excluding or limiting electoral participation simply compounds the already fragile social foundations of the democratic processes. While political entrepreneurship can find root in such an environment, the entire process strongly militates against any independent political representation of the poor, and hence, any independent leverage over the setting of policy or programme priorities of the national or local government. Notwithstanding the largely violence-free parliamentary elections in 1991, it is too early to argue that a qualitative transition has taken place in this regard.

The lack of electoral capacities does not, however, imply that the poor are only passive political subjects within society. One of the little reported features of political life at the local level is the numerous instances of spontaneous mobilisational politics around specific demands or grievances. Such mobilisational politics is mainly oriented towards acting as pressure groups on the district and sub-district administration to press popular demands requiring compensatory action by the state or to register grievances against gross anomalies in allocative and executive decisionmaking. Such mobilisational efforts can also take on the form of popular initiatives to act as crisis-coping mechanism in times of large-scale natural or social stress, such as flood.

The local-level mobilisational initiatives by the poor bespeaks of a dormant political capacity which, however, suffers from a crucial handicap in being systematically ignored by the national-level political process. In the absence of this wider political linkage, the effective significance of micro mobilisational politics lies not so much in agenda setting as in being a localised corrective pressure against administrative failures or implementation anomalies.

The Nature of the Policy Process

The limitations of representational and mobilisational politics as brought out above underline a crucial aspect of the socio-political reality in Bangladesh relevant to the poverty discussion, namely, that political and policy decisionmaking is to a critical extent subsumed within executive administration. Much more so than the political process per se, it is the agenda setting role of the executive leadership of the state on the one hand and the institutional prejudices of the machineries of administration on the other, which become the crucial variables to consider in assessing the priority accorded to poverty and the institutional potential to influence the poverty situation.

Prior to looking at the agenda setting role of the executive leadership, one needs to highlight the institutional prejudices of the administrative machineries. A major hurdle in the way of effective action for poverty-alleviation is the entrenched reality of an administrative structure which has been inherited as an unwelcome colonial legacy. By norms, jurisdictions and history, this bureaucratic state power is anything but participatory. More to the point, by the very logic of its institutional prejudices rooted in regulatory functions, it is inherently obstructive of the developmental goals which have been added to its function in the wake of independence. A crucial dichotomy which appears here is that between good intentions and unintended consequences. Programmes lacking nothing in good intentions but without sufficient cognition of the specific nature of the machinery of implementation are routinely generating ineffectual outcomes, subverted at the implementation stage by the entrenched ethos of an administrative machinery rooted in its colonial past. A dramatic illustration of this process was provided in the wake of the disastrous floods of 1988.

Impelled by its own populist rhetoric, the government at the close of 1988 declared its intention to safeguard the position of the small and marginal peasantry by declaring a legal bar on the transfer of rural land. The intention was to prevent unscrupulous land speculators from preying on the miseries of the peasantry. But without addressing the survival needs of these stricken households, such a measure merely added to bureaucratic complexities and in the event also failed to prevent land transfers. A survey carried out in one district at that time found that the letter of the law was being implemented in that no *sale* of land was being registered. However, during the sample period the number of *gift* transfers shot up and almost wholly substituted the decline in sale registration (Rahman, 1989). Realising soon the actual consequence of its action, the government in the event rescinded its order after two months.

The obstructive reality of an entrenched bureaucratic state has given rise to a situation where the *declarative intentions of policymakers* and *actual policy outcomes* may take on the character of *unrelated institutional processes*. This dichotomy between intentions and outcomes is all the more serious for Bangladesh where the absence of a hegemonic class allows for a multiplicity of declarative intentions at the policymaking centre. A key issue which, therefore, has to be borne in mind in devising policy packages is whether such policies reflect an adequate cognition of the institutional reality of the state structure. Without this, one will merely go on adding to the list of well-intentioned programmes which remain paper programmes.

The Boundary of State Concern

Going beyond declarative intentions per se, it becomes possible to see wherein lies the effective concern of the state on the poverty issue. The political reality today affords very little direct leverage of the poor over the policymaking process. However, they are not entirely without an impact, albeit in an indirect way. This stems from the fact that the policymaking centre has a relatively fluid class basis and as such remains susceptible to political challenges within an elite-conflict model. Both for the incumbent government and the discontented section of the political elite currently out of power, the poor appear as an important symbolic and social constituency which is not so much to be courted as to be denied to political contenders. Substantive concerns about poverty emerge in the context of such an elite-conflict model. Three strands of such concerns bear elaboration.

In the first, the pursuit of the poor as a symbolic and social constituency generates a profusion of populist rhetoric which cuts across the entire political spectrum. Indeed, in the recent past, it was the authoritarian state itself which appeared to hold the initiative in formulating this populist rhetoric. Such rhetoric spawns a stream of anti-poverty programmes which by the very logic of their origin routinely generate only ineffectual outcomes. A case in point is the creation of Debt Settlement Boards supposedly for relieving the debt burden of the rural poor. Not only has this programme become a dead-letter, a survey in March 1991 showed that the majority of rural population were not even aware that such a programme existed (Hossain et al., 1991).

The second strand of the state's concerns with the poor as a symbolic constituency is the rationale they provide for seeking high levels of foreign assistance. Without denying the existence of widespread poverty, there may be noted a tendency on the part of both the government and its political competitors to exaggerate poverty levels and ignore productivity gains if any. If this was meant only to ensure higher aid levels, there would be no objection in principle. However, estimates of poverty levels clearly also shape the policy responses of the government and here exaggerated estimates may produce flawed policy responses which are definitely not to the advantage of the poor. An illustration of this is provided by the exaggerated estimates of flood damages in 1987 and 1988 and the ill-planned food import policy which followed such estimates. Actual damage levels turned out to be much smaller than those publicised but because of an ill-planned expansion in food import, paddy prices in the ensuing season remained depressed much to the disadvantage of the small producers.

The third and final strand of the state's concern with poverty relates to the political lessons learnt from the famine of 1974. There is a widespread perception within the political elite of the country that the occurrence of a famine so soon after independence caused a massive crisis of legitimacy for the then government whose violent overthrow a year later was seen as an expression of this loss of legitimacy. The crisis of legitimacy due to a failure to contain the famine appears to have become for subsequent governments a crucial political concern. Out of this concern, compensatory food programmes for the poor has become the key growth area in state action on poverty, rising from 21 per cent of total public food distribution in 1982 to 48 per cent in 1989. The priority accorded to such programmes is underlined by the fact that the problem of implementation failures is anticipated by either providing for additional supervision or by bypassing the bureaucratic channel altogether as, for example, in the use of the armed forces for implementing post-flood relief in 1988 (Hossain et al., 1988).

With no independent political leverage on part of the poor to prod the policy process towards a poverty focus, effective attention to poverty-alleviation appears then to lie not so much in the area of macroeconomic management and the attendant growth process, but rather in targeted compensatory programmes aimed at averting any famine-type syndrome. Macro-management and crisis-management, thus, stand sharply contrasted as independent concerns of the state with the poor figuring only in the latter. The political economy of poverty appears to dictate no descent into famine but no definitive escape from the poverty situation either. Such is the institutional reality which we can ignore only at a greater cost to society if the debate on poverty is to transcend the level of ineffectual rhetorics.

References

Hossain et al., 1988, *The Economic Impact of 1988 Floods: A Field Survey*, BIDS, Dhaka.
———. et al., 1991, *BIDS Parliamentary Election Survey*, BIDS, Dhaka.
Rahman, H.Z., 1989, *A Case Analysis of the State Process in Bangladesh*, BIDS, Dhaka.
Rahman, H.S., 1990, 'Landscape of Violence: Local Election and Political Culture in Bangladesh', *Economic and Political Weekly*, November 24.

VI

Conclusions

17

Conclusions

HOSSAIN ZILLUR RAHMAN

Need for A Broader Focus

Notwithstanding two decades of 'poverty alleviation', widespread and acute rural poverty remains the single most important problem facing Bangladesh. Weaknesses in analytical understanding of poverty have compounded weaknesses in mobilisational and implementational capacities while the livelihood initiatives of the poor have had to contend with an opportunity frontier largely circumscribed by dysfunctional bureaucratic power. Twenty years after independence, there is an urgency to acknowledge and address these weaknesses not in the least because more effective guides to action are necessary.

The First-Order Concerns

Poverty is a multi-dimensional process. In arguing this, income and non-income dimensions are not posed as competing foci for the poverty debate. At stake rather is the adequate cognition of the core vulnerabilities which define the poverty experience in Bangladesh. Such vulnerabilities are best understood not from the standpoint of any exogenously defined list of 'basic needs' but from an informed enquiry into the ruling social concerns which capture the routine predicaments of the poor. While income or livelihood not surprisingly has been found to constitute one of these ruling concerns, our enquiry identified two such additional 'first-order' concerns. The first is the concern with insecurity and its constraining impact on the initiative space of the poor in their pursuit of livelihood and social dignity. The second is the concern with routine vulnerability to crisis which at the household level translates into a powerful set of downward mobility pressures which constantly threaten to overshadow incremental improvements in income.

Implementation as a Core Problem

The solution to poverty is not a matter of good intentions only. A particular weakness of the poverty debate in Bangladesh is the inadequate attention given to problems of implementation. Policy and programme formulation has routinely grown out of declarative intentions which lack adequate cognition of the machinery of implementation actually available. The consequence has been a succession of paper policies and paper programmes.

To a large extent, the developmental functions of the state has devolved upon an administrative machinery whose linchpin is the district administration created under colonial rule. The demands for development and participation have not meshed with the entrenched institutional procedures and ethos of this machinery with its inherited bias towards regulatory functions. Neither has the punitive hold of this regulatory administrative machinery over the initiative space of local society been effectively checked by any countervailing structures of local self-government. Such is the implementational reality which confronts the political and administrative intentions seeking a solution to poverty.

The perception of implementation failures as largely a problem of personal morality has tended to obscure the above features of the administrative environment in which policies and programmes on poverty are introduced. Yet, it is this very question of the administrative environment which appear to have a critical bearing on transforming implementation into a generalised problem for efforts at poverty-alleviation. Without addressing the generic roots of implementational failures, the debate on poverty is in danger of remaining a paper debate.

Poverty Indicators

While income is a very common concept, the methodological challenge is to capture it appropriately for any given context such as rural Bangladesh. Rural households are rarely able to depend on a single, substantive source of income as in the urban formal sector. Instead, they have to make do with a variety of petty self-employment and wage-employment activities. They have to operate in both market and non-market contexts. The economic opportunities available to them have marked seasonal variation. An important source of household sustenance come from direct appropriation of ecological reserves. The calculation of household income has to anticipate and take account of all of these specific features.

Income is an indirect measure of poverty. A direct measure is the level of malnutrition within a community. Ultimately, the very minimum objective of all development efforts is to assure the physical well-being of the population. Shortfalls in nutritional status specially that of children constitute an unambiguous if stark indicator of poverty.

A direct measure of poverty relates to the quality of the living environment in which households and individuals pass their daily existence. The most significant indicators here are the quality of housing, access to safe water and sanitation. Data suggests that these indicators which make up the non-food environment are no less significant than the food environment in determining people's well-being.

Poverty is not only a state of deprivation. It is equally importantly a state of vulnerability. For the female half of the population, vulnerability is perhaps a more central dimension of the poverty experience. As an aspect of poverty in Bangladesh, vulnerability translates into three critical indicators, namely, personal insecurity, crisis-proneness and coping capacities. The insecurity indicator relates to the level and potential for violence and intimidation within social and institutional life and the constraints which such an environment imposes on livelihood initiatives by the poor. The crisis and coping indicators adhere to the stability of household welfare and thereby illuminate poverty as a process.

Findings based on the Income Indicator

Level and Trend in Rural Poverty

Estimates of poverty for the year 1989-90 based on household income data puts the percentage population living in poverty at 55 per cent. A qualification to note here is that calculation of household incomes in countries like Bangladesh with large partially monetised rural economies suffer from some perennial under-reporting. Rural households routinely engage in a variety of expenditure-saving activities which do not show up in income calculations but which, if included, would increase household income estimates by 15 per cent on average according to our survey data. Once income estimates are adjusted by household expenditure data, the population living in poverty is seen to stand at 38 per cent in 1989-90.

Estimating trends in rural poverty is hampered by the fact that estimates for different periods have used different methods of calculation. Recalculating different estimates by a uniform method, it is seen that over the last two and a half decades, poverty has declined only marginally—from 44 per cent in 1963-64 to 38 per cent in 1989-90, by the per capita expenditure classification. There has, however, been considerable fluctuations around this horizontal trend line. Following a serious deterioration in the poverty situation in the early years of independence, there was a modest but sustained improvement from the late seventies right through to the mid-eighties. The consecutive floods of 1987 and 1988 led to worsening in the poverty situation with a sharp upswing in the poverty head count ratio in 1988-89. However, the rural economy appears to have recovered fast from this setback largely thanks to the survival efforts of the people themselves. This is reflected in the current poverty head count ratio which stands at 38 per cent by per capita expenditure classification.

Moderate and Extreme Poverty

The modest improvement in the poverty situation over the recent past marks an important differentiation within the ranks of poor. The poverty line income gives a measure of absolute poverty. But within the ranks of the absolute poor, we notice an even more extreme level of distress which can be categorised as extreme or 'hard core' poverty. Extremely poor households are seen to subsist on an income which is 40 per cent below the poverty line income. In the recent past, such households constituted over 40 per cent of the poor households.

What is disturbing is that the modest improvement in the poverty situation has largely benefitted the moderately poor while no serious dent has been made into the situation of the extremely poor. Indeed our survey data based on income classification shows that between 1987–88 and 1989–90 while aggregate poverty, i.e., extreme and moderate poverty taken together, has declined by 5 percentage points, extreme poverty over the same period has increased by 2 percentage point. It would appear that the impact of various government and non-government targeted programmes for the rural poor has beneficially touched on moderate poverty but has impacted little on extreme poverty. It is this tenacity of 'hard core' or extreme poverty which most starkly underlines the continuing gravity of the poverty situation in Bangladesh.

Between 1988 and early 1991, rural real wage registered a slight decline, a fact consistent with the slight deterioration in extreme poverty reported earlier. Over this period, money wage rate rose by 10 per cent but this was outstripped by the rise in the price of rice amounting to 17 per cent which led to a decline in the purchasing capacity of the wage-dependent poor. A point to note here, however, is that the wage component within the household income of the poor on average constitutes a relatively small proportion at around 25 per cent. This would caution against seeing rural wage as an overall monitor of poverty.

Composition of Household Income

The composition of household income underscores the diversity of sources from which rural households draw their sustenance. On average, 63 per cent of rural household income comes from agriculture while 37 per cent comes from various non-agricultural sources. Such a pattern is true not only in the aggregate but also at the individual household level. Indeed, even an individual member is often involved in diverse petty occupations. In terms of variation between poor and non-poor households, the composition of household income shows a broadly similar pattern. However, within the broad agricultural sector, some variation exists with the poor more dependent on labour income and the non-poor on cultivation income. The poor are also seen to make slightly more intensive use of kitchen gardens.

Interestingly, the percentage for remittance and service income is almost the same for both poor and non-poor households. Insofar as such income originates in urban or semi-urban occupations, it would appear that the poor are as much involved in the rural–urban linkage as the non-poor, albeit in different ends of the occupational scale.

An important escape route from poverty under current circumstances is via trade. It can be seen, however, that it is the non-poor households who have the advantage in this regard with trade accounting for 16 per cent of household income in their case vis-à-vis 9 per cent in the case of poor households. An argument clearly exists here for expanded programmes of capital support to poor households to strengthen their participation in trade activities.

Findings based on the Non-Income Indicators

The use of non-income indicators both confirm some of the features noted above and provide additional perspectives on the situation. Indicators of nutritional status show an overall improvement since the mid-seventies with considerable fluctuations in between. However, in 1990 the absolute situation remained very grim with 50 per cent of all under-5 children suffering from malnutrition. Female members in each age group fare worse than their male counterparts and there are also considerable variation between seasons and regions.

A point to emphasise here is that inter-temporal comparisons of non-income indicators is difficult because earlier surveys did not use such indicators. Only future surveys taking the 1990 findings as a base-line can adequately provide inter-temporal comparisons. Even for income and expenditure indicators, differences in methodology between surveys render such comparisons difficult. Comparable base-lines are, therefore, a critical necessity in the proper monitoring of poverty trends.

Considering the living environment, the housing indicator shows 60 per cent of rural households housed precariously in 1989–90. The housing indicator yields two even worse levels of vulnerability. 32 per cent of households enjoy only precarious single-structure unit while 10 per cent live in completely ramshackle structures of leaves and stray materials. This bottom 10 per cent of the rural population represents a floating underclass beyond the pale of settled communities. A priority programme of assistance which merits consideration here is the allocation of government owned khas land for housing such vulnerable households.

A heartening development which has occurred is the access to safe drinking water facilities: 1989–90 data report 87 per cent of rural households as enjoying access to safe drinking water as compared to BBS estimate of 53 per cent in 1981. Additional data reveal little inter-class variation in access indicating an across-the-board improvement in the situation.

On the critical health indicator, the picture in 1989–90 is a much more dismal one. Only 13 per cent of rural patients benefit from government health facilities. An earlier BIDS survey puts the corresponding figure for 1987–88 at 12 per cent. Thus, showing negligible improvement in public health security for the rural population. Nor does private health-care constitute any significant alternative source of health service. Only 18 per cent of deficit household patients managed to have any access to such services in 1989–90. In the absence of adequate access to health services, chronic or sudden illnesses invariably doom poor households to steep decline in income and welfare.

Available data also suggest very limited access of the rural population to education. The expansion of primary school facilities has been extremely slow in the late eighties with an increase of only 1.2 per cent during the Third Five Year Plan over the benchmark set by Second Five Year Plan. Official enrollment figures remain suspect and they omit the very high percentage of drop-outs.

Not only are rural households poor, they are also significantly crisis-prone which exacerbate the stability of household welfare and impair their livelihood initiatives. 76 per cent of all rural households were subject to at least one major household crisis in 1989–90 which was by Bangladesh standards a 'normal' year. 43 per cent of households were subject to two major household crisis.

Crisis which routinely befall Bangladesh rural households fall within three major categories: natural disasters, illness and insecurity. In 1989–90, 66 per cent of all rural households faced natural disaster crisis of one sort or another while 48 per cent or nearly half faced one or more illness crisis within the household. Interestingly, a quarter of households also faced various insecurity-related crisis. Needlessly to say, the onset of a household crisis strains the meagre reserves of poor households. Though networking and social solidarities play an important part in crisis-coping, in many cases a crisis is the precursor to a further decline in household welfare.

Differentiation of the Poor

The bulk of the poor households belong to the land-poor category. Functionally landless households contain 65 per cent of the poor while marginal land-owners contain another 21 per cent. An important point to note here is that poverty-alleviation interventions tend to focus only on the first category while an important segment of the poor belongs also to the ranks of marginal landholders with an ownership below 1.5 acres. This indicates a need to broaden the poverty-alleviation focus to cover this second category too.

Access of land through the tenancy market does not affect the poverty situation of landless households indicating no significant difference between landless tenants and landless workers. The same, however, is not true of marginal owners who combine self-cultivation with renting-in land.

In occupational terms, the poor are concentrated among the labour households, 85 per cent of whom fall within the poor category. The incidence of 'hard core' poverty, however, is greater among agricultural labour households compared to non-agricultural labour households. Among the non-farm poor, those who have some access to capital (i.e., traders) and those with better quality human resource (i.e., service-holders) are better-off than wage-labour households.

Education bears on the poverty situation in two important ways. Firstly, education contributes to the empowerment of the poor and thereby enhances their capacity to resist exploitation and achieve their rightful bargain in all economic transactions. Secondly, education can facilitate access to more remunerative employment opportunities. A caveat here is that while primary education is seen to carry a generally empowering function, the specific type of education received beyond the primary level in Bangladesh render any on-job application rather difficult. This implies a low correspondence between education and labour productivity. The benefits of secondary education and beyond for poor households, thus, come only in the distorted form of individual escapes into white-collar employment rather than through productivity increases in existing wage and self-employment avenues. The low correspondence between secondary education and productivity also means that drop-outs from this level become a liability for society. A high drop-out rate has also to be seen as indicating a low demand for such education in its current forms.[1]

The bulk of the poor are those without any formal schooling—55 per cent of all poor and 60 per cent of the 'hard core' poor. However, the impact of education on income is not a linear one. Incomes of poor households are found to benefit positively from primary education but are relatively unaffected by secondary or higher education. It is the incomes of the non-poor households which appear to benefit more from higher levels of education suggesting that higher education is more effective in raising rural incomes when it is combined with access to land and capital. Primary education, however, has a generally empowering function which impact positively on the incomes of the poor. Besides the need to substantially expand primary education, the above also suggests the importance of addressing the content of secondary and higher education with a view to achieving a higher correspondence between such education and productivity. The focus of change, in other words, has to be not only on supply-side problems of physical infrastructure but as importantly on demand-side problems bearing on curriculum and teaching methods.

The burden of poverty is seen to fall disproportionately on the female half of the population. On average, it is seen that females have a nutritional intake only 88 per cent that of males and 46 per cent of the wage rate earned by males. Only 29 per cent of females are literate compared to 45 per cent males. While 8 per cent of male headed households fall within the 'hard core' poor, the corresponding figure for female headed households is 33 per cent. Female headed households on average enjoyed an income which was 40 per cent below male headed households in 1988–89. Female headed and female managed households constituted 9 per cent of rural households and represent perhaps tne most vulnerable social group within rural society.

The Problem of Economic Graduation of the Poor: Need for a Refocusing of Priorities

A crucial finding of the current study relates to the problem of economic graduation of the poor. By economic graduation here is meant the distinction between incremental changes in household income resulting in cyclical mobility within the broad parameters of poverty and changes which lead to a definitive rise out of poverty. Rural households in Bangladesh have to contend with two analytically separate core problems. There is firstly the problem of an insufficiency of income. Secondly, there is an equally important problem of downward mobility pressures arising from a routine vulnerability to crisis. Under such a situation, incremental increases in household income of the poor are constantly overshadowed by threats of income erosion. Figure 17.1 underscores the resulting problem of cyclical mobility for the rural poor. Figure 17.1 is based on the self-evaluation of households. However, an almost similar pattern is also observed in Figure 10.1 which reports on inter-class mobility based on income measures between the years 1987–88 and 1989–90. Figure 7.3 describes the nature of income erosion pressures which hamper the prospects of economic graduation of the poor. Such pressures originate in three broad categories of factors, namely, life-cycle factors such as death or loss of earners and increase in the number of dependents, crisis factors, such as natural disasters, illness and insecurity, and structural factors, such as lack of growth, inflation and bad initial conditions.

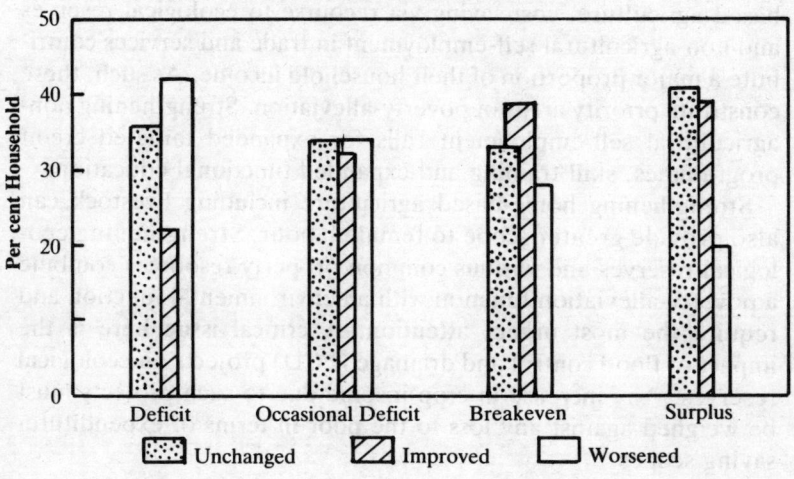

FIGURE 17.1
The Problem of Economic Graduation: Nature of Household Mobility over the Eighties as per Self-Evaluation

The importance of Figures 7.3 and 17.1 lie in illuminating downward mobility pressures or routine threats of income erosion as a crucial concern for the task of poverty-alleviation and in indicating the broad range of areas in which such pressures may be countered. Life-cycle factors underscore the importance of proper family planning so as not to be over-burdened by dependents. Crisis factors underscore the critical importance of three areas of action, firstly, disaster-management, secondly, an effective public health system, and thirdly, reform of the regulatory organs of the state, i.e., police and courts, and creation of effective local self-government to combat the structural sources of insecurity. Structural factors point towards the critical need for growth and human resource development through education.

Policy Implications

Rural poor do not enjoy substantive single income-sources but have rather to combine a variety of sources of sustenance. Only a quarter of the household income of the poor come from the wage-labour market indicating only a limited potential of alleviating poverty via improvements in this market in the near future. Home-based agriculture, cost-saving via recourse to ecological reserves and non-agricultural self-employment in trade and services contribute a major proportion of their household income. As such, these constitute priority areas of poverty-alleviation. Strengthening non-agricultural self-employment calls for expanded targeted credit programmes, skill training and expanded functional education.

Strengthening home-based agriculture including livestock can also provide greater scope to female labour. Strengthening ecological reserves and various common property resources combine a poverty-alleviation function with an environmental function and require the most urgent attention. A critical issue here is the impact of flood control and drainage (FCD) projects on ecological reserves. Any increase in crop income due to such projects must be weighed against any loss to the poor in terms of expenditure-saving scopes.

Targeted programmes for the poor primarily address the functionally landless. This is correct insofar as the functionally landless constitute a majority of the rural poor. However, substantial proportion of the poor also belong to the under 1.5 acres marginal owners. There is a clear need here to broaden the poverty-alleviation focus from the landless only and also bring marginal owners within the purview of targeted programmes, in particular credit programmes for small farms. Such credit programmes need not be conceived only as support for production but can also usefully embrace the area of marketing support.

Alleviating poverty requires not only raising incomes of the poor but also stabilising such incomes by countering downward mobility pressures. This calls for a two-pronged strategy, on one hand, to reduce crisis probabilities for poor households by addressing the macro origins of such probabilities, and on the other, to strengthen coping capacities at the individual and community levels.

Specific policy measures which such a strategy suggests here are (a) major improvements in primary health-care in particular by addressing the problem of service failure of existing facilities,[2] (b) empowerment through primary education with an emphasis not merely on physical infrastructure but on 'software' elements, such as curricula, teacher quality and non-structural facilities, (c) major reform of police, courts and other regulatory organs of the state on the one hand and strengthening community organisations and local self-government on the other. This will be critical in reducing the structural sources of insecurity and thereby serve to expand the initiative space of the poor and of society in general.

An additional measure to be considered here is the creation of a land bank targeted at marginal and small owners. Land sale or land mortgage are the most common distress response of marginal owners when faced with severe liquidity crisis originating in natural disasters or other household crises. Access to a land bank may protect such owners from the necessity of distress sale of their land assets. The challenge here, however, is not so much one of policy as of effective institution-building either within the government or the non-government arena.

Given the sharp differentiation within the ranks of the poor, targeted programmes of assistance need to be supplemented with safety nets for the most vulnerable of the rural poor, i.e., destitute women. Such programmes already exist and must be sustained. An additional consideration here is the bottom 10 per cent of the rural population identified by the housing indicator to be living in extreme vulnerability. The use of government owned khas land for housing such families may be seen as a necessary second safety net for the rural poor.

Another dimension of the differentiation of the poor with important policy implication is the regional and seasonal variation in poverty. The pattern of agricultural growth in Bangladesh thus far has served to contain the early summer lean season but has done little to allay the suffering of the poor during the autumn lean season. Such seasonal crisis routinely assume extreme forms in certain regional pockets which suffer from very adverse land-man ratio and poor resource-base. Programmes based on 'safety net' considerations must acknowledge such area-wise concentration of distress in their overall focus and allocations. Special projects, such as employment guarantee schemes can usefully be considered for such pockets.

Over and above the foregoing measures, a major dent in the problem of poverty will also require a sustained growth process. While a number of macro variables are relevant here, a priority area for action identified in this study in this context is physical infrastructure. Three key areas here are irrigation, rural electrification and good transportation. Irrigation was found to contribute substantially to a reduction in poverty nearly halving the level of extreme poverty in villages with irrigation compared to villages without. Rural electrification reduces the cost of irrigation and facilitates the development of the rural non-farm sector the latter in particular, having a pronounced impact on the poverty situation including that of extreme poverty. Effective transportation expands general economic activity and was found to add 13 per cent to the income of poor households. The attention to improved transportation does not necessarily point towards land transportation exclusively. A major revamping of the river system of Bangladesh and river transportation also constitute a priority focus here.

The focus on infrastructure carries important implications for a crucial growth variable, namely, agriculture and non-agriculture linkage. A sustained growth process demands the maximisation of such linkage effects. An institutional consideration in this regard is the promotion of local growth centres. In the long run, the growth potential of existing urban centres may be overwhelmed by poverty-led rural–urban exodus if sufficient economic opportunities fail to materialise in the countryside itself. A focus on decentralised urbanisation may be crucial here in which existing thana facilities may play a useful role.

Finally, there is a question of addressing the problem of field-level implementation failures. Insofar as such failures critically originate in a machinery of district administration with an inherited bias towards regulatory functions, the question of countervailing structures of local self-government demands priority inclusion in the poverty agenda. Such structures need to be conceived not as subordinate arms of administration but as the key foundations of a participatory political process with a countervailing supervisory potential over executive and allocative decisionmaking up to the district level.

Notes

1. Hossain Zillur Rahman, 1992, *The State of Basic Social Services in Bangladesh*, BIDS.
2. Ibid.

The Contributors

Hossain Zillur Rahman combines degrees in economics, political and historical sociology to explore innovative answers to the complex challenges of poverty and democratic transition in the contemporary era. Since 1989, he has been the leader of a major research programme on poverty analysis at the Bangladesh Institute of Development Studies, Dhaka. The current volume is the first major output of this programme. Hossain Zillur has written on agrarian dynamics in the *Journal of Peasant Studies* and on political violence in the *Economic and Political Weekly*. He is a contributor to Teodor Shanin (ed.), *Peasants and Peasant Societies* (Blackwell, 1987). He has also edited a volume on field research methodology. Hossain Zillur Rahman is currently completing a 2-volume set, *Law and Disorder*, a sociological analysis of British colonial rule and *Fractured Polity*, a theoretical treatise on politics under post-colonial conditions.

Mahabub Hossain is the former Director General of the Bangladesh Institute of Development Studies at Dhaka. He previously worked as a Staff Economist at the Pakistan Institute of Development Economics at Karachi and has been a visiting Research Fellow at the International Food Policy Research Institute, Washington DC and the Institute of Developing Economics, Tokyo. He is currently working as Head of the Social Sciences Division at the International Rice Research Institute, Philippines. He has worked on various aspects of rural development including the role of technology, infrastructure, credit and the informal sector. His recent works on the Grameen Bank, Green Revolution and Rural Infrastructure have been published as IFPRI Research Reports. He is the co-author of the book *Strategy of Development in Bangladesh*, published by Macmillan in association with OECD Development Centre.

Binayak Sen is a Research Fellow at the Bangladesh Institute of Development Studies (BIDS). Dr. Sen's published works include articles on poverty measurement, monitoring and alleviation, on privatisation and industrial finance, rural informal credit, economic and social history. He has co-authored a number of books, such as *Debt Default to the Development Finance Institutions: The Crisis of State Sponsored Entrepreneurship in Bangladesh; The Decade of Stagnation: The State of Bangladesh Economy in the 1980s;* and *Modernisation at Bay: Structure and Change in Bangladesh*. He is currently working in the World Bank as a coresearcher in the study entitled *Social Impact of Structural Adjustment in the Developing Countries*.

Shamim Hamid is a Research Fellow at the Bangladesh Institute of Development Studies. Her research focus has been on gender issues, national income accounting and the application of complex computer techniques in socioeconomic analysis. She is currently in Rome.

Omar Haider Chowdhury is a Senior Research Fellow at the Bangladesh Institute of Development Studies, Dhaka. He has worked on various aspects of macroeconomic policy and rural development including nutrition, role of infrastructure, fiscal policy and taxation.

Index

abject poverty, 74
absolute poverty, 46, 48, 52
adjustment, 193; aspects of, 199–215
administrative environment, 284
administrative machinery, 276
adult literacy rate, 133; *see also*, literacy
age, difference between married couple, 147; of the household, 186, 187; and poverty level of household, 143
agrarian structure, 36
agriculture(al), 294; activity, 80; Census, 34; development, 36; income from, 59, 60, 62, 288; slack season, 51; technology, 32, 33, 36, 198, 202, 203, 257, 262, 264, 270; wage labourers, 60, 62
Agricultural Sector Review, 178
Akhter, F., 151
Alam, S., 178
aman crop, 235, 240; damages to, 246; impact of floods on, 238, 239
annual household income, 227
annual savings, 228
anthropometry, 76, 85–89; child, 86–87, 89, 90
anticipated crisis, 114, 115–21; response to, 118
anti-poor bias, 262, 264
Arif, F., 178
Ashad, M., 151

asset, access to, 29, 197; of earning members by sex, 136; ownership, 182; structure, and living environment, 35

'banded mobility', 217
Bangladesh Bureau of Statistics (BBS), 28, 40, 42, 44, 46, 99, 101, 108, 195, 289
Bangladesh Institute of Development Studies (BIDS), 28, 36, 43, 44, 78, 85, 86, 87, 89, 99, 108, 133, 137, 195
Bangladesh Labour Force Survey, 178
Bangladesh Population Census Sample Survey, 178
Bangladesh Rural Development Board (BRDB), 198
boro crop, 51, 52, 235
borrowings, 247; from friends and relatives, 205
Bruce, J., 133, 152
buffer capacity, crisis and, 125, 130
business activity, trend in, 248–49

calorie intake, 93
calorie requirements, 272
capital, access to, 198–99
casual wage labour, 213, 214
Chen, M., 151
child (children), anthropometry, 35, 86–87, 89, 90, 92; nutritional

level of, 86, 87, 88, 89, 90, 94; population, 179
Chittagong division, 118, 236, 253; poverty level in, 68; trend in business activity in, 248
Chowdhury, Omar Haider, 74
'chronic deficit' households, 212, 213, 214; and housing facilities, 108; landless, 200; medical assistance to, 102
chronic and transient poverty, 173–74
clothing, 135; adequate, 99–101; basic, 183
commercial exploitation, of ecological reserves, 233
commodity credit, 126
common property resources, 24, 294; food from, 66, 67
community facilities, 24
community forestry, 233
community organisation, 294
consumer durables, 183
consumer prices, rural, 47
consumption expenditure, 44
consumption level, 99
contract labour, 142, 214, 215
coping capacity, 285
credit, access to, 35; advances, pattern of distribution of, 206; facility, 126; from shopkeepers-cum-lenders, 205; programme, 294
credit market(s), deprivation of, to poor, 272; dynamics, 35; informal adjustment through, 203–209
crisis, 25, 35; as dimension of poverty, 25; of entitlement, 243; expenditure, 120; factors, and downward mobility, 128, 129; and insecurity, 113ff; proneness, of rural household by land ownership and occupational status, 122; vulnerability to, 284, 285
'crop-gleaning', 222, 223, 227
croping capacity, crisis and, 124–26
croping intensity, 34
cultivator households, 71
cyclone, 125, 237

dadan trade advances, 205
daily earnings, 235, 236
daily wage workers, 141, 142
data sources, 40–42; on nutrition, 76–77
debt bondage, 234, 251
Debt Settlement Boards, 278
decolonisation, 23
de facto households, 178, 179, 180
deficit, group, 214; households, 213; –proneness, 115–21; status of household, 134, 184
de jure households, 178, 180, 182
development activities, 48
Dhaka division, lower sales in, 252–53; poverty level in, 68; trend in business activity in, 248–49
diarrhoea, 243, 246
dietary intake, 35; inadequate, 75–76, 78, 90
disadvantage, females as economic, 178, 184
discrimination, of women, 148
diseases, 77; pattern by land ownership categories, 105
dislocation, 193
dissaving, 125
distress conditions, 251, 252
distress households, 240, 241, 242
distress loans, 126
distress sales, of household assets, 126
domestic help, women as, 141, 142
downward mobility, 25, 284, 294
dowry, 149
drinking water, safe, 93, 102, 184, 272, 285, 289
drop-outs, from school, 106
droughts, 46, 242
drought-prone villages, 70
Dwyer, D., 133, 152

ecological reserves, 24, 294; access to, 230, 231, 232; appropriation of, 285; and expenditure, 221
ecological vulnerability, 36
economic condition, 147, 247; of women, 148

economic dependency ratio, 136, 179, 186, 187, 188
economic mobility, 127
economic revival, 252
economy, diversification of, 36
education, 99, 105–107, 289, 295; and rural income, 257, 258, 259, 262, 264, 271–72; of women, 94
elderly persons, 189
electoral violence, 274–75
electricity, access to, and income, 258, 262, 264, 265, 269
electrification, 269, 271, 296
elite-conflict model, 277
emergency loans, risk insurance through, 207–209
employment, generation programme, 71, 72; opportunities, 269; rate, 188
enrollment, in school, 105, 106, 289
Expanded Immunisation Programmes (EPI), 104, 106
expenditure, on protein-rich food, 42
expenditure-saving, activities, 150, 286; fuel use and, 222, 223, 224, 225, 227, 231, 233; to household welfare, 226–30; household participation in, 223–26; scope, 35, 222–23, 230–31
expenditure schedule, 44
extreme poverty, 71
extremely poor households, 287

family labour, surplus, 67
family size, 257
famine, of 1974, 278
farm households, income from, 58
farming, 180
female headed households, 177ff; characteristics of, 179–84; definition of, 178–79; stratification of, 184–88
female labour force, 137, 140, 142, 211, 212, 258, 259
female members, households with food shortage and high number of, 134
female population, 113

firewood collection, 224, 226
fishery (fishing), 43, 222, 223, 224, 226, 227, 230, 231
Five Year Plans, Second, 289; Third, 289
floods, 46, 286; control and drainage projects, 294; damage due to, 243, 246; damages in 1987 and 1988, 278; impact of, 51, 238, 239, 242, 243; and loss in crop production, 71; -prone villages, poverty in, 68, 70
food, aid, 71; chronic shortage in, 183; consumption, 77–82; deficit, 67, 71; expenditure, 42; import policy, 278, programme, for poor, 278; production, and consumption, 80; production, regional, 91; purchases, 247; shortage, higher number of females and, 134
food intake, 66, 81–82; 91; age-sex composition of 80; gender bias in, 80, 81, 82, 91; shortage, in, 240, 241; variations in, 80, 81; see also, per capita food intake
Food For Work (FFW), 71, 72
foodgrain prices, 72
foreign assistance, 278
Foster-Greer-Torbecke (FGT) measures, of poverty, 49, 50
functionally landless households, 194, 195, 197, 294

gastro-intestinal diseases, 104
gender bias, 75; in food intake, 80, 81, 82, 91
gender differential, 29
gender dimensions, of poverty, 132ff
gender disparities, baseline, 133–36; in labour force, 137–42; in lifecycle pattern, 142–47
girls, poor nutritional status of, 92
Gomez, F., 86
government, of Bangladesh, relief efforts by, 251; role of, 26
Grameen Bank, 151, 203

green revolution, 235, 262
gross domestic product, sector-wise growth rate of, 41
growth, and equity, 93

half-needs, 252
Hamid, Shamim, 132, 150, 177
Haque, T., 40
'hard core' poor, 70, 71, 184, 195, 197, 267, 268, 269, 270, 272, 287
harvest time, 235
head count ratio, and poverty, 45, 46–49, 66, 67
health care, 24, 130, 289, 295; access to, 99, 101–105; hazards, 103; status, 94, 149–50
height and weight, malnutrition and, 85
homestead forestry, 233
homestead resources, 222
Hossain, Mahabub, 28, 57, 203, 257, 278
house-building materials, collection of, 222, 223, 224, 225, 226, 227, 233
houses, damages due to floods to, 243, 246
housing, 24, 99, 107–10, 186, 272, 285; changes in conditions of, 110
household assets, distress sale of, 243, 247, 250
household behaviour, 24
household economic status, 127
household expenditure, 35, 42, 43, 67
household income, 35; contribution of labour to, 259; of poor and non-poor, 262–64; structure of, 58–61; *see also*, income
household product account, 42
household savings, 227
household size, 179
household structure, 35
Household Expenditure Surveys (HES), 28, 40, 42, 43, 44, 51, 99
Human Development Index (HDI), 133

hunger, 25, 74

illiteracy rate, 134
illness-related crisis, 124; and expenditure on, 120
immortality, 121
implementation, problems of, 284
immunisation programme, 272
incidence of poverty, 46, 49, 65–70; by geographical division, 68; by production environments, 69, 70; by self-evaluation, 68
income, 24, 29, 133; determinants of, 257–62; distribution, 62, 65; –earning activities, 150, 188, 189, 193, 211; dimensions, of poverty, 57ff; household, 42–43, 180–82, 287–88; inequality in, 58, 61–65; land-owned and, 211, 213, 258, 259; measures of poverty, 24, 26, 285; from non-farm sector, 40; of poor and non-poor households, 66, 262–64; sources of, 135, 18–82, 285, 286; structure and distribution of household, 57ff; under reporting of, 57
India, 39, 133; head-count ratio for, 49
industrial activities, rural, 61
inequality, 132, 271
infectious diseases, 104
influenza, 103, 104
informal sector, 41
infrastructure, physical, 32, 257, 258, 262, 296; and poverty, 265–70, 271
inheritance, 143, 149; denial of, to mothers, 147; rights of women, 152
injurious contracts, 250
injustice, 121
inputs, modern, 203
insecurity, 25, 284, 285; crisis and, 113ff, 120, 121, 122
Institute of Nutrition and Science (INFS), 78, 87, 89
institutional credit, access to, 198, 199

inter-class mobility, and land stability, 218
intra-household distribution, of assets, 136
irrigation, 265-68, 296; infrastructure, and poverty, 267-68
Islam, M., 178
Islamic marriage contract, 147

Jahan, R., 151
Jain, D., 132
Jamalpur, floods in, 246
Jodha, N.S., 39

Kabeer, N., 39
Khulna division, 118; landholding size in, 68; lower sales in, 253; poverty levels in, 67, 68; trend in business activity in, 248
kinship, lineages, and supplying loans, 208, 209; network, in tenancy market, 202
Kushtia district, food intake in, 80

labour, contracts, 247; distribution of, and sources of income, 140; and income, 264; by poverty level, 140; power, 93, 272; services, 58
Labour Force Survey (LFS), 137
labour households, deficit-prone among, 116, 118; going without any work, 235
labour market, 60, 61; participation, 35; rural, 272; women's participation in, 150
land, assets, access to, 193; assets, distress sale of, 295; bank, 295; -person ratio, 32; poverty trap, 217; -stability, 215, 216, 217; tenancy market, 35; transfer, bar on, 276
landholding, size, 266, 268, 269
landowning groups, and access to clothing, 100-101; credit advances of, 206; disease pattern by, 105; and housing condition, 107-109; and ownership of prestigeous items, 111; and sanitary facilities, 102
land owership, 32, 33, 34, 181, 186, 187, 197, 257; location, of deficit households, 1941 rural income and, 258-59, 262; status, 122, 123, 127
landless, deficit-proneness among, 116; functionally, 269
landless household, 34, 40, 194, 195, 197; adequate clothing in, 100; enrollment ratio in, 106; tenancy market and, 201
land-poor group, 200, 205, 212, 266; dependency of, on tenancy market, 201
land-poor households, 62, 197; and land stability, 217
Lathum, M.C., 86
leafy vegetables, collection of, 224, 226
lean seasons, in Bangladesh, 235-37
life expectancy, 133
liquid assets, 110
liquidity crisis, 295
literacy rate, 32, 134; adult, 133; of women, 150, 152
livelihood, 25, 284
livestock, grazing, 222; income from, 140-41; ownership, 182, 192-96; sector, 43
living environment, 285
living standard, 29, 39, 184, 186; indicators of, 99ff
loan, 199
local self-government, 26, 294

macro-management, 26
Magura district, food intake in, 80
male labour force, 140, 142
malnutrition, 74, 77, 86, 92, 94, 288; age-sex structure of, 84; calorie-protein, 83, 85; severity of, 89, 92
manual labour, 212
marginal landowners, 197, 198
marital status, 134, 135
markets, participation in, 200; prices, wage rates and, 244-45

mature households, 188
media exposure, 135
medicare facility, 93, 102, 103
methodological issues, 42–45
migrant male household heads, 178
migration, 117, 149, 177, 188, 189; distress, 40; rural–urban, 266
minimum labour wages, 141
mobilisational politics, 274, 275
mobility, 25, 133, 193; aspects of, 215–19; downward, 126–30; upward, 201, 215
'moderate distress', 247
moderate poor, 71
monitoring of poverty process, 28
Mora Kartik, 234
morbidity, 104, 272
multiple occupation pattern, 210

Nari Swanirbhar Parishad, 151
National Accounts data, 42
National Accounts Statistics, 41
National Income Commission, 41
natural calamities, 120, 129; and impact on agricultural production, 237–39
Netrokona, crisis to cattle fodder in, 246
network support, 126
Niger, 133
'no deficit', 200
non-agricultural activities, 258, 264; income from, 40, 61, 62, 271
non-agricultural wage labour, 141
non-farm activities, 32, 41, 258, 259, 262, 264, 271, 296
non-farm households, income of, 58
non-income measures, of poverty, 24, 25, 288
non-governmental organisations (NGOs), 151, 203, 204
non-institutional credit, 204
non-land assets, access to, 195–98
'non-poor' households, 174
non-sampling errors, 37–38
nutrition(al), 24, 35, 82–83, 85; dimensions of poverty, 74ff; intake, of inter- and intra-household

distribution, 83, 85, 92; status, 76, 85, 86, 87, 88, 89, 90, 94, 285; sex bias in, 89–90

'occasional deficit', 200
occupation(al), 257; category, 115, 116; mobility, 264; multiple, 180; pattern, 140, 141; status, 122, 123
ornaments, access to valuable, 110

Pabna region, floods in, 246
Pakistan, head-count ratio for, 49
participation rate, age specific, 137
patron, -client politics, 274; support, 126
pauperisation, 190
per capita, cloth availability, $112n$; expenditure data, 46; food intake, 77, 78, 80; income, 40, 41, 61, 65, 67; land ownership, 62; minimum diet, 46; nutrient intake, 82
personal insecurity, 25
petty trade, 235, 236
piece-rate jobs, 214
policy implications, 294–96
policy process, nature of, 275–75
political economy, of poverty-alleviation, 274ff
political process, poor in, 274–77
poor, households, 287; identifying, 75
Population Census, 1981, 29, 32
Population Census Sample Survey, 178
population pressure, 231
poultry, income from, 140
poverty, -alleviation, 24, 26, 198, 233, 270–73, 276, 283, 294; aspects of, 135, 152; definition of, 39, 74; determinants of, 257; experience, 23, 25; income measures of, 24, 26, 285; indicators of, 285; infrastructure and, 265–70; level of household, 180, 181; line expenditure, 67; line, people living below, 46, 48, 174; moderate and extreme,

287; non-income dimension of, 24; nutritional dimension of, 74ff; process, crisis and insecurity and, 126; rural, 23, 44, 99, 234, 283; situation, changes in, 71–72; trap, 174; trends from 1963–64 to 1989–90, 39ff
pressure groups, 275
prestige items, access to, 110–12
primary health care, 104, 272
primary school, 105, 106
production environment constraints, and incidence of poverty, 70
productive time, on expenditure-saving activities, 231
productivity, of land, 258
Proshika, 151
protein-calorie malnutrition, 91
protein-energy malnutrition (PEM), 74, 76
public expenditure, 93
purchasing capacity, of poor, 287; decline in, 52
purchasing power, 239–41, 247, 251
pure tenants, 201

radio, listening to, 135
Rahman, A., 40
Rahman, Hossain Zillur, 23, 28, 39, 113, 178, 221, 234, 274, 283
Rajshahi division, 118, 236, 241–42; lower sales in, 249, 253; poverty level in, 67
Rangpur, 247, 251; deficit in, 243
reforms, 26
regional dimension, of poverty, 29
remarriage, 148, 149
remittance, 61, 288
reproductive role, of women, 151
research, 37
resource-poor households, and crisis, 124; and ecological reserves, 229
risk insurance, 209
rural economy, 34, 46, 286
rural labour market, 211, 213
rural poverty, 23, 44, 234, 283; level and trends in, 286; *see also* poverty

Saldert, C., 178
sales, decline in, 251, 253–54
sanitation, 24, 93, 101–105, 285
Scone, N., 86
seasonal crisis, 235, 252, 295
seasonal deficit, 115–21
seasonal dimension, of poverty, 29, 51–53
'seed-fertiliser-water' technology, 258, 266
self-employment, 24, 57, 150, 189, 213, 272
self-sufficiency, in food, 93
Sen, A., 132
Sen, Binayak, 39, 99, 193, 203, 257
service, -delivery, 26; 'category', 118; income from, 61, 288; sector, 214, 215
sex-bias, in nutrition status, 89–90, 92
shelter, *see* housing
small farm households, 269
small landowning groups, 198
social dignity, 284
social marginalisation, of women, 151
social mobilisation, 26
social sector expenditure, 35, 106
social security, 39, 272, 273
Socioeconomic Development Programme for Women, 151
Soptogram, 151
Sri Lanka, head-count ratio for, 49
standard of living, 135
starvation, 74, 251
state, and poverty issue, 277–79
Streeten, Paul, 75
'structural constraints', 202
structural factors, and downward mobility, 128, 129
'stunting' growth, 86, 87, 89, 92
supplementary food, 222, 223
survey modules, 34–37
susceptibility, to crisis, 25
sustenance, 294
symbolic and social constituency, 277, 278

targeted credit programmes, 203
Targetted Employment Generation Programme, 72

Task Force Report, 40–41
television, access to, 135
tenancy, cultivation, 32; market, adjustments through, 200–203; and technology, 258, 270; variable, 262; system, 32
trade, income from, 61, 288
transport facilities, 258, 262, 265, 269–70, 296
trickle-down programme, 272
tubewell water, 102

unanticipated crisis, 114, 120–24
underemployment, 210
unemployment, rate of women, 149
University of Dhaka, 78
urban retail prices, 44, 45
urbanisation, 296
USAID, 269
United States Department of Health, Education and Welfare, 78

village(s), politics, 121; of study, 31, 32
violence, 113, 114
Vulnerable Group Development (VGD), programmes, 71, 118
vulnerable poor households, 209

vulnerability, 113, 114, 251, 284, 285

wage, dependent households, 247; employment, 24, 197, 198, 214; labour, 150, 182, 235; labour by sex, 143; labour households, 140; for male labour from non-poor households, 141; rates, and market prices, 244–45; rates, real, 72
War of Liberation, 46
Waring, M., 152
water resource development, 266
Waterlow, J.C., 86
weight, for-age, 89; and height of children, 92, 96, 97, 98
welfare, 39, 114, 227; and ecological reserves, 229
widowers, 147, 148
widows, 147, 148, 149, 177; households headed by, 189
women, aspects of poverty and, 152; in development programmes, 151; as household heads, 149, 189; inheritance denial to, 147–49; multiple occupation of, 141
Woolf, V., 153

THE UNIVERSITY OF MICHIGAN

DATE DUE

DEC 2 8 2000